GEORGE BERNARD SHAW

Modern Critical Views

These and other titles in preparation

Modern Critical Views

GEORGE BERNARD SHAW

Edited and with an introduction by
Harold Bloom
Sterling Professor of the Humanities
Yale University

CHELSEA HOUSE PUBLISHERS ◊ 1987
New York ◊ New Haven ◊ Philadelphia

© 1987 by Chelsea House Publishers,
a division of Chelsea House Educational Communications, Inc.,
  95 Madison Avenue, New York, NY 10016
  345 Whitney Avenue, New Haven, CT 06511
  5014 West Chester Pike, Edgemont, PA 19028

Introduction © 1987 by Harold Bloom

Printed and bound in the United States of America

∞ The paper used in this publication meets the minimum
requirements of the American National Standard for
Permanence of Paper for Printed Library Materials,
Z39.48-1984.

Library of Congress Cataloging-in-Publication Data
George Bernard Shaw.
    (Modern critical views)
    Bibliography: p.
    Includes index.
    1. Shaw, Bernard, 1856–1950—Criticism and interpretation.
I. Bloom, Harold.   II. Series.
PR5367.G43   1987   822'.912   86–24460
ISBN 0–87754–649–5 (alk. paper)

Contents

Editor's Note

This book gathers together a representative selection of the most useful criticism of the plays of George Bernard Shaw. The critical essays are reprinted here in the chronological order of their original publication, except for the "Introduction to Shaw" by Stanley Weintraub, which I have placed after my own introduction. I am grateful to Marena Fisher for her erudition and judgment in aiding me to edit this volume.

My introduction, after considering Shaw's copious intellectual debts, offers critical readings of *Man and Superman, Major Barbara, Pygmalion,* and *Saint Joan,* in the hope of arriving at a freshly balanced estimate both of Shaw's limitations, and of his varied achievement as a comic melodramatist. Shaw's biography is examined in close relation to his works by Stanley Weintraub, an essential essay because of Shaw's incessant self-concern.

I have gone all the way back to the early years of our century in order to benefit by G. K. Chesterton's account of Shaw's work as a critic of art, drama, and music, because Chesterton remains unmatched in his shrewd and genial early insights into Shaw. Eric Bentley, dean of contemporary Shavians, follows with his sympathetic defense of *Pygmalion* as Shaw's particularly personal play.

John Bull's Other Island is seen by Frederick P. W. McDowell as another Shavian world beautifully represented, properly reflective both of Shaw's Irish background and of his comic genius at its most intense. Louis Crompton, studying *Caesar and Cleopatra,* finds in it a deft conversion of all tragic possibilities into the eternal dramatic strength of farce.

Shaw's politics, the supposed polemical basis for his dramatic art, are surveyed by Martin Meisel, who centers upon the plays of 1890 to 1920, including the celebrated Unpleasant Plays, Pleasant Plays, and Plays for Puritans. *Candida,* that shrewd subversion of the Victorian domestic ethos, is analyzed by Margery M. Morgan, while Charles Berst examines the fiercer *Heartbreak House* as the great instance of "Shavian Expressionism." Another great polemical tract, the epic cycle of *Back to Methuselah*, receives a similar intensive study by Maurice Valency.

In an exegesis by J. L. Wisenthal, *Major Barbara* is neatly related to Blake's *Marriage of Heaven and Hell*, with its vision of progression through humanized contraries. Another kind of archetypal reading, feminist rather than Blakean, is exemplified by a reading of *Man and Superman* as carried through by Sally Peters Vogt. Shaw's history play *Saint Joan* is defended by Nicholas Grene whose analysis should be compared with the rather harsher estimate in my introduction.

This volume ends with a delightful return to early Shaw by Barbara M. Fisher, who gives us *Fanny's First Play* as a Shavian experiment or testing ground for those later triumphs in attempting (if not accomplishing) the reconciliation of the rival claims of morality and art.

Introduction

"With the single exception of Homer there is no eminent writer, not even Sir Walter Scott, whom I despise so entirely as I despise Shakespear when I measure my mind against his." Shaw, obsessive polemicist, would write anything, even that unfortunate sentence. No critic would wish to measure Shaw's mind against Shakespeare's, particularly since originality was hardly Shaw's strength. Shavian ideas are quarried from Schopenhauer, Nietzsche, Ibsen, Wagner, Ruskin, Samuel Butler, Shelley, Carlyle, Marx (more or less), William Morris, Lamarck, Bergson—the list could be extended. Though an intellectual dramatist, Shaw essentially popularized the concepts and images of others. He continues to hold the stage and might appear to have earned his reputation of being the principal writer of English comic drama since Shakespeare. Yet his limitations are disconcerting, and the experience of rereading even his most famous plays, after many years away from them, is disappointingly mixed. They are much more than period pieces, but they hardly seem to be for all time. No single comedy by Shaw matches Wilde's *Importance of Being Earnest* or the tragic farces of Beckett.

Eric Bentley best demonstrated that Shaw viewed himself as a prose prophet in direct succession to Carlyle, Ruskin, and Morris. This is the Shaw of the prefaces, of *Essays in Fabian Socialism*, of *Doctors' Delusions, Crude Criminology, Sham Education*. Only the prefaces to the plays are still read, and of course they are not really prefaces to the plays. They expound Shaw's very odd personal religion, the rather cold worship of Creative Evolution. Of this religion, one can say that it is no more bizarre than most, and less distasteful than many, but it is still quite grotesque. To judge religions by aesthetic criteria may seem perverse, but what others are relevant for poems, plays, stories, novels, personal essays? By any aesthetic standard, Shaw's heretical faith is considerably less interesting or impressive than D. H. Lawrence's barbaric vitalism in *The Plumed Serpent* or even Thomas Hardy's negative homage to the Immanent Will in *The Dynasts*.

G. K. Chesterton, in his book on Shaw (1909), observed that the heroine of *Major Barbara*

> ends by suggesting that she will serve God without personal hope, so that she may owe nothing to God and He owe everything to her. It does not seem to strike her that if God owes everything to her He is not God. These things affect me merely as tedious perversions of a phrase. It is as if you said, "I will never have a father unless I have begotten him."

"He who is willing to do the work gives birth to his own father," Kierkegaard wrote, and Nietzsche mused: "If one hasn't had a good father, then it is necessary to invent one." Shaw was neither a Darwinian nor a Freudian and I think he was a bad Nietzschean, who had misread rather weakly the sage of *Zarathustra*. But in his life he had suffered an inadequate father and certainly he was willing to do the work. Like his own Major Barbara, he wished to have a God who would owe everything to G. B. S. That requires a writer to possess superb mythopoeic powers, and fortunately for Shaw his greatest literary strength was as an inventor of new myths. Shaw endures in a high literary sense and remains eminently readable as well as actable because of his mythmaking faculty, a power he shared with Blake and Shelley, Wagner and Ibsen. He was not a stylist, not a thinker, not a psychologist, and utterly lacked even an iota of the uncanny Shakespearean ability to represent character and personality with overwhelming persuasiveness. His dialogue is marred by his garrulous tendencies, and the way he embodied his ideas is too often wearisomely simplistic. And yet his dramas linger in us because his beings transcend their inadequate status as representations of the human, with which he was hopelessly impatient anyway. They suggest something more obsessive than daily life, something that moves and has its being in the cosmos we learn to call Shavian, a comic version of Schopenhauer's terrible world dominated by the remorseless Will to Live.

As a critic, Shaw was genial only where he was not menaced, and he felt deeply menaced by the Aesthetic vision, of which his Socialism never quite got free. Like Oscar Wilde and Wilde's mentor Walter Pater, Shaw was the direct descendant of Ruskin, and his animus against Wilde and Pater reflects the anxiety of an ambitious son toward rival claimants to a heritage. Pater insisted upon style, as did Wilde, and Shaw has no style to speak of, not much more, say, than Eugene O'Neill. Reviewing Wilde's *An Ideal Husband* on January 12, 1895, for Frank Harris's *Saturday Review,* Shaw was both generous and just:

Mr. Wilde, an arch-artist, is so colossally lazy that he trifles even with the work by which an artist escapes work. He distils the very quintessence, and gets as product plays which are so unapproachably playful that they are the delight of every play-goer with twopenn'orth of brains.

A month later, confronted by *The Importance of Being Earnest: A Trivial Comedy for Serious People,* Shaw lost his composure, his generosity, and his sense of critical justice:

> I cannot say that I greatly cared for The Importance of Being Earnest. It amused me, of course; but unless comedy touches me as well as amuses me, it leaves me with a sense of having wasted my evening. I go to the theatre to be moved to laughter, not to be tickled or bustled into it; and that is why, though I laugh as much as anybody at a farcical comedy, I am out of spirits before the end of the second act, and out of temper before the end of the third, my miserable mechanical laughter intensifying these symptoms at every outburst. If the public ever becomes intelligent enough to know when it is really enjoying itself and when it is not, there will be an end of farcical comedy. Now in The Importance of Being Earnest there is plenty of this rib-tickling: for instance, the lies, the deceptions, the cross purposes, the sham mourning, the christening of the two grown-up men, the muffin eating, and so forth. These could only have been raised from the farcical plane by making them occur to characters who had, like Don Quixote, convinced us of their reality and obtained some hold on our sympathy. But that unfortunate moment of Gilbertism breaks our belief in the humanity of the play.

Would it be possible to have a sillier critical reaction to the most delightful comic drama in English since Shakespeare? Twenty-three years later, Shaw wrote a letter (if it is that) to Frank Harris, published by Harris in his *Life of Wilde* (1918), and then reprinted by Shaw in his *Pen Portraits and Reviews*. Again Wilde was an artist of "stupendous laziness," and again was indicted, this time after his death, for heartlessness:

> Our sixth meeting, the only other one I can remember, was the one at the Café Royal. On that occasion he was not too preoc-cupied with his danger to be disgusted with me because I, who had praised his first plays handsomely, had turned traitor over

The Importance of Being Earnest. Clever as it was, it was his first really heartless play. In the others the chivalry of the eighteenth-century Irishman and the romance of the disciple of Théophile Gautier (Oscar was old-fashioned in the Irish way, except as a critic of morals) not only gave a certain kindness and gallantry to the serious passages and to the handling of the women, but provided that proximity of emotion without which laughter, however irresistible, is destructive and sinister. In The Importance of Being Earnest this had vanished; and the play, though extremely funny, was essentially hateful. I had no idea that Oscar was going to the dogs, and that this represented a real degeneracy produced by his debaucheries. I thought he was still developing; and I hazarded the unhappy guess that The Importance of Being Earnest was in idea a young work written or projected long before under the influence of Gilbert and furbished up for Alexander as a potboiler. At the Café Royal that day I calmly asked him whether I was not right. He indignantly repudiated my guess, and said loftily (the only time he ever tried on me the attitude he took to John Gray and his more abject disciples) that he was disappointed in me. I suppose I said, "Then what on earth has happened to you?" but I recollect nothing more on that subject except that we did not quarrel over it.

Shaw remains unique in finding *The Importance of Being Earnest* (of all plays!) "essentially hateful." A clue to this astonishing reaction can be found in Shaw's outraged response to Max Beerbohm's review of *Man and Superman,* as expressed in his letter to Beerbohm, on September 15, 1903:

You idiot, do you suppose I dont know my own powers? I tell you in this book as plainly as the thing can be told, that the reason Bunyan reached such a pitch of mastery in literary art (and knew it) whilst poor Pater could never get beyond a nerveless amateur affectation which had not even the common workaday quality of vulgar journalism (and, alas! didnt know it, though he died of his own futility), was that it was life or death with the tinker to make people understand his message and see his vision, whilst Pater had neither message nor vision & only wanted to cultivate style, with the result that of the two attempts I have made to read him the first broke down at the tenth sentence & the second at the first. Pater took a genteel walk up

Parnassus: Bunyan fled from the wrath to come: that explains
the difference in their pace & in the length they covered.

Poor Pater is dragged in and beaten up because he was the apostle of
style, while Bunyan is summoned up supposedly as the model for Shaw,
who also has a message and a vision. It is a little difficult to associate *The
Pilgrim's Progress* with *Man and Superman*, but one can suspect shrewdly
that Pater here is a surrogate for Wilde, who had achieved an absolute
comic music of perfect style and stance in *The Importance of Being Earnest*.
Shavians become indignant at the comparison, but Shaw does poorly when
one reads side by side any of the *Fabian Essays* and Wilde's extraordinary
essay "The Soul of Man under Socialism." Something even darker happens
when we juxtapose *Man and Superman* with *The Importance of Being
Earnest*, but then Shaw is not unique in not being able to survive such a
comparison.

II

Everything about *Man and Superman*, paradoxical as the play was to
begin with, now seems almost absurdly problematical. The very title cannot
mean (any more) what Shaw doubtless intended it to mean: the Superman
of Nietzsche, Zarathustra, the heroic vitalist who prophesies the next phase
of Creative Evolution, the next resting place of that cold God, the Life
Force. Nietzsche's Zarathustra, as Shaw blandly chose never to see, is a
god-man who is free of what Freud came to call the Over-I (superego), the
shadow or spectre of bad conscience that hovers above each separate self.
But Shaw's Superman is simply Bunyan's Pilgrim writ large and brought
(supposedly) up to date, Shaw being about as much an immoralist as Bunyan.
Nietzsche transvalued all values (perhaps) or tried to (in some moods),
and at the least developed an extraordinary perspectivism that really does
call every stance—rhetorical, cosmological, psychological—into question.
Shaw was interested neither in rhetoric (which he dismissed as Paterian
"style") nor in psychology (Associationist or Freudian), and his cosmological speculations, though mythologically powerful, are informed primarily
by his post-Ruskinian and only quasi-Marxist political economics. His
Fabian socialism marries the British Protestant or Evangelical sensibility
(Bunyan, Carlyle, Ruskin) to philosophical speculation that might transcend
Darwinian-Freudian scientism (Schopenhauer, Lamarck, Nietzsche,
Bergson). Such a sensibility is moral and indeed Puritanical, so that Shaw
always remained in spirit very close to Carlyle rather than to Nietzsche
(who despised Carlyle and loved Emerson for his slyly immoralistic Self-

Reliance). Shaw's Superman, alas, in consequence looks a lot more like Thomas Carlyle crying out "work, for the night cometh in which no man can work" than he does like Zarathustra-Nietzsche urging us: "Try to live as though it were morning."

In Shaw's defense, he took from the Nietzschean metaphor of the Superman what he most needed of it: a political and therefore literal reading, in which the Superman is nothing but what Shaw called "a general raising of human character through the deliberate cultivation and endowment of democratic virtue without consideration of property or class." That is a boring idealization, from an aesthetic or epistemological perspective, but pragmatically it is indeed what we most require and never will attain, which is why doubtless we must perish as a civilization. Such a consideration, fortunately, has nothing to do with *Man and Superman* as a farce and a sexual comedy, or with its glory, the extraordinary inserted drama of dialectic and mythology, "Don Juan in Hell," certainly the outstanding instance of a play-within-a-play from Shakespeare to Pirandello.

The preface to *Man and Superman* is a dedicatory epistle to the drama critic Arthur Bingham Walkley and is a piece of Shavian outrageousness, particularly in promising far more than the play can begin to deliver. Shakespeare, perpetual origin of Shavian aesthetic anxiety, is associated with Dickens as being obsessed with the world's diversities rather than its unities. Consequently, they are irreligious, anarchical, nihilistic, apolitical, and their human figures are lacking in will. Against them, Shaw ranges Bunyan, Nietzsche, and himself—the artist-philosophers! Shakespeare did not understand virtue and courage, which is the province of the artist-philosophers.

The shrewdest reply one could make to Shaw is to contrast Shakespeare's Falstaff (whom Shaw praises) to Nietzsche's Zarathustra. Which is the Superman, embodiment of the drive to live, person free of the superego? Hamlet, to Shaw, is an inadequate Don Juan, since he is famously irresolute. The sadness is that the Don Juan we will see debating the Devil in Hell is only (at best) a wistful impersonation of Hamlet, who remains the West's paradigm of intellectuality even as Falstaff abides forever as its paradigm of wit.

Yet this epistle commencing *Man and Superman* is one of Shaw's grandest performances, reminding us of how soundly he trained as a Hyde Park soapbox orator, a splendid preparation for a polemical playwright of ideas. In the midst of his perpetual advertisements for himself, he utters a poignant credo:

Now you cannot say this of the works of the artist-philosophers. You cannot say it, for instance, of The Pilgrim's Progress. Put your Shakespearian hero and coward, Henry V and Pistol or Parolles, beside Mr Valiant and Mr Fearing, and you have a sudden revelation of the abyss that lies between the fashionable author who could see nothing in the world but personal aims and the tragedy of their disappointment or the comedy of their incongruity, and the field preacher who achieved virtue and courage by identifying himself with the purpose of the world as he understood it. The contrast is enormous: Bunyan's coward stirs your blood more than Shakespear's hero, who actually leaves you cold and secretly hostile. You suddenly see that Shakespear, with all his flashes and divinations, never understood virtue and courage, never conceived how any man who was not a fool could, like Bunyan's hero, look back from the brink of the river of death over the strife and labor of his pilgrimage, and say "yet do I not repent me"; or, with the panache of a millionaire, bequeath "my sword to him that shall succeed me in my pilgrimage, and my courage and skill to him that can get it." This is the true joy in life, the being used for a purpose recognized by yourself as a mighty one; the being thoroughly worn out before you are thrown on the scrap heap; the being a force of Nature instead of a feverish selfish little clod of ailments and grievances complaining that the world will not devote itself to making you happy. And also the only real tragedy in life is the being used by personally minded men for purposes which you recognize to be base. All the rest is at worst mere misfortune or mortality: this alone is misery, slavery, hell on earth; and the revolt against it is the only force that offers a man's work to the poor artist, whom our personally minded rich people would so willingly employ as pandar, buffoon, beauty monger, sentimentalizer and the like.

Shakespeare then is not a prophet or at least does not himself suffer personally the burden of his prophecy. Bunyan and Shaw are prophets, and if they suffer, then also they experience the "true joy in life . . . the being a force of Nature." The passage has in it the accent of Carlyle, except that Carlyle rendered it with more gusto in his sublimely outrageous style, and Carlyle (not being in direct competition with Shakespeare) set Shakespeare first among the artist-prophets, higher even than Goethe. We are moved by

Shaw, yet he has not the rhetorical power to overwhelm us (however dubiously) as Carlyle sometimes does.

Why has Shaw, of all dramatists, written a play about Don Juan Tenorio, or John Tanner, as he is called in *Man and Superman*? And in what way is the bumbling Tanner, cravenly fleeing the Life Force that is Ann Whitefield, a Don Juan? A crafty ironist, Shaw knows that all Don Juans, whether literary or experiential, are anything but audacious seducers. Poor Tanner is a relatively deliberate Shavian self-parody, and is all too clearly an Edwardian gentleman, a pillar of society, and very much a Puritan. He is all superego, and from the start is Ann's destined victim, her proper and inevitable husband, the father of her children. She will let him go on talking; she acts, and that is the end of it. The true Don Juan does not like women, which is why he needs so many of them. Tanner adores and needs Ann, though perhaps he will never know how early on the adoration and the need commenced in him.

Don Juan, as Shaw revises the myth, is Faust (whom Shaw calls the Don's cousin). He is the enemy of God, in direct descent from Faust's ancestor, Simon Magus the first Gnostic, who took the cognomen of Faustus ("the favored one") when he moved his campaign of charlatanry to Rome. Shaw's Don Juan is Prometheus as well as Faust, and so is an enemy not so much of God as of Jehovah (Shelley's Jupiter in *Prometheus Unbound*) the sky-tyrant, the deity of finance capitalism, repressive sexual morality, and institutional or historical Christianity.

It is manifest that *Man and Superman* does not have a Faustian or Promethean hero in the absurdly inadequate though amiable John Tanner. Tanner is, as Eric Bentley economically observes, a fool and a windbag, all-too-human rather than Don Juan Tenorio the Superman. But Shaw gives him a great dream: "Don Juan in Hell." Again Bentley is incisive: "Take away the episode in hell, and Shaw has written an anti-intellectual comedy." I would go a touch further and say: "Take away the episode in hell, and Shaw has written a very unfunny comedy." Though it can be directed and acted effectively, most of the play singularly lacks wit; its paradoxes are sadly obvious. But the paradoxes of "Don Juan in Hell" continue to delight and disturb, as in the contrast between the erotic philosophies of Don Juan and the Statue:

> DON JUAN: I learnt it by experience. When I was on earth, and
>   made those proposals to ladies which, though universally
>   condemned, have made me so interesting a hero of legend,
>   I was not infrequently met in some such way as this. The

lady would say that she would countenance my advances, provided they were honorable. On inquiring what that proviso meant, I found that it meant that I proposed to get possession of her property if she had any, or to undertake her support for life if she had not; that I desired her continual companionship, counsel, and conversation to the end of my days, and would take a most solemn oath to be always enraptured by them: above all, that I would turn my back on all other women for ever for her sake. I did not object to these conditions because they were exorbitant and inhuman: it was their extraordinary irrelevance that prostrated me. I invariably replied with perfect frankness that I had never dreamt of any of these things; that unless the lady's character and intellect were equal or superior to my own, her conversation must degrade and her counsel mislead me; that her constant companionship might, for all I knew, become intolerably tedious to me; that I could not answer for my feelings for a week in advance, much less to the end of my life; that to cut me off from all natural and unconstrained intercourse with half my fellowcreatures would narrow and warp me if I submitted to it, and, if not, would bring me under the curse of clandestinity; that, finally, my proposals to her were wholly unconnected with any of these matters, and were the outcome of a perfectly simple impulse of my manhood towards her womanhood.

ANA: You mean that it was an immoral impulse.

DON JUAN: Nature, my dear lady, is what you call immoral. I blush for it; but I cannot help it. Nature is a pandar, Time a wrecker, and Death a murderer. I have always preferred to stand up to those facts and build institutions on their recognition. You prefer to propitiate the three devils by proclaiming their chastity, their thrift, and their loving kindness; and to base your institutions on these flatteries. Is it any wonder that the institutions do not work smoothly?

THE STATUE: What used the ladies to say, Juan?

DON JUAN: Oh, come! Confidence for confidence. First tell me what you used to say to the ladies.

THE STATUE: I! Oh, I swore that I would be faithful to the death; that I should die if they refused me; that no woman could ever be to me what she was—

ANA: She! Who?

THE STATUE: Whoever it happened to be at the time, my dear. I
    had certain things I always said. One of them was that even
    when I was eighty, one white hair of the woman I loved
    would make me tremble more than the thickest gold tress
    from the most beautiful young head. Another was that I
    could not bear the thought of anyone else being the mother
    of my children.

DON JUAN [*revolted*]: You old rascal!

THE STATUE [*stoutly*]: Not a bit; for I really believed it with all
    my soul at the moment. I had a heart: not like you. And it
    was this sincerity that made me successful.

DON JUAN: Sincerity! To be fool enough to believe a ramping,
    stamping, thumping lie: that is what you call sincerity! To
    be so greedy for a woman that you deceive yourself in your
    eagerness to deceive her: sincerity, you call it!

THE STATUE: Oh, damn your sophistries! I was a man in love, not
    a lawyer. And the women loved me for it, bless them!

Does Shaw take sides? Don Juan, advance guard for the Superman,
presumably speaks for the dramatist, but our sympathies are divided, or
perhaps not called upon at all. I hear the stance of Shelley's *Epipsychidion*
taken up in Don Juan's rhetoric, probably as a deliberate allusion on Shaw's
part. The Statue though, splendid fellow, speaks the universal rhetoric of all
ordinary men in love, and his rather dialectical "sincerity" has its own
persuasiveness. Much trickier, and a larger achievement, is Shaw's management of the fencing match between the Shavian Don Juan and that Wildean-
Paterian Aesthete, the Devil. Shaw's lifelong animus against Pater, and his
repressed anxiety caused by Wilde's genius as an Anglo-Irish comic dramatist, emerge with authentic sharpness and turbulence as Don Juan and the
Devil face off. They are as elaborately courteous as Shaw and Wilde always
were with one another, but their mutual distaste is palpable, as pervasive as
the deep dislike of Shaw and Wilde for each other's works, ideas, and
personalities:

THE DEVIL: None, my friend. You think, because you have a
    purpose, Nature must have one. You might as well expect it
    to have fingers and toes because you have them.

DON JUAN: But I should not have them if they served no purpose.
    And I, my friend, am as much a part of Nature as my own
    finger is a part of me. If my finger is the organ by which I

grasp the sword and the mandoline, my brain is the organ by which Nature strives to understand itself. My dog's brain serves only my dog's purposes; but my own brain labors at a knowledge which does nothing for me personally but make my body bitter to me and my decay and death a calamity. Were I not possessed with a purpose beyond my own I had better be a ploughman than a philosopher; for the plough-man lives as long as the philosopher, eats more, sleeps bet-ter, and rejoices in the wife of his bosom with less misgiving. This is because the philosopher is in the grip of the Life Force. This Life Force says to him "I have done a thousand wonderful things unconsciously by merely willing to live and following the line of least resistance: now I want to know myself and my destination, and choose my path; so I have made a special brain—a philosopher's brain—to grasp this knowledge for me as the husbandman's hand grasps the plough for me. And this" says the Life Force to the philos-opher "must thou strive to do for me until thou diest, when I will make another brain and another philosopher to carry on the work."

THE DEVIL: What is the use of knowing?

DON JUAN: Why, to be able to choose the line of greatest advan-tage instead of yielding in the direction of the least resis-tance. Does a ship sail to its destination no better than a log drifts nowhither? The philosopher is Nature's pilot. And there you have our difference: to be in hell is to drift: to be in heaven is to steer.

THE DEVIL: On the rocks, most likely.

DON JUAN: Pooh! which ship goes oftenest on the rocks or to the bottom? the drifting ship or the ship with a pilot on board?

THE DEVIL: Well, well, go your way, Señor Don Juan. I prefer to be my own master and not the tool of any blundering uni-versal force. I know that beauty is good to look at; that music is good to hear; that love is good to feel; and that they are all good to think about and talk about. I know that to be well exercised in these sensations, emotions, and studies is to be a refined and cultivated being. Whatever they may say of me in churches on earth, I know that it is universally admitted in good society that the Prince of Darkness is a gentleman; and that is enough for me. As to your Life Force,

which you think irresistible, it is the most resistable thing in
the world for a person of any character. But if you are
naturally vulgar and credulous, as all reformers are, it will
thrust you first into religion, where you will sprinkle water
on babies to save their souls from me; then it will drive you
from religion into science, where you will snatch the babies
from the water sprinkling and inoculate them with disease
to save them from catching it accidentally; then you will
take to politics, where you will become the catspaw of corrupt functionaries and the henchman of ambitious hum-
bugs; and the end will be despair and decrepitude, broken
nerve and shattered hopes, vain regrets for that worst and
silliest of wastes and sacrifices, the waste and sacrifice of the
power of enjoyment: in a word, the punishment of the fool
who pursues the better before he has secured the good.

DON JUAN: But at least I shall not be bored. The service of the
Life Force has that advantage, at all events. So fare you well,
Señor Satan.

THE DEVIL [*amiably*]: Fare you well, Don Juan. I shall often
think of our interesting chats about things in general. I wish
you every happiness: heaven, as I said before, suits some
people. But if you should change your mind, do not forget
that the gates are always open here to the repentant prod-
igal. If you feel at any time that warmth of heart, sincere
unforced affection, innocent enjoyment, and warm, breathing, palpitating reality—

This is hardly fair to the Devil, whose Paterian sense of repetition is a
powerful answer to the Idealism of Schopenhauer's Life Force, and whose
Ecclesiastes-like vision of vanity does not exclude the holiness of the heart's
affections. Don Juan regards the Devil as a sentimentalist, but the Creative
Evolution preached by the Shavian Don now seems precisely the sentimentality of a lost world. By a paradox that Shaw would not have enjoyed, the
Aesthetic vision of Pater and Wilde now appears to be Ruskin's abiding
legacy, while Shaw's Fabian Evolutionism would seem to have been a
Ruskinian dead end. *Man and Superman* is effective enough farce, and its
"Don Juan in Hell" is more than that, being one of the rare efforts to turn
intellectual debate into actable and readable drama. Yet *Man and Superman*
survives as theater; if you want an artist-philosopher in social comedy, then
you are better off returning to the sublime nonsense and Aesthetic vision of

The Importance of Being Earnest, a play that Shaw so curiously condemned as being "heartless."

III

Shaw initially planned to call *Major Barbara* by the rather more imposing title of *Andrew Undershaft's Profession.* The play has been so popular (deservedly so) that we cannot think of it by any other title, but the earlier notion would have emphasized Undershaft's strength and centrality. He dwarfs Cusins, and dominates Barbara, as much during her rebellion against him as in her return. And he raises the fascinating question of Shaw's own ambivalence toward the Socialist ideal, despite Shaw's lifelong labor in behalf of that ideal. Undershaft may be the archetype of the capitalist as amoral munitions-monger, but his arms establishment dangerously resembles a benign state socialism, and the drama moves finally in a direction equally available for interpretation by the extreme Left or the extreme Right.

Despite his ignorance of Freud, Shaw in *Major Barbara* (1905) wrote a drama wholly consonant with Freud's contemporary works, *The Interpretation of Dreams* and *Three Essays on the Theory of Sexuality.* Consider the first amiable confrontation of Barbara and her father Undershaft, who has not seen her since she was a baby:

> UNDERSHAFT: For me there is only one true morality; but it might not fit you, as you do not manufacture aerial battleships. There is only one true morality for every man; but every man has not the same true morality.
>
> LOMAX [*overtaxed*]: Would you mind saying that again? I didnt quite follow it.
>
> CUSINS: It's quite simple. As Euripides says, one man's meat is another man's poison morally as well as physically.
>
> UNDERSHAFT: Precisely.
>
> LOMAX: Oh, that! Yes, yes, yes. True. True.
>
> STEPHEN: In other words, some men are honest and some are scoundrels.
>
> BARBARA: Bosh! There are no scoundrels.
>
> UNDERSHAFT: Indeed? Are there any good men?
>
> BARBARA: No. Not one. There are neither good men nor scoundrels: there are just children of one Father; and the sooner they stop calling one another names the better. You neednt talk to me: I know them. Ive had scores of them through my

hands: scoundrels, criminals, infidels, philanthropists, missionaries, county councillors, all sorts. Theyre all just the same sort of sinner; and theres the same salvation ready for them all.

UNDERSHAFT: May I ask have you ever saved a maker of cannons?

BARBARA: No. Will you let me try?

UNDERSHAFT: Well, I will make a bargain with you. If I go to see you tomorrow in your Salvation Shelter, will you come the day after to see me in my cannon works?

BARBARA: Take care. It may end in your giving up the cannons for the sake of the Salvation Army.

UNDERSHAFT: Are you sure it will not end in your giving up the Salvation Army for the sake of the cannons?

BARBARA: I will take my chance of that.

UNDERSHAFT: And I will take my chance of the other. [*They shake hands on it.*] Where is your shelter?

BARBARA: In West Ham. At the sign of the cross. Ask anybody in Canning Town. Where are your works?

UNDERSHAFT: In Perivale St Andrews. At the sign of the sword. Ask anybody in Europe.

LOMAX: Hadnt I better play something?

BARBARA: Yes. Give us Onward, Christian Soldiers.

LOMAX: Well, thats rather a strong order to begin with, dont you know. Suppose I sing Thourt passing hence, my brother. It's much the same tune.

BARBARA: It's too melancholy. You get saved, Cholly; and youll pass hence, my brother, without making such a fuss about it.

LADY BRITOMART: Really, Barbara, you go on as if religion were a pleasant subject. Do have some sense of propriety.

UNDERSHAFT: I do not find it an unpleasant subject, my dear. It is the only one that capable people really care for.

Barbara, having replaced the absent Undershaft by God the Father in his Salvation Army guise, begins by accepting her phallic father as one more sinner to be saved. Their prophetic interchange of signs—daughterly cross and fatherly sword—bonds them against the mother, as each stands for a version of the only subject that the capable Shaw really cares for: religion as the Life Force, Creative Evolution. The daughter and the father, in mutual recognition, have commenced upon their inevitably narcissistic dance of repressed psychosexual courtship. Cusins shrewdly sums up the enigma in his act 2 dialogue with Undershaft:

> UNDERSHAFT: Religion is our business at present, because it is through religion alone that we can win Barbara.
> CUSINS: Have you, too, fallen in love with Barbara?
> UNDERSHAFT: Yes, with a father's love.
> CUSINS: A father's love for a grown-up daughter is the most dangerous of all infatuations. I apologize for mentioning my own pale, coy, mistrustful fancy in the same breath with it.

Undershaft's love for Barbara is conversionary and therefore complex; its aim is to transform family romance into societal romance. After three quarters of a century, G. K. Chesterton remains much the best of Shaw's early critics, but he insisted upon a weak misreading of Undershaft's (and Shaw's) scheme:

> The ultimate epigram of *Major Barbara* can be put thus. People say that poverty is no crime; Shaw says that poverty is a crime; that it is a crime to endure it, a crime to be content with it, that it is the mother of all crimes of brutality, corruption, and fear. If a man says to Shaw that he is born of poor but honest parents, Shaw tells him that the very word "but" shows that his parents were probably dishonest. In short, he maintains here what he had maintained elsewhere: that what the people at this moment require is not more patriotism or more art or more religion or more morality or more sociology, but simply more money. The evil is not ignorance or decadence or sin or pessimism; the evil is poverty. The point of this particular drama is that even the noblest enthusiasm of the girl who becomes a Salvation Army officer fails under the brute money power of her father who is a modern capitalist. When I have said this it will be clear why this play, fine and full of bitter sincerity as it is, must in a manner be cleared out of the way before we come to talk of Shaw's final and serious faith. For this serious faith is in the sanctity of human will, in the divine capacity for creation and choice rising higher than environment and doom; and so far as that goes, *Major Barbara* is not only apart from his faith but against his faith. *Major Barbara* is an account of environment victorious over heroic will. There are a thousand answers to the ethic in *Major*

Barbara which I should be inclined to offer. I might point out
that the rich do not so much buy honesty as curtains to cover
dishonesty: that they do not so much buy health as cushions to
comfort disease. And I might suggest that the doctrine that poverty degrades the poor is much more likely to be used as an
argument for keeping them powerless than as an argument for
making them rich. But there is no need to find such answers to
the materialistic pessimism of *Major Barbara*. The best answer
to it is in Shaw's own best and crowning philosophy.

Is the environment of Undershaft's "spotlessly clean and beautiful hill-
side town" of well-cared-for munitions workers victorious over Barbara's
heroic will? Has the sanctity of human will, its divine capacity for creation
and choice, been violated by Undershaft playing the part of Machiavel?
Who could be more Shavian than the great Life Forcer, Undershaft, who
cheerfully provides the explosives with which the present can blast itself into
the future, in a perhaps involuntary parody of Creative Evolution? How far
is Undershaft from the Caesar of *Caesar and Cleopatra*? The questions are
so self-answering as to put Chesterton, splendid as he is, out of court.

But that still gives us the problem of Barbara's conversion: to what
precisely has she come? The scene of her instruction is a characteristic
Shavian outrage, persuasive and absurd. Cusins asks Undershaft the crucial
question as to his munitions enterprise: "What drives the place?"

> UNDERSHAFT [*enigmatically*]: A will of which I am a part.
> BARBARA [*startled*]: Father! Do you know what you are say-
> ing; or are you laying a snare for my soul?
> CUSINS: Dont listen to his metaphysics, Barbara. The place is
> driven by the most rascally part of society, the money hunt-
> ers, the pleasure hunters, the military promotion hunters;
> and he is their slave.
> UNDERSHAFT: Not necessarily. Remember the Armorer's Faith. I
> will take an order from a good man as cheerfully as from a
> bad one. If you good people prefer preaching and shirking
> to buying my weapons and fighting the rascals, dont blame
> me. I can make cannons: I cannot make courage and con-
> viction. Bah! you tire me, Euripides, with your morality
> mongering. Ask Barbara: she understands. [*He suddenly
> reaches up and takes Barbara's hands, looking powerfully
> into her eyes.*] Tell him, my love, what power really means.
> BARBARA [*hypnotized*]: Before I joined the Salvation Army, I

was in my own power; and the consequence was that I never knew what to do with myself. When I joined it, I had not time enough for all the things I had to do.

UNDERSHAFT [*approvingly*]: Just so. And why was that, do you suppose?

BARBARA: Yesterday I should have said, because I was in the power of God. [*She resumes her self-possession, withdrawing her hands from his with a power equal to his own.*] But you came and shewed me that I was in the power of Bodger and Undershaft. Today I feel—oh! how can I put it into words? Sarah: do you remember the earthquake at Cannes, when we were little children?—how little the surprise of the first shock mattered compared to the dread and horror of waiting for the second? That is how I feel in this place today. I stood on the rock I thought eternal; and without a word of warning it reeled and crumbled under me. I was safe with an infinite wisdom watching me, an army marching to Salvation with me; and in a moment, at a stroke of your pen in a cheque book, I stood alone; and the heavens were empty. That was the first shock of the earthquake: I am waiting for the second.

There will not be a second shock, nor need there be. The dialectic of Barbara's conversion is all there in the single moment when Undershaft speaks of "a will of which I am a part" and Barbara is startled into the realization that her two fathers, Undershaft and God, are one. The realization is confirmed in the covenant of power that springs up between father and daughter as Undershaft takes Barbara's hands, while hypnotizing her through the will of which he is a part. Having been driven by one version of the Life Force, she yields now to another, but it is the same force. We somehow wish to find Shavian irony here, but there is less than we seek to find. What we discover is Shavian cruelty at Barbara's expense. Yielding her will to Undershaft sends Barbara into a massive regression, which calls into question her Christian idealism at the play's opening. A baby clutching at her mother's skirt, poor Barbara ends as the most reduced and humiliated heroine anywhere in Shaw. Why is he so harsh to so vivacious a figure, exuberant in her early idealism?

Eric Bentley observes accurately that "Barbara's final conversion has much less force than her previous disillusionment." This is useful as far as it goes, but Bentley is too fond of Shaw to see and say that her final conversion destroys her as an adult. *Major Barbara* is not a text for feminists, and if it can be construed as one for socialists, then they are very unsocial socialists indeed. Undershaft was a brilliant indication of where Shaw was heading, toward Carlyle's worship of heroes, strong men who would impose socialism because the Superman still waited to be born. Playful, wise, and charming, Undershaft nevertheless is a dangerous vision of the father-god enforcing the will of Creative Evolution. One remembers that Shaw, though knowing better, always retained a fondness for Stalin.

Nothing is got for nothing, and Shaw makes Barbara pay the price for this extravagant triumph of the religion of power. To be reconciled with the father, she becomes a child again, in a very curious parody of the Christian second birth. Perhaps she is a Shavian self-punishment that masquerades as a Nietzschean will revenging itself against time. Her pathetic dwindling remains a dark tonality at the conclusion of one of Shaw's most enduring farces.

IV

Part of the lovely afterglow of *Pygmalion* (1913) resides in its positioning both in Shaw's career and in modern history. The First World War (1914–1918) changed Shaw's life and work, and nothing like so effective and untroubled a comedy was to be written by him again. If we seek his strong plays after *Pygmalion,* we find *Heartbreak House* (1916), *Back to Methuselah* (1921), *Saint Joan* (1923), and *Too True to be Good* (1932), none of them free of heavy doctrine, tendentious prophecy, and an unpleasant ambivalence toward human beings as they merely are. Fifty-eight and upon the heights of his comedic inventiveness, Shaw reacted to the onset of a catastrophic war with his bitter satiric pamphlet *Common Sense About the War,* which denounced both sides and called for instant peace.

British reaction, justifiably predictable, was hostile to Shaw until late 1916, when the increasing slaughter confirmed the accuracy of his prophetic views. By war's end, Shaw's public reputation was more than restored, but an impressively impersonal bitterness pervades his work from *Heartbreak House* until his death. *Pygmalion,* hardly by design, is Shaw's farewell to the Age of Ruskin, to an era when that precursor prophet, Elijah to his Elisha, cried out in the wilderness to the most class-ridden of societies. Since Great Britain now, in 1986, is more than ever two nations, Shaw's loving fable of class distinctions and of a working girl's apotheosis, her rise into hard-won self-esteem, has a particular poignance that seems in no immediate danger of vanishing.

Pygmalion manifests Shaw's mythopoeic powers at their most adroit, and it is certainly Shaw himself who is still central and triumphant both in the film (which he wrote) and in the musical *My Fair Lady*. Mythmaking most affects us when it simultaneously both confirms and subverts sexual stereotypes, which is clearly Shaw's dramatic advantage over such male vitalists as D. H. Lawrence or the entire coven of literary feminists, from Doris Lessing to Margaret Atwood.

The best judgment of *Pygmalion* as drama that I have encountered is again Eric Bentley's:

> It is Shavian, not in being made up of political or philosophic discussions, but in being based on the standard conflict of vitality and system, in working out this conflict through an inversion of romance, in bringing matters to a head in a battle of wills and words, in having an inner psychological action in counterpoint to the outer romantic action, in existing on two contrasted levels of mentality, both of which are related to the main theme, in delighting and surprising us with a constant flow of verbal music and more than verbal wit.

That is grand, but is *Pygmalion* more "an inversion of romance," more a *Galatea,* as it were, than it is a *Pygmalion*? Shaw subtitled it "A Romance in Five Acts." All romance, literary or experiential, depends upon enchantment, and enchantment depends upon power or potential rather than upon knowledge. In Bentley's reading, Eliza acquires knowledge both of her own vitality and of something lacking in Higgins, since he is incarcerated by "system," by his science of phonetics. This means, as Bentley severely and lucidly phrases it, that Higgins is suspect: "He is not really a life-giver at all." The title of the play, and its subtitle, are thus revealed as Shaw's own interpretive ironies. Higgins is not Pygmalion, and the work is not a romance.

That Eliza is more sympathetic than Higgins is palpably true, but it remains his play (and his film, though not his musical). In making that assertion, I do not dissent wholly from Bentley, since I agree that Higgins is no life-giver, no Prometheus. Shaw after all has no heroes, only heroines, partly because he is his own hero, as prophet of Creative Evolution, servant only of God, who is the Life Force. Higgins is another Shavian self-parody, since Shaw's passion for himself was nobly unbounded. The splendid Preface to *Pygmalion,* called *A Professor of Phonetics,* makes clear that Shaw considers Higgins a man of genius, a composite of Shaw himself, Henry Sweet who was Reader of Phonetics at Oxford, and the poet Robert Bridges, "to whom perhaps Higgins may owe his Miltonic sympathies," as Shaw slyly added.

Higgins, like Carlyle and Shaw, is a fierce Miltonist, an elitist who adopts toward women that great Miltonic maxim (so beloved by literary feminists): "He for God only, she for God in him," where the reference is to Adam and Eve in their relation to Milton's God. The myth of Shaw's *Pygmalion* is that of Pygmalion and Galatea, but also that of Adam and Eve, though as a Shavian couple they are never to mate (at least in Shaw's interpretation). Shaw rewrote some aspects of his *Pygmalion* in the first play, *In the Beginning,* of his *Back to Methuselah* cycle. There Adam and Eve repeat, in a sadly less comedic tone, the contrast between Higgins and Eliza:

> ADAM: There is a voice in the garden that tells me things.
> EVE: The garden is full of voices sometimes. They put all sorts of thoughts into my head.
> ADAM: To me there is only one voice. It is very low; but it is so near that it is like a whisper from within myself. There is no mistaking it for any voice of the birds or beasts, or for your voice.
> EVE: It is strange that I should hear voices from all sides and you only one from within. But I have some thoughts that come from within me and not from the voices. The thought that we must not cease to be comes from within.

Like Adam, Higgins hears the inner voice only, which is the Miltonic response to reality. Eve, like Eliza, hears the voice of the Life Force. Yet Adam, like Higgins, is no slave to "system." They serve the same God as Eve and Eliza, but they cannot accommodate themselves to change even when they have brought about change, as Higgins has worked to develop Eliza, and wrought better than, at first, he has been able to know or to accept, or ever be able to accept fully.

The famous final confrontation of Higgins and Eliza is capable of several antithetical interpretations, which is a tribute to Shaw's dialectical cunning, as he too wrought better (perhaps) than he knew, but then he truly was a Pygmalion:

> HIGGINS [*wondering at her*]: You damned impudent slut, you! But it's better than snivelling; better than fetching slippers and finding spectacles, isn't it? [*Rising*] By George, Eliza, I said I'd make a woman of you; and I have. I like you like this.

LIZA: Yes: you turn round and make up to me now that I'm not afraid of you, and can do without you.

HIGGINS: Of course I do, you little fool. Five minutes ago you were like a millstone round my neck. Now youre a tower of strength: a consort battleship. You and I and Pickering will be three old bachelors instead of only two men and a silly girl.

Mrs Higgins returns, dressed for the wedding. Eliza instantly becomes cool and elegant.

MRS HIGGINS: The carriage is waiting, Eliza. Are you ready?

LIZA: Quite. Is the Professor coming?

MRS HIGGINS: Certainly not. He cant behave himself in church. He makes remarks out loud all the time on the clergyman's pronunciation.

LIZA: Then I shall not see you again, Professor. Goodbye. [*She goes to the door.*]

MRS HIGGINS [*coming to Higgins*]: Goodbye, dear.

HIGGINS: Goodbye, mother. [*He is about to kiss her, when he recollects something.*] Oh, by the way, Eliza, order a ham and a Stilton cheese, will you? And buy me a pair of reindeer gloves, number eights, and a tie to match that new suit of mine. You can choose the color. [*His cheerful, careless, vigorous voice shews that he is incorrigible.*]

LIZA [*disdainfully*]: Number eights are too small for you if you want them lined with lamb's wool. You have three new ties that you have forgotten in the drawer of your washstand. Colonel Pickering prefers double Gloucester to Stilton; and you dont notice the difference. I telephoned Mrs Pearce this morning not to forget the ham. What you are to do without me I cannot imagine. [*She sweeps out.*]

MRS HIGGINS: I'm afraid youve spoilt that girl, Henry. I should be uneasy about you and her if she were less fond of Colonel Pickering.

HIGGINS: Pickering! Nonsense: she's going to marry Freddy. Ha ha! Freddy! Freddy!! Ha ha ha ha ha!!!!! [*He roars with laughter as the play ends.*]

Shaw, in an epilogue to the play, married Eliza off to Freddy and maintained Higgins and Eliza in a perpetual transference, both positive and negative, in which Higgins took the place of her father, Doolittle:

That is all. That is how it has turned out. It is astonishing how much Eliza still manages to meddle in the housekeeping at Wimpole Street in spite of the shop and her own family. And it is notable that though she never nags her husband, and frankly loves the Colonel as if she were his favorite daughter, she has never got out of the habit of nagging Higgins that was established on the fatal night when she won his bet for him. She snaps his head off on the faintest provocation, or on none. He no longer dares to tease her by assuming an abysmal inferiority of Freddy's mind to his own. He storms and bullies and derides; but she stands up to him so ruthlessly that the Colonel has to ask her from time to time to be kinder to Higgins; and it is the only request of his that brings a mulish expression into her face. Nothing but some emergency or calamity great enough to break down all likes and dislikes, and throw them both back on their common humanity—and may they be spared any such trial!— will ever alter this. She knows that Higgins does not need her, just as her father did not need her. The very scrupulousness with which he told her that day that he had become used to having her there, and dependent on her for all sorts of little services, and that he should miss her if she went away (it would never have occurred to Freddy or the Colonel to say anything of the sort) deepens her inner certainty that she is "no more to him than them slippers"; yet she has a sense, too, that his indifference is deeper than the infatuation of commoner souls. She is immensely interested in him. She has even secret mischievous moments in which she wishes she could get him alone, on a desert island, away from all ties and with nobody else in the world to consider, and just drag him off his pedestal and see him making love like any common man. We all have private imaginations of that sort. But when it comes to business, to the life that she really leads as distinguished from the life of dreams and fancies, she likes Freddy and she likes the Colonel; and she does not like Higgins and Mr Doolittle. Galatea never does quite like Pygmalion: his relation to her is too godlike to be altogether agreeable.

Shaw is clearly Pygmalion-Higgins here, and Mrs. Patrick Campbell is Galatea-Eliza. Mrs. Campbell, the actress who first played Eliza, had jilted Shaw definitively the year before *Pygmalion* opened in London, thus ending their never-consummated love affair. The price of being the prophet of Creative Evolution, in art as in experience, is that you never do get to make love to the Life Force.

V

Saint Joan (1923) is a work written against its own literary age, the era of Proust, Joyce, Kafka, and above all others, Freud. It seems astonishing that *Saint Joan* is contemporary with Eliot's *The Waste Land* (1922). Eliot, whose own once-fashionable neo-Christianity now seems a refined super-stition, rejected Shaw with his customary generosity of spirit: "The potent ju-ju of the Life Force is a gross superstition." That might be Stagumber crying out as he drags Joan out to be burned in Shaw's play, but then Eliot had become more English than the English. Luigi Pirandello, Shaw's peer as dramatist (as Eliot was not; *Murder in the Cathedral* weirdly concludes with a blatant imitation of the end of *Saint Joan*) made the inevitably accurate comment on the play, which is that it could as well have been called *Saint Bernard Shaw:*

> Joan, at bottom, quite without knowing it, and still declaring herself a faithful daughter of the Church, is a Puritan, like Shaw himself—affirming her own life impulse, her unshakable, her even tyrannical will to live, by accepting death itself.

That "tyrannical will to live" is once again Shaw's revision of Schopenhauer by way of Ruskin and Lamarck—the only wealth is life, as Ruskin taught, and the will creatively modifies the evolution of life in the individual, as Shaw strongly misread Lamarck. Eric Bentley, always the brilliantly sympathetic defender of Shaw, reads *Saint Joan* as a triumphant resolution of Shaw's worn-out agon between system and vitality, between society and the individual, a resolution that is comprised of an exactly equal sympathy for the old antagonists. The sympathy cannot be denied, but the play is overwhelmingly Protestant and its rhetoric wars against its argu-ment, and so takes the side of Joan.

What precisely *is* Joan's religion, which is to ask: Can we make a coherent doctrine out of the religion of Bernard Shaw—his religion as a dramatist rather than as G. B. S. the polemicist and public personality? Did he indeed believe that what he called the Evolutionary Appetite was "the only surviving member of the Trinity," the Holy Spirit? Milton, Shaw's greatest precursor as exalter of the Protestant Will and its holy right of private judgment, had invoked that Spirit as one that descended, in prefer-

ence to all temples, in order to visit the pure and upright heart—of John
Milton in particular. We know how prophetically serious Milton was in this
declaration, and his sublime rhetoric persuades us to wrestle with his self-
election. But what are we to do with Shaw, whose rhetoric perhaps can
beguile us sometimes but never can persuade?

Joan, like Shaw, does very well without either God the Father or Jesus
Christ His Son. Though her ghost concludes the epilogue by addressing the
"God that madest this beautiful earth," she does not intend her auditor to
be the Jehovah of Genesis. Her initial divine reference in the play is to
"orders from my Lord," but immediately she tells us that "that is the will of
God that you are to do what He has put into my mind," which means that
her own will simply is the will of God. Since she is, like Shaw, an Anglo-Irish
Protestant, she never once invokes Jesus or His Mother. Instead, she listens
to the voices of "the blessed saints Catherine and Margaret, who speak to
me every day," and who might as well be girls from her own village. Her
battle cry is: "Who is for God and His Maid?" And her last words, before
she is pushed off stage to the stake, make clear that she is Shaw's substitute
for Jesus of Nazareth:

> His ways are not your ways. He wills that I go through the fire
> to His bosom; for I am His child, and you are not fit that I should
> live among you. This is my last word to you.

In the queer but effective *The Adventures of the Black Girl in Her
Search for God*, Shaw has his surrogate, whose "face was all intelligence,"
explain to the black girl his doctrine of work: "For we shall never be able
to bear His full presence until we have fulfilled all His purposes and become
gods ourselves. . . . If our work were done we should be of no further use:
that would be the end of us." Carlyle would have winced at our becoming
gods ourselves, but the gospel of labor remains essentially Carlyle's and
Ruskin's. Defending *The Black Girl* in a letter to a friendly but pugnacious
Abbess, Shaw associated himself with the prophet Micah and refused to
take as his idea of God "the anti-vegetarian deity who, after trying to
exterminate the human race by drowning it, was coaxed out of finishing the
job by a gorgeous smell of roast meat." That is good enough fun, but we
return to *Saint Joan* to ask a question that has nothing in common with the
Anglo-Catholic Eliot's indictment of a gross superstition. Vocabulary aside,
is Joan at all interested in God, any God at all? Is Shaw?

If the term "God" is to retain any crucial aspect of its Biblical range of
reference, then Joan and Shaw could not care less. The Life Force has no
personality, whereas Jehovah most certainly does, however uncomfortable

it makes us. Is Joan anything except an embodiment of the Life Force? Has Shaw endowed her with a personality? Alas, I think not. The play holds the stage, but that will not always be true. Shaw's rhetoric is not provident or strong enough to give us the representation of a coherent psychology in Joan. The figure of the first few scenes has nothing in common with the heroine who repudiates her own surrender at the trial, or with the shade of a saint who appears to the King of France in his dream that forms the epilogue. No development or unfolding authentically links the country girl with the martyr.

Shaw's bravura as a dramatist saves the play as a performance piece, but cannot make it into enduring literature. Its humor works; its caricatures amuse us; its ironies, though too palpable, provoke analysis and argument. But Joan, though she listens to voices, cannot change by listening to her own voice speaking, which is what even the minor figures in Shakespeare never fail to do. Creative Evolution, as a literary religion, could not do for Shaw what he could not do for himself. In *Saint Joan,* he fails at representing persons, since they are more than their ideas.

STANLEY WEINTRAUB

Introduction to Shaw

In his preface to *Man and Superman,* one of his most ambitious works, Bernard Shaw declared, "This is the true joy in life, the being used for a purpose recognized by yourself as a mighty one; the being thoroughly worn out before you are thrown on the scrap heap; the being a force of Nature instead of a feverish selfish little clod of grievances complaining that the world will not devote itself to making you happy." Practicing what he preached, Shaw lived his ninety-four years fully and forcefully. Beginning late as a playwright, he became nevertheless the most significant English dramatist since the seventeenth century, although the theatre was only one of his many careers. And he was more than the best comic dramatist of his time, for some of his greatest work for the stage has a high purpose and a prose beauty unmatched by his theatrical contemporaries. Among his other roles he was the most trenchant pamphleteer since Swift, the most readable music critic in English, the best theatre critic of his generation, a prodigious lecturer and essayist on politics, economics, religion, and society, and possibly the most prolific letter writer in literature. All of these facets of G. B. S.—and more—are illuminated in this volume.

Born in Dublin on July 26, 1856, G. B. S. was the third child and only son of the middle-aged George Carr Shaw and his young wife, Lucinda. Technically he belonged to the Protestant "ascendancy"—the landed Irish gentry—but his father (first a sinecured civil servant and then an unsuccessful corn merchant) was little more than an amiable drunkard, and young

---

From *The Portable Bernard Shaw,* edited by Stanley Weintraub. © 1977 by Viking Penguin, Inc.

Shaw grew up in a "downstart" atmosphere of genteel impecuniosity, which he felt was more humiliating than to be born poor and have pretensions to nothing more. After being tutored by a clerical uncle, he attended—briefly—both Protestant and Catholic day schools (the latter an experience repugnant to him in the extreme), and before he was sixteen he was working in a land agent's office, having derived his most practical education outside the classroom.

The Shaw ménage was a curious one. George Carr Shaw counted for little. His wife had turned for consolation not only to music, but also to her music teacher, George John Vandeleur Lee, a mesmeric figure in Irish music circles. By 1866 Lee shared a house in Dublin with the Shaws as well as a cottage on Dalkey Hill, overlooking Dublin Bay, a setting that provided the young Shaw with the beginnings of an aesthetic sensibility. Art he found in abundance at the National Gallery in Dublin, and music pervaded the household, since Lee trained singers and rehearsed operas and oratorios. Shaw absorbed what he could, often accompanying on the piano or acting as Lee's factotum. At the estate office of Uniacke Townshend, Shaw joylessly handled the collections and the accounts, and sang arias to relieve the tedium. Escape finally came when his mother and sisters abandoned George Carr Shaw in Dublin and followed Lee to London in 1875. Determined to make his way in literature, but not knowing how—except that London was the place in which to make the attempt—G. B. S. followed the next year.

In his twenties Shaw endured unrelieved frustration and poverty, yet he never became embittered. For a while he produced ghost-written musical criticism for Lee, but his only other job, which he found through an aunt late in 1879, was with the Edison Telephone Company of London. He seized the opportunity of the company's consolidation with a competing firm to leave in mid-1880, and this marked the end of his nonliterary employment. Living with his mother and elder sister Lucy (Agnes had died in 1876), he depended upon their pound a week from a family bequest, mailed from Dublin by George Carr Shaw, and his mother's earnings as a music teacher. He spent his days in the British Museum Reading Room, writing novels and reading what he had missed at school, and his nights in search of additional self-education through the free lectures and debates that characterized the intellectual ferment of contemporary middle-class London. And he became a vegetarian: such a diet was cheap and Shelley had subscribed to the philosophy. Eventually it became a passionate commitment.

Shaw's fiction failed, utterly. The semiautobiographical and aptly titled *Immaturity*, written in 1879 (but not published until 1930) was Shaw's own *David Copperfield*, with a flavor both reminiscent of Dickens and anticipatory of Gissing. Its sometimes sober, sometimes satirical evocation of the mid-Victorian milieu put off every publisher in London. The next four novels, similarly refused, soon padded out propagandist magazines edited by Shaw's socialist friends. *The Irrational Knot* (1880; serialized 1885–87) Shaw later pronounced a forerunner of Henrik Ibsen, of whom he had not yet heard, for the hero marries at the beginning and walks out on the heroine at the end. Its characters, hardly more than animated theories, were each endowed with an "original morality" that publishers' readers found "disagreeable," "perverse," and "crude." With half-hearted job hunting still fruitless, Shaw began *Love Among the Artists* (1881; serialized 1887–88), which reflected, in the neglect of "a British Beethoven" among dilettantes and mediocrities, Shaw's passionate belief in his own large talents and his frustration at being thwarted. Midway through the manuscript in 1881 he was stricken during a smallpox epidemic in London, but he stubbornly completed the unsalable novel and the next year began still another, *Cashel Byron's Profession* (1882; serialized 1885–86). Its exuberance belied Shaw's lack of success and its theme, "immoral" and "retrograde" professions—in this case, prizefighting—as an indictment of society, anticipated such early plays as *Mrs Warren's Profession*. In 1901 Shaw spoofed his own novel in a burlesque Elizabethan blank-verse adaptation which he called *The Admirable Bashville*.

The socialism in *Cashel Byron* was an afterthought, most of it daubed in for its appearance in a magazine after an 1882 lecture by the radical American economist Henry George had spurred him to a reading of Marx. Shaw was ready to become a socialist disciple, but found difficulty in selecting a group to join from among many splinter parties in London. Meanwhile, the new gospel became the stimulus for his last novel, *An Unsocial Socialist* (1883; serialized 1884). Intended as "a gigantic grapple with the whole social problem," it broke down under the weight of its incongruities, which included a runaway husband, a finishing school for girls, and ponderous paraphrases from *Das Kapital* among passages of sparkling Shavian dialogue. A fragment written and abandoned in 1887–88 was his final false start in fiction, except for a few minor short stories and a witty, *Candide*-like novella he wrote in 1932, *The Adventures of the Black Girl in Her Search for God*. His strength, he had discovered, lay in dialogue. He was not, he later announced, "a plot-monger."

The story of the Black Girl, told simply in fable fashion, came to Shaw as a result of his meeting in England with an authentic female missionary, and then finding himself in South Africa in the appropriate setting for his story; but it summed up his own attitude toward religions, and his own faith, more accessibly than he had ever done before. He reviewed the gods of man from Jehovah to Science, and closed with a blending of rationalism and mysticism which had appeared in his plays and his "lay sermons" and essays since the turn of the century. Despite its unconventional religion and some denunciations from English pulpits, it was a Christmas season best-seller.

Notwithstanding his early failure in fiction, the 1880s was the decade in which Shaw found himself. He became a spell-binding orator, a polemicist, even tentatively a playwright. He became the force behind the newly founded (1884) Fabian Society, a middle-class Socialist group which aimed at the transformation of English society not through revolution but through "permeation" (in Sidney Webb's term) of the nation's intellectual and political life. Adept at committee work, Shaw involved himself in every aspect of Fabian activities, most visibly as editor of what proved to be one of the classics of British radicalism, *Fabian Essays in Socialism* (1889), to which he also contributed two sections. Through the Fabians, too, he assisted at the birth of the Labour Party in 1893 and helped Fabian-supported candidates campaign in municipal and parliamentary elections.

Shaw's experience as a pamphleteer and platform speaker helped forge the forceful prose of his missionary books *The Quintessence of Ibsenism* (1891; revised 1913), *The Perfect Wagnerite* (1898), *The Sanity of Art* (1895; revised 1908), *The Common Sense of Municipal Trading* (1904; revised 1908)—the result of his years, from 1897–1903, as Vestryman and Borough Councillor of St. Pancras Parish, London)—and of his later tracts and polemics as well as the prefaces and dialogue for his plays. His John Tanner of *Man and Superman* was good-humored Shavian satire of this political aspect of himself. Although Tanner combined the personalities of socialist theoretician Sidney Webb and socialist agitator Henry Hyndman, Shaw's protagonist (the Don Juan of the "Interlude in Hell") also combined the Don Juan and the polemical sides of his creator. Tall, pale, and red-bearded, G. B. S. was a striking figure in a debate or on the stump, and for years he not only attended every public lecture he could within commuting distance of London, but also spoke without fee two or three times a week to groups of any political or religious persuasion interested in hearing him, often paying his own expenses to get there. According to Beatrice Webb, nearly every "advanced" female in London "worshipped at the Shavian shrine," for his romantic Irish wit and charm won those not captured by his dialectical skill or his ideas. And he spoke on street corners, in parks and public squares, at the docks, or in the traditional London halls where liberal or radical causes could be espoused, offering—usually from note cards—

extemporaneous treatises, lectures, and lay sermons on topics ranging from municipal reform to modern theology. In 1933, in his seventy-seventh year, Shaw gave his last public lecture—at the Metropolitan Opera House in New York, on a rare visit to the United States. "I regard the platform as obsolete," he told an interviewer; "the microphone's the thing. It is foolish to talk to a few hundred when you can talk to millions." By then he had already perfected his radio speaking style, which was warm and informal and directed at audiences of all ages and interests; one of his talks, entitled "School," was even intended for Sixth Form students. At ninety he gave his last B.B.C. broadcast—this time for television.

Although Shaw's journalism quickly became an extension of his platform role, he began writing book reviews in the *Pall Mall Gazette* (1885–88) and art criticism in the *World* (1886–88) because a young drama critic, William Archer, who became a lifelong friend, provided the contacts and because Shaw needed the bread-and-butter income. "I did not throw myself into the struggle for life," he once joked. "I threw my mother into it. I was not a staff to my father's old age: I hung on to his coat tails." Until his thirtieth year, he had lived off his mother's earnings as a music teacher while he struggled to make a career as a writer, and it was finally music that made the career possible, for Shaw finally found himself through brilliant, and often brilliantly digressive, musical columns in the *Star* (signed by "Corno di Bassetto"—basset horn) from 1888 to 1890 and in the *World* (as "G. B. S.") from 1890 to 1894. In his reviews, he confessed, he was always "electioneering. . . . Never in my life have I penned an impartial criticism; and I hope I never may." He campaigned for better music and better performances, and declared that "a criticism written without personal feeling is not worth reading. It is the capacity for making good or bad art a personal matter that makes a man a critic." But, he added, he went beyond personal feeling, for it was the "passion for artistic perfection—the noblest beauty of sight, sound and action—" that made him seem "diabolically unfair" to performers who were trying their best.

When Shaw transferred his attentions to the drama his strategy remained the same. "If my head had not been full of Ibsen and Wagner in the nineties," he confessed, "I should have been kinder and more reasonable in my demands. Also, perhaps, less amusing." Recruited by Frank Harris to the *Saturday Review* as a theatre critic (1895–98), Shaw carried on in its columns a campaign to displace the artificialities and hypocrisies of the Victorian stage (or "Sardoodledom" as he called it) with a theatre of vital ideas. It required also the unmasking of "Bardolatry," as Shaw described the pompous and reverential portrayal of Shakespeare, whom he admired beyond all other dramatists, but whose words, he insisted, were not holy writ but only lines for players to speak. It required a contemporary drama of wit and substance to replace the melodramas and farces which were the staple of the commercial theatre, but other than the comedies of Wilde and the dramas of Ibsen, there was little around which Shaw could rally.

With his talk about a "New Drama" threatening to conclude with the humiliating confession that in England, at least, modern theatre was "only a figment of the revolutionary imagination," Shaw determined that the situation could not be further endured: "I had rashly taken up the case; and rather than let it collapse I manufactured the evidence." That effort became his primary activity during the 1890s. The strain—for his critical and political work went on unabated—sapped his strength to such an extent, however, that a minor foot infection, haphazardly cared for in bachelor fashion, developed into necrosis of the bone and required serious surgery. Since playwriting had, by then, become more important to him than play criticism, the event provided him with an excuse for his "Valedictory" as drama columnist, a sprightly essay written from his bed and introducing his hand-picked successor, "the incomparable Max" Beerbohm, a young man in his middle twenties whose major piece of criticism had been two columns in the *Saturday Review* taking issue with Shaw's own *Mrs Warren's Profession*.

In 1898, during his recuperation, Shaw married his unofficial nurse, Charlotte Payne-Townshend (1857–1943), an Irish heiress and friend of Beatrice and Sidney Webb. It was an unusual marriage, for at Charlotte's insistence it remained unconsummated. Although the couple was childless, they established a series of surrogate-parent relationships, with such men as actors Granville Barker and Robert Loraine and writer-soldier T. E. Lawrence, which seemed to satisfy an otherwise unfulfilled need. As Shaw confessed to Frank Harris, he had been financially unable as a young man to maintain a mistress or a marriage and his sexual initiation, with an aggressive widow, did not occur until he was twenty-nine. After that time, he enjoyed a number of affairs (two simultaneous ones are satirized in his play *The Philanderer* which was written in 1893 but not performed until 1903), but eventually his passions subsided, concentrating themselves into female friendships which were mostly epistolary. The chief exception was his relationship with Mrs. Stella Patrick Campbell (1865–1940), the Eliza Doolittle of his *Pygmalion* in 1914. His ardor for Mrs. Campbell nearly wrecked his marriage in 1912. Thereafter, however, his correspondences cooled, concluding with an almost fatherly flirtation with American actress Molly Tompkins, which began when Shaw was nearly seventy, and a nearly brotherly one (in every sense of the word) with Sister Laurentia McLachlan, a Benedictine nun, which ended only with Shaw's death. As he wrote in the preface to a volume of his correspondence with actress Ellen Terry (1931), "only on paper has mankind ever yet achieved glory, beauty, truth, knowledge, virtue and abiding love."

The Shaws' marriage lasted until Charlotte's death in 1943. In many ways she had become a substitute mother who compensated for a childhood marked by neglect that G. B. S. in later years preferred to make light of rather than expose the wound, although his plays are replete with ineffective mothers—and fathers. When Charlotte died of a lingering illness, Shaw, who was frail and feeling the effects of World War II privations, made a permanent retreat from his apartment in bomb-wracked London to his country home at Ayot St. Lawrence, a village in Hertfordshire where he had lived since 1906. He died there at the age of 94 on November 2, 1950, having continued to write and to maintain the crusty "G. B. S." persona to the end.

"The Celebrated G. B. S.," Shaw once wrote, "is about as real as a pantomime ostrich. . . . I have played my game with a conscience. I have never pretended that G. B. S. was real: I have over and over again taken him to pieces before the audience to shew the trick of him." Yet having put on his jester's cap and bells to call attention to himself, he became the captive of his public reputation. The real Shaw, according to J. B. Priestley, "was courteous, kind, generous, shy rather than impudent, physically strong and courageous, yet rather timid and prudish in his relations with the world of food and drink, sex or hearty male companionship or conviviality, no dramatist for the Mermaid Tavern." Much of that real Shaw emerges in his private letters, which show a warm, waggish, witty human being, sometimes sentimental, often selfless, always sincere, whether his strategy utilized Irish blarney, Anglo-Saxon candor, or Shavian paradox. But G. B. S. to the outside world was ruthless as a critic, devastating in wit, irreverent about people, careless of feelings, impudent toward convention, iconoclastic toward institutions, hyperbolic for effect, cold-blooded about politics, secondhand as a thinker—a Mephistopheles-Machiavelli (as Andrew Undershaft in *Major Barbara* is charged) who boasted that he was better than Shakespeare. Few understood the humane vision that articulated what Shaw wrote and did better than his great friend and ideological opposite G. K. Chesterton, who still early in Shaw's career wrote, "Here was a man who could have enjoyed art among the artists, who could have been the wittiest of the flaneurs; who could have made epigrams like diamonds and drunk music like wine. He has instead labored in a mill of statistics and crammed his mind with all the most dreary and most filthy details, so that he can argue on the spur of the moment about sewing-machines or sewage, about typhus fever or two-penny tubes."

Although Shaw had been experimenting in the drama since his early twenties, not until William Archer suggested a collaboration in 1884 (he to supply the plot, G. B. S. the dialogue) did serious work begin. Even then the project was abandoned when Shaw used up all the projected plot in hardly more than half the play; but eight years later, in 1892, Shaw completed it on his own for J. T. Grein's fledgling Independent Theatre. *Widowers' Houses* had only two performances but created a newspaper sensation all out of proportion to its merits, for it was a dramatized socialist tract on slum landlordism redeemed in part by what Shaw had learned about ironic comedy from Ibsen and Dickens. The romantic predicament of the lovers (who find that both their incomes derive from exploitation of the poor) becomes an economic one and the "happy ending" in which they agree to live happily ever after on their tainted money could not please an audience expecting the threadbare sentimental conventions exploited even by the most daring new playwrights.

Unafraid to satirize himself, or even the new movements he championed, Shaw then in *The Philanderer* invented an "Ibsen Club" and ironically treated the "New Woman." But no one was willing to produce the play, and Shaw, undeterred, began a third, *Mrs Warren's Profession* (1893; performed 1902). This time the Lord Chamberlain as Censor of Plays refused it a license, although its ostensible subject, organized commercial prostitution, was treated remorselessly and without the titillation afforded by fashionable comedies about "fallen women" which long had been the West End's stock in trade. To make his seriousness certain, Shaw drew his Mrs Warren as a vulgarly flashy woman who found that being proprietor of her own body was more advantageous than sweating for a pittance in a factory or a pub, and turned her realization into a chain of profitable brothels. Her daughter Vivie, whose discovery of the facts behind her fashionable Newnham College education sets up the situation of the play, discovers, too, that she cannot look sentimentally for very long at daughterly duty or economic rationalizations. The result is a play with a sardonic thesis built upon the paradox of a form of prostitution meant to symbolize not just social and economic guilt but all the ways in which human beings prostitute their humanity for gain. Labeling as "unpleasant" three of the plays in his first collection, the two-volume edition *Plays, Pleasant and Unpleasant* (1898), Shaw explained that "their dramatic power is being used to force the spectator to face unpleasant facts. No doubt all plays which deal sincerely with humanity must wound the monstrous conceit which it is the business of romance to flatter."

The four "pleasant" plays of the companion volume were Shaw's attempt to find the producers and audiences his mordant comedies put off. "To me," he explained in the preface to the second volume, "[both] the tragedy and comedy of life lie in the consequences, sometimes terrible, sometimes ludicrous, of our persistent attempts to found our institutions on the ideals suggested to our imaginations by our half-satisfied passions, instead of on a genuinely scientific natural history." *Arms and the Man* (1894), in a spoof-Balkan setting, satirized romantic falsifications of love, war, and upward mobility, and was itself romanticized (unauthorized by Shaw) in the Oscar Straus operetta *Der tapfere Soldat* (1908), translated as *The Chocolate Soldier* (1909). *Candida* (1894; performed 1897) seemed to be a conventional comedy-drama about a husband, wife, and young interloper, complete with a happy ending in which the sanctity of the hearth is upheld and the interloper ejected into the night. Beneath the surface, however, the wife—who represents herself in a *tour de force* "auction scene" as being compelled to choose between her stuffy but high-minded clergyman husband (a well-meaning Christian Socialist) and a hysterical and immature young poet—chooses the best of all possible worlds for herself, and the poet renounces what Shaw later called "the small beer of domestic happiness" for the larger creative purpose he senses within himself. The two other "pleasant" plays were of lighter weight. The one-act *The Man of Destiny* (1895; performed 1897) Shaw described as "a bravura piece to display the virtuosity of two performers," but it was more than that. Shaw's antidote to the "older, coarser Napoleon" of earlier plays, this was his first study in greatness. In *You Never Can Tell* (1896; performed 1899) Shaw spun out his themes about parent-child relationships, the equality of women in society, and the power of the sex instinct—the latter bringing together an amorist of uncertain confidence and an impregnably rational New Woman.

Three Plays for Puritans (1901) packaged Shaw's continued output, again with what became the traditional Shavian preface—an introductory essay in an electric prose style dealing as much with the themes suggested by the plays as with the plays themselves. The texts of the plays, made available to the wider reading public for whom his plays were generally inaccessible even when produced, included—a Shaw innovation—stage directions and descriptions in narrative form rather than in brief directorial jargon. *The Devil's Disciple* (1896; performed 1897), a play set in New Hampshire during the American Revolution and written as an inversion of traditional Victorian melodrama, has been accepted by most audiences, eager to fulfill expectations, as authentic melodrama. Dick Dudgeon, however, the black sheep of his family because he rejects Puritan masochism and hypocrisy, appears to be heroically taking the place of a rebel minister whom the English condemn to the gallows, but he manages to do the right things for the wrong reasons. He acts, not in Sydney Carton fashion (Shaw's inspiration for the scene was the final episode of *A Tale of Two Cities*), out of love for the Rev. Anderson's wife, as she supposes, but spontaneously, out of some instinctive imperative. As with Caesar and other significant Shavian characters, virtue is a quality, not an achievement.

Caesar and Cleopatra (1898; performed 1901) was Shaw's first attempt at a play of Shakespearean scope for a heroic actor, in this case Sir Johnston Forbes-Robertson. By choosing a sixteen-year-old Cleopatra, rather than Shakespeare's thirty-eight-year-old temptress of Antony, and a Caesar in Egypt who has not yet been enticed into the domestic demagoguery against which Brutus reacts, Shaw seemingly evades the "Better than Shakespear?" challenge of his preface. His feline Cleopatra, however, is a logical precursor to Shakespeare's voluptuous one; and G. B. S.'s aging Caesar, as much philosopher as soldier in this mentor-disciple play, is meant to be a study in credible magnanimity and "original morality," rather than a superhuman hero on a stage pedestal—in Shaw's words, a hero "in whom we can recognize our own humanity." A serio-comic chronicle play which rises to prose-poetic eloquence and wisdom, it may be the best theatrical work written in English in the nineteenth century. Its companion piece in *Three Plays for Puritans, Captain Brassbound's Conversion* (1899; performed 1900), is subtitled "An Adventure" and appears to be little more than that. Here, too, however, are serious themes, particularly that of revenge as misplaced justice, lurking amid the musical-comedy plot about an aristocratic Englishwoman (a role written for Ellen Terry) among brigands in turn-of-the-century Morocco.

In *Man and Superman* (1901–02; performed 1905) Shaw "took the legend of Don Juan in its Mozartian form and made it a dramatic parable of Creative Evolution. But being then at the height of my invention and comedic talent, I decorated it too brilliantly and lavishly. I surrounded it with a comedy of which it formed only one act, and that act was so episodical (it was a dream which did not affect the action of the piece) that the comedy could be detached and played by itself. . . . Also I supplied the published work with an imposing framework consisting of a preface, an appendix called *The Revolutionist's Handbook*, and a final display of aphoristic fireworks. The effect was so vertiginous, apparently, that nobody noticed the new religion in the centre of the intellectual whirlpool." Although Henri Bergson's *Creative Evolution* (1907) was still unwritten, Shaw used the term in a Bergsonian sense to describe the purposeful and eternal movement toward ever higher organisms he saw to be a more satisfactory explanation of the nature of things than "blind" Darwinian evolution, and one which restored a sense of divinity to the universe besides. Subtitled "A Comedy and a Philosophy," the play on the surface is Shaw's equivalent to Congreve's *The Way of the World* (1700), even to a brilliant last-act proposal scene, a comedy of manners about the relations between the sexes in which a resourceful young woman, Ann Whitefield, determines to capture her man, the reluctant John Tanner, who is a social philosopher and socialist propagandist. The action provides the basis for a series of interlocking debates and discussions in which Shaw explored the intellectual climate of the new century. It provides, too, the frame for the nonrealistic third act "Don Juan in Hell" dream scene, often played separately and independently, in which mythic counterparts to four characters in *Man and Superman*, Don Juan Tenorio, Doña Ana, the Commander (Ana's father), and the Devil play out a dramatic quartet that is spoken theatre at its most operatic. Shaw's early operatic education at the hands of his mother and Lee never left him, nor did the effect of his years as a music critic, and he often not only cast his own plays according to the timbre of voice needed, but also shaped his scenes into recitatives, arias, and vocal ensembles. In the duets and arias of the Devil and Don Juan, twentieth-century literature for the stage attained a height in its first years that it would seldom reach again.

At W. B. Yeats's request, Shaw wrote *John Bull's Other Island* (1904) for the Abbey Theatre, Dublin, but the Abbey directors, worried about audience reaction to the wit and honesty of its picture of Ireland, used the excuse of casting difficulties to avoid producing it. Yet Shaw had written into this play of contemporary Anglo-Irish relations, for exhibition to an Irish audience, a comic Englishman as absurd as the comic Irishmen so often seen on the London stage in those days. Although its politics have become dated, the play when performed as a period piece remains a shrewd examination of the Irish character, as well as—in Father Keegan—one of Shaw's earliest explorations of the religious rebel as saint. While performances of his earlier plays in Central Europe had already established him on the continent as a major dramatist, it was the Vedrenne-Barker London production of *John Bull,* including a Command Performance for Edward VII, which finally established Shaw's stage reputation in England. He had backed John Vedrenne's and Harley Granville Barker's management of the Royal Court Theatre, Sloane Square, not only with his own capital but with his own plays as well, and in the years of their association (1904 through

1907), with Barker both acting and directing, a skilled repertory group grew up which gave Shavian drama many of its finest moments. His plays soon drew box-office receipts to such an extent that the Court management, while experimenting with the work of other contemporary dramatists, found it necessary to produce Shaw 701 times (in eleven plays) out of 988 total performances. He had arrived.

Through the medium of high comedy Shaw continued to explore the religious consciousness and to point out society's complicity in its own evils. In *Major Barbara* (written and performed in 1905), Barbara Undershaft, a major in the Salvation Army, discovers that her estranged father, a munitions manufacturer, may be a dealer in Death, but that his principles and practice, however unorthodox, are religious in the highest sense, while those of the Salvation Army require the hypocrisies of often-false public confession and the donations of the distillers and the armorers against which it piously inveighs. Indebted to Plato (*The Republic*) and Euripides (*The Bacchae*) as well as to dozens of other sources, including the lives of such contemporary armaments makers as Nobel and Krupp, it is one of Shaw's most intellectually complex plays, yet ironically also one of his most moving, particularly in its second-act Salvation Army shelter scene (peopled with Dickensian characters) in which Barbara recants her adopted faith.

With his place in the English theatre secure, Shaw began shifting after *Major Barbara* to theatrical experiments already foreshadowed in earlier plays. In *The Doctor's Dilemma* (1906), he produced a comedy with a serio-comic death scene, a satire upon the medical profession (representing the self-protection of professions in general) and upon both the artistic temperament and the public's inability to separate it from the artist's achievement. If Shaw failed to create a convincing artistic genius in the tubercular and double-dealing painter Louis Dubedat, it may be not that he could not depict one, but rather that he aimed at depicting the self-advertising frauds who use the license of "genius" to bilk a world baffled by the artistic temperament.

Other plays of the prewar period ranged from self-described potboilers to an attempt to create a discussion-drama which might best be described as serious farce. *Getting Married* (1907–8), *Misalliance* (1909; performed 1910), and *Fanny's First Play* (1911) are examples of the genre—dramatized debates on marriage, parents and children, and women's rights, respectively. *Misalliance* has since shown remarkable vivacity in revival as a period farce, while the thinner *Fanny's First Play* set a first-run box-office record unequaled by any other Shavian play—622 performances. *The Shewing-up of Blanco Posnet* (1909), set in an improbable American "Wild

West," concerned the conversion of a horse thief, aptly subtitled "A Sermon in Crude Melodrama." *Androcles and the Lion* (1912) more successfully handled true and false religious exaltation, combining the traditions of miracle play and Christmas pantomime and transforming the fable of the Greek slave and the Roman lions into a philosophical farce about early Christianity. Its central theme—recurrent in Shaw—is that one must have something worth dying for, a purpose outside oneself, in order to make life worth living. Lavinia, its heroine—like Father Keegan and Barbara Undershaft before her—is a step toward Shaw's Joan of Arc.

Pygmalion (1912; first performed 1913 in Vienna) was claimed by Shaw to be a didactic play about phonetics, and its anti-heroic middle-aged hero, Henry Higgins, is a fanatical phonetician; however, the play is a high and humane comedy about love and class and human dignity—the story of a Cockney flower girl trained to pass as a lady and of the repercussions of the "experiment's" success. Possibly Shaw's comedic masterpiece, and certainly his funniest and most popular play, *Pygmalion* has been both filmed (1938), winning an Academy Award for Shaw (who wrote the screenplay), and turned into a musical, in 1956, as *My Fair Lady*.

The play's London success in 1914 outraged as well as delighted Shaw. Sir Herbert Beerbohm Tree, the Henry Higgins of the production, having played a lifetime of romantic endings, had devised a way to distort Shaw's ironic and ambiguous conclusion without altering a word; in the interval between the last lines of the play and the last lowering of the curtain he would provide by demonstrative affection for Eliza a broad hint that matrimony was in store for the professor and his pupil. Shaw was furious at the Cinderella suggestion and wrote to Tree telling him what he thought of the performance. "My ending makes money; you ought to be grateful," Tree answered smugly. Shaw fired back, "Your ending is damnable: you ought to be shot." And to prevent future fairy-tale endings Shaw wrote an unsentimental short-story epilogue for the published play which "proved" that Eliza would marry the weak Freddy Eynsford Hill and open a successful flower shop with money proffered from Colonel Pickering. "It does not follow in the least," Shaw defended himself to his Edinburgh printer, William Maxwell, nearly twenty years later, "that Liza and Higgins were sexually insensible to each other, or that their sensibility took the form of repugnance . . . ; but the fact stands that their marriage would have been a revolting tragedy and that the marriage with Freddy is the natural and happy ending to the story." But no one acts an undramatized prose epilogue, and Shaw's bittersweet ending to the actual play leaves the Higgins-Eliza relationship more dramatically at its appropriate—and unsettled—point.

The 1914–18 war, which followed immediately upon the success of *Pygmalion*, was a watershed for Shaw. At first he stopped writing plays, producing instead in the first days of the war a lengthy Swiftian pamphlet, *Common Sense About the War* (1914), which called Britain and its allies equally culpable with the Germans and which argued for negotiation and peace. It sold more than 75,000 copies and made him internationally notorious. "It is an established tradition," Shaw wrote years afterward, that he was "a pro-German, a Pacifist, a Defeatist, a Conscientious Objector, and everything that any enemy of his country can be without being actually shot as a traitor. Nothing could be more absolutely wide of the truth." The common sense of his, and similar, arguments prevailed only when the nation was ground down by astronomical—and futile—casualties and home-front austerities, but until 1917 unreason reigned, even to the extent that some of his antiwar speeches were erased from history by newspaper censorship, and he himself was ejected from the Dramatists' Club, although he was its most distinguished member. As the tide of public opinion turned, the Government's measure of Shaw's usefulness shifted as well, and in early 1917 he was even invited to Flanders to report from the front (*Daily Sketch*, March 6–8, 1917, reprinted in *What I Really Wrote About the War*, 1931). By the end of the war he was not that persecuted but proud figure, a major prophet whom his own people refused to honor, but a confirmed oracle, a prophet who had survived into his own time. Explaining the metamorphosis, T. S. Eliot afterward remarked that "it might have been predicted that what he said then would not seem so subversive or blasphemous now. The public has accepted Mr. Shaw not by recognizing the intelligence of what he said then, but by forgetting it; we must not forget that at one time Mr. Shaw was a very unpopular man. He is no longer the gadfly of the commonwealth; but even if he has never been appreciated, it is something that he should be respected."

The unforgetful Shaw translated his experience of 1914–18 (including a Zeppelin raid) into a dozen plays, sometimes defiantly, sometimes unobtrusively. *Heartbreak House* (written 1916–17; performed 1920) became the classic Shavian presentation of the spiritual bankruptcy of the generation responsible for the war, a departure for him in that he combined high discursive comedy with an almost Strindbergian symbolism, producing a somber vision owing much in mood to Chekhov's *Cherry Orchard* while owing its elderly leading figure, as well as much else, to Shakespeare's *Lear*. Captain Shotover is eighty-eight and half mad; and although he tries to recall the heroine from a cynical despair induced by disillusioned love, his own sense of foreboding (he warns that the country must "learn navigation") is expressed in his having turned his skills as an inventor to military uses. At the end there is an air raid which causes casualties and destruction, yet there is no other sign (except for a character playing several bars of "Keep the Home Fires Burning" on his flute in the last act) that the action takes place in wartime. The drama's culminating horror lies, however, not in exploding bombs, but in the comments of two jaded and once lovesick women at the curtain, one saying of the unseen and anonymous raiders in the sky, "But what a glorious experience! I hope they'll come again tomorrow night," and the other (*"radiant at the prospect,"* in Shaw's stage directions) agreeing, "Oh, I hope so." Thanatos has replaced Eros.

Back to Methuselah (1918–20; performed 1922) was Shaw's attempt to keep from falling into "the bottomless pit of an utterly discouraging pessimism." A cycle of five linked plays (*In the Beginning, The Gospel of the Brothers Barnabas, The Thing Happens, The Tragedy of an Elderly Gentleman, As Far as Thought Can Reach*), it created a parable of "Creative Evolution" which progresses from the Garden of Eden to A.D. 31,920, a "Metabiological Pentateuch" which drew imaginatively upon Genesis, Plato, Swift, and dozens of other sources, including the war in progress (all but the last part was begun before 1918), with the aim of creating a work of the magnitude of Wagner's *Ring*. The first and most poetic play, from Adam and Eve (and the Serpent) to Cain and Abel, dramatizes the need to overcome death by the renewal of birth, and the need to have aspirations beyond mere subsistence. (Serpent: "You see things; and say "Why?' But I dream things that never were; and I say "Why not?' ") Cain, having killed his brother and resenting his plodding father, discovers that he does not know what he wants "except that I want to be something higher and nobler than this stupid old digger." "Man need not always live by bread alone," says Eve. "There is something else." Finding the something else—and the means to it—motivates the cycle.

The second part takes place in the years just after the First World War, and is an indictment of the generation that created the war ("Burge" is Lloyd George, and "Lubin" is Asquith). But in it, too, Conrad Barnabas makes the discovery that sufficient longevity to learn from experience— perhaps three hundred years—might be willed. (The superman is here no longer thought of as attainable through eugenic breeding, Shaw's earlier thesis, and comes with a leap in the third play.) Two undistinguished characters from the second play prove to be still alive in A.D. 2170, and longevity has given them wisdom. In the fourth play, set in A.D. 3000, an elderly gentleman from the now-shrinking race of short-livers confronts the conflicting manners and motives of the passionless and ascetic long-livers, who possess extraordinary powers over nature, but—to the Gentleman—no soul. Nevertheless, although he is warned that he will very likely die of discouragement, he wants to remain in the land of his ancestors (the scene is the shore of Galway Bay), rather than return to the distant land in which his vanishing breed is confined. "If I go back," he pleads, like Gulliver among the Houyhnmnmns, "I will die of disgust and despair. . . . It is the meaning of life, not of death, that makes banishment so terrible to me." He stays, and dies. In the remote fifth play, with its science-fiction overtones, humans are born fully developed from eggs and live lives of contemplative ecstasy achieved through creative use of intellect after a brief adolescent phase of physical pleasure. Through satire which ranges from bright to bleak and through his futuristic characters, Shaw had progressed from examining in the first plays how mankind had found itself in its present predicament to speculating in the closing parts of the cycle about the uncertain values of escaping from "this machinery of flesh and blood." An uneven work, it is compounded of the prosaic as well as the poetic, and it is dated as well as enlarged by the topical references in the middle plays. *Back to Methuselah* is nevertheless ennobling in vision although awkward as a total theatre experience.

Convinced that the long cycle had exhausted his creative energies, Shaw anticipated, as he approached seventy, that he had ended his career as a playwright; however, the canonization of Joan of Arc in 1920 had reawakened within him ideas for a chronicle play about the warrior saint which had never quite been abandoned. For G. B. S. it would not have been enough to depict Joan as the sentimental heroine of a melodrama arrayed against a stage full of stock villains. Neither the militant nor the martyr in Joan were as important to him as her symbolizing the possibilities of the race. Thus for Shaw, the Maid is not only Catholic saint and martyr but Shavian saint and martyr, a combination of practical mystic, heretical saint, and inspired genius. For this reason Shaw made the conflict as irreconcilable as did Sophocles in his *Antigone*. To give Joan's greatness of soul credibility he had to make her adversaries credible, which meant that Shaw—with more courage than the Vatican itself—had to rehabilitate Cauchon and his clerical colleagues much as Joan herself had been rehabilitated nearly five centuries earlier. As Hegel—whom Shaw had read—suggested, the truly tragic is not to be found in the conflict between right and wrong, but in that between right and right. Joan as the superior being (in the Inquisitor's words), "crushed between those mighty forces, the Church and the Law," is the personification of the tragic heroine, but to Shaw it was not sufficient for his theme. Tragedy was not enough: thus the Epilogue begins with Shavian wit and moves inexorably to litany, transforming the play from a tragedy of inevitability to the embodiment of the paradox that human-kind fears—and often kills—its saints and its heroes and will go on doing so until the very qualities it fears become the general condition of man.

Acclaim for *Saint Joan* (1923; performed 1924) resulted in a Shavian apotheosis. Even the Nobel Prize committee could no longer look away, and Shaw received the Prize for Literature in 1925, an honor almost certainly given because of *Joan*. To the consternation of the grantors, he wrote to the Royal Swedish Academy to "discriminate between the award and the prize. For the award I have nothing but my best thanks. But after the most careful consideration I cannot persuade myself to accept the money. My readers and audiences provide me with more than sufficient money for my needs; and as to my renown it is greater than is good for my spiritual health. Under these circumstances the money is a lifebelt thrown to a swimmer who has already reached the shore in safety."

The dream-epilogue to *Saint Joan* had continued Shaw's explorations into tragicomic and nonrealistic symbolism. His last fourteen plays would intensify this aspect of his work, which involved broad, caricatured impersonations, sometimes of Aristophanic extravagance, on which Shaw based a theatre of disbelief. These characterizations were deliberately designed to destroy Ibsenesque verisimilitude by regularly reminding the audience that these were performances in a theatre, not life in a three-walled room or realistic exterior.

During a six-year theatrical silence Shaw worked on his Collected Edition of 1930–38 and the encyclopedic *Intelligent Woman's Guide to Socialism, Capitalism, Sovietism, and Fascism* (1928), an idiosyncratic essay on political economy replete with ironic Shavian asides on education, marriage, religion, law, population, patriotism—and himself. The emphasis upon government led to his Platonic "political extravaganza" *The Apple Cart* (1928; performed 1929), a futuristic comedy which emphasized Shavian inner conflicts between his lifetime of radical politics and his essentially conservative mistrust of the common man's ability to govern himself. Later plays even included apocalyptic imagery, Shaw warning that the 1914–18 war was about to be repeated. The deliberately absurd *Too True to be Good* (1931; performed 1932) is a dream-fantasy including a Bunyanesque prophet, a Lawrence of Arabia caricature, and a burglar-turned-preacher who (as the curtain closes upon him) suggests Shaw confronting his own obsolescence. *On the Rocks* (1933) predicts the collapse of parliamentary government in a proto-fascist, depression-ridden England. *The Simpleton of the Unexpected Isles* (1934; performed 1935), in a futuristic South Seas setting, satirizes a eugenic solution to human problems and ends with a spoof Day of Judgment. *The Millionairess* (1932–34; performed 1936), a "Jonsonian comedy" according to the subtitle, is a knockabout farce which probes the human type of "born boss," while *Geneva* (1936–38; revised 1947) translates the problem into contemporary political terms, lampooning the futile League of Nations as well as dictators Hitler, Mussolini, and Franco, all of whom appear on the stage under nearly invisible disguises. That the despots are treated so lightly suggests that Shaw's flirtation with dictatorships, which arose out of his 1914–18 disillusionment with democracies, was slow in dying, the one with Stalin stubbornly enduring to the end. *In Good King Charles's Golden Days* (1938–39), his last prewar play, is a throwback to the mood of *The Apple Cart,* a warm yet discursive high comedy in which Charles II, Newton, Fox, Nell Gwynn, and others in "a true history which never happened" debate leadership, science, art, and religion. Eloquent, humorous, and intermittently moving, it dwells further upon the major preoccupation of Shaw's final period. "The riddle of how to choose a ruler is still unanswered," says Charles, "and it is the riddle of civilization." As a result, at eighty-eight he published his final long tract, the discursive yet incisive and aptly named *Everybody's Political What's What* (1944).

After a second wartime stage hiatus Shaw produced several plays in his nineties. *Buoyant Billions* (begun 1936–1937; completed 1945–47; performed 1948), subtitled "a comedy of no manners," concerned the peregrinations of Junius, a self-styled "world-betterer." *Farfetched Fables* (1948; performed 1950) is a farce in six short scenes, in which Shaw attempted to see into a timeless future which, in his post-atomic outlook, is much different from that envisioned in the *As Far as Thought Can Reach* finale of *Back to Methuselah.*

Shakes versus Shav (1949) is a brief puppet play in which the two playwrights confront each other and gently challenge the greatness of each other's works, Shaw reaffirming his once-shaken evolutionary optimism in the face of Shakespeare's alleged pessimism. They even debate each other's lines, as Aristophanes in *The Frogs* once toyed with Aeschylus and Euripides. Still, at the curtain, "Shav" appeals, "Peace, jealous Bard:/We are both mortal. For a moment suffer/My glimmering light to shine." A last playlet, *Why She Would Not* (1950), a fantasy with flashes of the earlier Shaw in evidence, combines the "born boss" theme with the duel of sex, but has more historical than dramatic interest. As G. B. S. had written in the preface to *Buoyant Billions,* "As long as I live I must write." He did.

Visiting Shaw's house at Ayot St. Lawrence on behalf of the National

Trust, to which G. B. S. had willed it, Sir Harold Nicolson was dubious about the government's accepting the unpretentious former rectory. "I am not happy about it," he noted in his diary. "I do not think that Shaw will be a great literary figure in 2000 A.D." But despite that glum prediction in 1950, Bernard Shaw's "glimmering light" is likely to illuminate stages—and minds—well into the next century, and after.

G. K. CHESTERTON

The Critic

It may often be remarked that mathematicians love and understand music more than they love or understand poetry. Bernard Shaw is in much the same condition; indeed, in attempting to do justice to Shakespeare's poetry, he always calls it "word music." It is not difficult to explain this special attachment of the mere logician to music. The logician, like every other man on earth, must have sentiment and romance in his existence; in every man's life, indeed, which can be called a life at all, sentiment is the most solid thing. But if the extreme logician turns for his emotions to poetry, he is exasperated and bewildered by discovering that the words of his own trade are used in an entirely different meaning. He conceives that he understands the word "visible," and then finds Milton applying it to darkness, in which nothing is visible. He supposes that he understands the word "hide," and then finds Shelley talking of a poet hidden in the light. He has reason to believe that he understands the common word "hung"; and then William Shakespeare, Esquire, of Stratford-on-Avon, gravely assures him that the tops of the tall sea waves were hung with deafening clamours on the slippery clouds. That is why the common arithmetician prefers music to poetry. Words are his scientific instruments. It irritates him that they should be anyone else's musical instruments. He is willing to see men juggling, but not men juggling with his own private tools and possessions—his terms. It is then that he turns with an utter relief to music. Here is all the same fascination and inspiration, all the same purity and plunging force as in poetry; but not requiring any verbal confession that light conceals things or that

From *George Bernard Shaw*. © 1910 by Devin Adair Publishers, Inc. Hill & Wang, 1956.

darkness can be seen in the dark. Music is mere beauty; it is beauty in the abstract, beauty in solution. It is a shapeless and liquid element of beauty, in which a man may really float, not indeed affirming the truth, but not denying it. Bernard Shaw, as I have already said, is infinitely far above all such mere mathematicians and pedantic reasoners; still his feeling is partly the same. He adores music because it cannot deal with romantic terms either in their right or their wrong sense. Music can be romantic without reminding him of Shakespeare and Walter Scott, with whom he has had personal quarrels. Music can be Catholic without reminding him verbally of the Catholic Church, which he has never seen, and is sure he does not like. Bernard Shaw can agree with Wagner, the musician, because he speaks without words; if it had been Wagner the man he would certainly have had words with him. Therefore I would suggest that Shaw's love of music (which is so fundamental that it must be mentioned early, if not first, in his story) may itself be considered in the first case as the imaginative safety-valve of the rationalistic Irishman.

This much may be said conjecturally over the present signature; but more must not be said. Bernard Shaw understands music so much better than I do that it is just possible that he is, in that tongue and atmosphere, all that he is not elsewhere. While he is writing with a pen I know his limitations as much as I admire his genius; and I know it is true to say that he does not appreciate romance. But while he is playing on the piano he may be cocking a feather, drawing a sword or draining a flagon for all I know. While he is speaking I am sure that there are some things he does not understand. But while he is listening (at the Queen's Hall) he may understand everything including God and me. Upon this part of him I am a reverent agnostic; it is well to have some such dark continent in the character of a man of whom one writes. It preserves two very important things—modesty in the biographer and mystery in the biography.

For the purpose of our present generalisation it is only necessary to say that Shaw, as a musical critic, summed himself up as "The Perfect Wagnerite"; he threw himself into subtle and yet trenchant eulogy of that revolutionary voice in music. It was the same with the other arts. As he was a Perfect Wagnerite in music, so he was a Perfect Whistlerite in painting; so above all was a perfect Ibsenite in drama. And with this we enter that part of his career with which this book is more specially concerned. When Mr. William Archer got him established as dramatic critic of the *Saturday Review,* he became for the first time "a star of the stage"; a shooting star and sometimes a destroying comet.

On the day of that appointment opened one of the very few exhilarating and honest battles that broke the silence of the slow and cynical collapse of the nineteenth century. Bernard Shaw the demagogue had got his cart and his trumpet; and was resolved to make them like the car of destiny and the trumpet of judgment. He had not the servility of the ordinary rebel, who is content to go on rebelling against kings and priests, because such rebellion is as old and as established as any priests or kings. He cast about him for something to attack which was not merely powerful or placid, but was unattacked. After a little quite sincere reflection, he found it. He would not be content to be a common atheist; he wished to blaspheme something in which even atheists believed. He was not satisfied with being revolutionary; there were so many revolutionists. He wanted to pick out some prominent institution which had been irrationally and instinctively accepted by the most violent and profane; something of which Mr. Foote would speak as respectfully on the front page of the *Freethinker* as Mr. St. Loe Strachey on the front page of the *Spectator*. He found the thing; he found the great unassailed English institution—Shakespeare.

But Shaw's attack on Shakespeare, though exaggerated for the fun of the thing, was not by any means the mere folly or firework paradox that has been supposed. He meant what he said; what was called his levity was merely the laughter of a man who enjoyed saying what he meant—an occupation which is indeed one of the greatest larks in life. Moreover, it can honestly be said that Shaw did good by shaking the mere idolatry of Him of Avon. That idolatry was bad for England; it buttressed our perilous self-complacency by making us think that we alone had, not merely a great poet, but the one poet above criticism. It was bad for literature; it made a minute model out of work that was really a hasty and faulty masterpiece. And it was bad for religion and morals that there should be so huge a terrestrial idol, that we should put such utter and unreasoning trust in any child of man. It is true that it was largely through Shaw's own defects that he beheld the defects of Shakespeare. But it needed some one equally prosaic to resist what was perilous in the charm of such poetry; it may not be altogether a mistake to send a deaf man to destroy the rock of the sirens.

This attitude of Shaw illustrates of course all three of the divisions or aspects to which the reader's attention has been drawn. It was partly the attitude of the Irishman objecting to the Englishman turning his mere artistic taste into a religion; especially when it was a taste merely taught him by his aunts and uncles. In Shaw's opinion (one might say) the English do not really enjoy Shakespeare or even admire Shakespeare; one can only say, in the strong colloquialism, that they swear by Shakespeare. He is a mere god; a thing to be invoked. And Shaw's whole business was to set up the

things which were to be sworn by as things to be sworn at. It was partly
again the revolutionist in pursuit of pure novelty, hating primarily the oppression of the past, almost hating history itself. For Bernard Shaw the
prophets were to be stoned after, and not before, men had built their sep-
ulchres. There was a Yankee smartness in the man which was irritated at the
idea of being dominated by a person dead for three hundred years; like
Mark Twain, he wanted a fresher corpse.

These two motives there were, but they were small compared with the
other. It was the third part of him, the Puritan, that was really at war with
Shakespeare. He denounced that playwright almost exactly as any contemporary Puritan coming out of a conventicle in a steeple-crowned hat and
stiff bands might have denounced the playwright coming out of the stage
door of the old Globe Theatre. This is not a mere fancy; it is philosophically
true. A legend has run round the newspapers that Bernard Shaw offered
himself as a better writer than Shakespeare. This is false and quite unjust;
Bernard Shaw never said anything of the kind. The writer who he did say
was better than Shakespeare was not himself, but Bunyan. And he justified
it by attributing to Bunyan a virile acceptance of life as a high and harsh
adventure, while in Shakespeare he saw nothing but profligate pessimism,
the *vanitas vanitatum* of a disappointed voluptuary. According to this view
Shakespeare was always saying, "Out, out, brief candle," because he was
only a ballroom candle; while Bunyan was seeking to light such a candle as
by God's grace should never be put out.

It is odd that Bernard Shaw's chief error or insensibility should have
been the instrument of his noblest affirmation. The denunciation of
Shakespeare was a mere misunderstanding. But the denunciation of
Shakespeare's pessimism was the most splendidly understanding of all his
utterances. This is the greatest thing in Shaw, a serious optimism—even a
tragic optimism. Life is a thing too glorious to be enjoyed. To be is an
exacting and exhausting business; the trumpet though inspiring is terrible.
Nothing that he ever wrote is so noble as his simple reference to the sturdy
man who stepped up to the Keeper of the Book of Life and said, "Put down
my name, Sir." It is true that Shaw called this heroic philosophy by wrong
names and buttressed it with false metaphysics; that was the weakness of
the age. The temporary decline of theology had involved the neglect of
philosophy and all fine thinking; and Bernard Shaw had to find shaky
justifications in Schopenhauer for the sons of God shouting for joy. He
called it the Will to Live—a phrase invented by Prussian professors who
would like to exist, but can't. Afterwards he asked people to worship the
Life-Force; as if one could worship a hyphen. But though he covered it with

crude new names (which are now fortunately crumbling everywhere like bad mortar) he was on the side of the good old cause; the oldest and the best of all causes, the cause of creation against destruction, the cause of yes against no, the cause of the seed against the stony earth and the star against the abyss.

His misunderstanding of Shakespeare arose largely from the fact that he is a Puritan, while Shakespeare was spiritually a Catholic. The former is always screwing himself up to see truth; the latter is often content that truth is there. The Puritan is only strong enough to stiffen; the Catholic is strong enough to relax. Shaw, I think, has entirely misunderstood the pessimistic passages of Shakespeare. They are flying moods which a man with a fixed faith can afford to entertain. That all is vanity, that life is dust and love is ashes, these are frivolities, these are jokes that a Catholic can afford to utter. He knows well enough that there is a life that is not dust and a love that is not ashes. But just as he may let himself go more than the Puritan in the matter of enjoyment, so he may let himself go more than the Puritan in the matter of melancholy. The sad exuberances of Hamlet are merely like the glad exuberances of Falstaff. This is not conjecture; it is the text of Shakespeare. In the very act of uttering his pessimism, Hamlet admits that it is a mood and not the truth. Heaven *is* a heavenly thing, only to him it seems a foul congregation of vapours. Man *is* the paragon of animals, only to him he seems a quintessence of dust. Hamlet is quite the reverse of a sceptic. He is a man whose strong intellect believes much more than his weak temperament can make vivid to him. But this power of knowing a thing without feeling it, this power of believing a thing without experiencing it, this is an old Catholic complexity, and the Puritan has never understood it. Shakespeare confesses his moods (mostly by the mouths of villains and failures), but he never sets up his moods against his mind. His cry of *vanitas vanitatum* is itself only a harmless vanity. Readers may not agree with my calling him Catholic with a big C; but they will hardly complain of my calling him catholic with a small one. And that is here the principal point. Shakespeare was not in any sense a pessimist; he was, if anything, an optimist so universal as to be able to enjoy even pessimism. And this is exactly where he differs from the Puritan. The true Puritan is not squeamish: the true Puritan is free to say "Damn it!" But the Catholic Elizabethan was free (on passing provocation) to say "Damn it all!"

It need hardly be explained that Bernard Shaw added to his negative case of a dramatist to be depreciated a corresponding affirmative case of a dramatist to be exalted and advanced. He was not content with so remote a comparison as that between Shakespeare and Bunyan. In his vivacious weekly articles in the *Saturday Review*, the real comparison upon which everything turned was the comparison between Shakespeare and Ibsen. He early threw himself with all possible eagerness into the public disputes about the great Scandinavian; and though there was no doubt whatever about which side he supported, there was much that was individual in the line he took. It is not our business here to explore that extinct volcano. You may say that anti-Ibsenism is dead, or you may say that Ibsen is dead; in any case, that controversy is dead, and death, as the Roman poet says, can alone confess of what small atoms we are made. The opponents of Ibsen largely exhibited the permanent qualities of the populace; that is, their instincts were right and their reasons wrong. They made the complete controversial mistake of calling Ibsen a pessimist; whereas, indeed, his chief weakness is a rather childish confidence in mere nature and freedom, and a blindness (either of experience or of culture) in the matter of original sin. In this sense Ibsen is not so much a pessimist as a highly crude kind of optimist. Nevertheless the man in the street was right in his fundamental instinct, as he always is. Ibsen, in his pale Northern style, is an optimist; but for all that he is a depressing person. The optimism of Ibsen is less comforting than the pessimism of Dante; just as a Norwegian sunrise, however splendid, is colder than a Southern night.

But on the side of those who fought for Ibsen there was also a disagreement, and perhaps also a mistake. The vague army of "the advanced" (an army which advances in all directions) were united in feeling that they ought to be the friends of Ibsen because he also was advancing somewhere somehow. But they were also seriously impressed by Flaubert, by Oscar Wilde and all the rest who told them that a work of art was in another universe from ethics and social good. Therefore many, I think most, of the Ibsenites praised the Ibsen plays merely as *choses vues,* æsthetic affirmations of what can be without any reference to what ought to be. Mr. William Archer himself inclined to this view, though his strong sagacity kept him in a haze of healthy doubt on the subject. Mr. Walkley certainly took this view. But this view Mr. George Bernard Shaw abruptly and violently refused to take.

With the full Puritan combination of passion and precision he informed everybody that Ibsen was not artistic, but moral; that his dramas were didactic, that all great art was didactic, that Ibsen was strongly on the side of some of his characters and strongly against others, that there was preaching and public spirit in the work of good dramatists; and that if this were not so, dramatists and all other artists would be mere panders of intellectual debauchery, to be locked up as the Puritans locked up the stage players. No one can understand Bernard Shaw who does not give full value to this early revolt of his on behalf of ethics against the ruling school of *l'art pour l'art.* It is interesting because it is connected with other ambitions in the man, especially with that which has made him somewhat vainer of being a Parish Councillor than of being one of the most popular dramatists in Europe. But its chief interest is again to be referred to our stratification of the psychology; it is the lover of true things rebelling for once against merely new things; it is the Puritan suddenly refusing to be the mere Progressive.

But this attitude obviously laid on the ethical lover of Ibsen a not inconsiderable obligation. If the new drama had an ethical purpose, what was it? and if Ibsen was a moral teacher, what the deuce was he teaching? Answers to this question, answers of manifold brilliancy and promise, were scattered through all the dramatic criticisms of those years on the *Saturday Review.* But Bernard Shaw had already dealt with these things somewhat more systematically before he began to discuss Ibsen only in connection with the current pantomime or the latest musical comedy. It is best in this matter to turn back to a previous summary. In 1891 had appeared the brilliant book called *The Quintessence of Ibsenism,* which some have declared to be merely the quintessence of Shaw. However this may be, it was in fact and profession the quintessence of Shaw's theory of the morality or propaganda of Ibsen.

The book itself is much longer than the book that I am writing; and as is only right in so spirited an apologist, every paragraph is provocative. I could write an essay on every sentence which I accept and three essays on every sentence which I deny. Bernard Shaw himself is a master of compression; he can put a conception more compactly than any other man alive. It is therefore rather difficult to compress his compression; one feels as if one were trying to extract a beef essence from Bovril. But the shortest form in which I can state the idea of *The Quintessence of Ibsenism* is that it is the idea of distrusting ideas, which are universal, in comparison with facts, which are miscellaneous. The man whom he attacks throughout he calls "The Idealist"; that is the man who permits himself to be mainly moved by a moral generalisation. "Actions," he says, "are to be judged by their effect on happiness, and not by their conformity to any ideal." As we have already seen, there is a certain inconsistency here; for while Shaw had always chucked all ideals overboard the one he had chucked first was the ideal of happiness. Passing this however for the present, we may mark the above as the most satisfying summary. If I tell a lie I am not to blame myself for having violated the ideal of truth, but only for having perhaps got myself into a mess and made things worse than they were before. If I have broken my word I need not feel (as my fathers did) that I have broken something inside me, as one who breaks a blood vessel. It all depends on whether I have broken up something outside me; as one who breaks up an evening party. If I shoot my father the only question is whether I have made him happy. I must not admit the idealistic conception that the mere shooting of my father might possibly make me unhappy. We are to judge of every individual case as it arises, apparently without any social summary or moral ready-reckoner at all. "The Golden Rule is that there is no Golden Rule." We must not say that it is right to keep promises, but that it may be right to keep this promise. Essentially it is anarchy; nor is it very easy to see how a state could be very comfortable which was Socialist in all its public morality and Anarchist in all its private. But if it is anarchy, it is anarchy without any of the abandon and exuberance of anarchy. It is a worried and conscientious anarchy; an anarchy of painful delicacy and even caution. For it refuses to trust in traditional experiments or plainly trodden tracks; every case must be considered anew from the beginning, and yet considered with the most wide-eyed care for human welfare; every man must act as if he were the first man made. Briefly, we must always be worrying about what is best for our children, and we must not take one hint or rule of thumb from our fathers. Some think that this anarchism would make a man tread down mighty cities in his madness. I think it would make a man walk down the street as if he were walking on eggshells. I do not think this experiment in opportunism would end in frantic licence; I think it would end in frozen timidity. If a man was forbidden to solve moral problems by moral science or the help of mankind, his course would be quite easy—he would not solve the problems. The world instead of being a knot so tangled as to need unravelling, would simply become a piece of clockwork too complicated to be touched. I cannot think that this untutored worry was what Ibsen meant; I have my doubts as to whether it was what Shaw meant; but I do not think that it can be substantially doubted that it was what he said.

In any case it can be asserted that the general aim of the work was to exalt the immediate conclusions of practice against the general conclusions of theory. Shaw objected to the solution of every problem in a play being by its nature a general solution, applicable to all other such problems. He disliked the entrance of a universal justice at the end of the last act; treading down all the personal ultimatums and all the varied certainties of men. He disliked the god from the machine—because he was from a machine. But even without the machine he tended to dislike the god; because a god is more general than a man. His enemies have accused Shaw of being anti-domestic, a shaker of the roof-tree. But in this sense Shaw may be called almost madly domestic. He wishes each private problem to be settled in private, without reference to sociological ethics. And the only objection to this kind of gigantic casuistry is that the theatre is really too small to discuss it. It would not be fair to play David and Goliath on a stage too small to admit Goliath. And it is not fair to discuss private morality on a stage too small to admit the enormous presence of public morality; that character which has not appeared in a play since the Middle Ages; whose name is Everyman and whose honour we all have in our keeping.

ERIC BENTLEY

Pygmalion: *A Personal Play*

Reviewing Shaw's first decade in the theatre, one can see that, taking up the materials of the theatre as he found them, and enriching them with thoughts and attitudes he had learnt from life and literature, Shaw created a new type of comedy. Compare any of his plays with the kind of play he is parodying or otherwise modifying and his own contribution to the drama will be evident. Were we to have entered a theatre in 1900 the things that would have struck us in a Shaw play, assuming that we were sympathetic enough to notice them, would have been—in order of their saliency—the endlessly witty and eloquent talk, the wideness of reference in the dialogue, the incredible liveliness of the characters, the swift tempo, the sudden and unexpected reverses (especially anti-climaxes), in a phrase, the unusual energy coupled with the unusual intellect. And the gist of the early reviews is that, though it wasn't drama, it was something as serious as it was entertaining, as brilliant as it was funny. The more intelligent reviewers began by gravely observing that it wasn't drama and ended by saying precisely the opposite. Shaw is not a dramatist, says one, but a preacher and satirist—"incidentally, no doubt, he often gives us very good drama indeed." "The chief characteristics of Mr. Bernard Shaw's plays," says another, "are not precisely dramatic," yet he goes on to say of the new drama, "the special mode of its manifestation does belong to the stage." "As a conscientious critic," says a third, "I have pointed out that Mr. Shaw's abundance of ideas spoils his plays. I may add as a man,"

From *Bernard Shaw 1856–1950*. © 1947, 1957 by New Directions Publishing Co. © renewed 1975 by Eric Bentley.

he somewhat disarmingly goes on, "that to me it is their great attraction."

It all boils down to the fact that Shaw's plays were good in an unfamiliar way. What was new about them? Though this question has been partly answered already it may be of interest to recall Shaw's own answer. He located the newness of Ibsen (and for "Ibsen," throughout *The Quintessence of Ibsenism,* we should read "Shaw") in two things: his naturalism and his use of discussion. The naturalism is arrived at primarily by the replacement of romance and melodrama by "natural history." This entails a vast extension of subject matter. Invariably naturalism has meant an extension of subject matter, so to say, downwards—towards the inclusion of low life and animal passions. Shaw made this extension in his Unpleasant Plays. A more characteristically Shavian extension of subject matter was the extension *upwards* in the Pleasant Plays and the *Three Plays for Puritans,* an extension towards the inclusion of the higher passions—the passion for beauty, for goodness, for control. Sardoodledom had removed from the theatre most of the serious interests of civilized men. Nobody did more than Shaw to bring them all back. And nobody brought them back more entertainingly.

As for the use of discussion, Shaw observes that the conventional nineteenth-century play consisted of an exposition, a complication, and a denouement, but that Ibsen, in *A Doll's House,* replaced the denouement by a discussion, and thus made the essential technical innovation in modern drama. Luckily Shaw goes on to qualify this over-simplification with the observation that the new element of discussion may sometimes be found at the beginning (one thinks of *The Apple Cart*) or in the middle (one thinks of *Man and Superman*) or it may interpenetrate the whole action—one thinks of a dozen Shaw plays. As so often, Shaw's critical comment is too simple to cover his practice. A Shavian play is not to be equated with a non-Shavian play plus discussion. The truth is far more complicated. Shaw is perfectly capable of writing a *drame* which is as personal and emotional as one of Ibsen's. He has also written much disquisitory dialogue. Personal plays—such as *Candida*—and discussion plays—such as *Getting Married*—are, in fact, the twin poles of Shavian drama. Without denying the existence of either, one should see that the bulk of Shaw's plays are on middle ground between the poles.

Another distinction is called for. There are broadly two different kinds of discussion in Shavian drama. The one has become a byword because, until Shaw proved the contrary, everyone denied that it could be dramatic. I refer to the discussion of problems for their inherent interest. "Don Juan in Hell," "The Doctrine of the Brothers Barnabas," *In Good King Charles's Golden Days* are instances. In these nothing is more important than the discussion itself. The other type of discussion is more usual on the stage— discussion as an emanation of conflict between persons. Shaw is expert at writing verbal duels in which the acerbity and the interest derive not from the questions discussed but from situation and character. The discussions in *Major Barbara* and *John Bull's Other Island* are of this type. Of course our two types are again twin poles, and most of Shavian dialogue is between the extremes. It is therefore not enough to say, on the one hand, that Shaw makes the ideas themselves dramatic, for this implies that he eschews drama of character and situation. It is not enough to say, on the other hand, that Shaw after all wrote *Candida,* for this implies that Shaw is at his best only when he is closest to conventional patterns, only when the discussions never venture far from the human crisis that is being enacted. One must take particular cases to see how Shaw is drawn now to one magnetic pole, now to another, and how at his best he feels and expresses tension from the pull of both. To analyse particular plays will also afford an opportunity of illustrating other points that so far have remained mere generalizations.

Pygmalion is a characteristic instance of a personal play. And it is characteristic that many people think of it as very disquisitory. At least it at first seems to conform to Shaw's formula: exposition, complication, discussion. But let us take a closer look.

Pygmalion is the story, in five acts, of Henry Higgins's attempt to make a duchess out of a flower girl. Act 1 is really a sort of prologue in which the two main characters encounter each other. The action proper starts in act 2 when Higgins decides to make the experiment. In act 3 the experiment reaches its first stage when Eliza appears in upper-class company behaving like an imperfectly functioning mechanical doll. Readers of Bergson will understand why this scene gets more laughs than all the others put together, so that to the groundlings the rest of the play seems a prolonged anti-climax. Has not Shaw blundered? What ought to be the climax seems to have been left out: it is between acts 3 and 4 that Eliza is finally passed off as a duchess at an ambassador's party. Would not Sarcey have called this the *scène à faire?* When the curtain goes up on act 4 all is over; Eliza has triumphed. Higgins is satisfied, bored, and wondering what to do next. The comedy is over. But there are two more acts!

"The play is now virtually over but the characters will discuss it at length for two Acts more." Such is the curtain line of act 1 in a later Shaw play. It is one of those Shavian jokes which appear to be against Shaw but are really against the vulgar opinion of Shaw. The two acts that follow (in

Too True To Be Good) are *not* a discussion of what happens in act 1. Nor are the last two acts of *Pygmalion* as purely disquisitory as they at first seem.

Certainly, the big event occurs between the acts, and the last two acts *are* a "discussion" of the consequences. But the discussion is of the second of the types defined above: it is not so much that the consequences are discussed as that the consequences are worked out and determined by a conflict that is expressed in verbal swordplay. There is no pretence of objectivity. Each character speaks for himself, and speaks, not as a contributor to a debate, but as one whose life is at stake. Eliza is talking to free herself. Higgins is talking to keep his domination over her. The conclusion of conversations of this kind is not the statement of a principle (as in Plato's symposia or even Shaw's *Getting Married*) but the making of a decision. Ibsen's Nora slams the door, his Ellida decides to stay at home. What happens to Eliza? What *can* happen, now that the flower girl is a duchess, the statue a flesh-and-blood Galatea?

In the original romance, so lyrically revived by Shaw's friend William Morris, Pygmalion marries Galatea. Might not something of the kind be possible for Shaw, since Pygmalion is a life-giver, a symbol of vitality, since in Eliza the crime of poverty has been overcome, the sin of ignorance cancelled? Or might not Higgins and Eliza be the "artist man" and "mother woman" discussed in *Man and Superman*? They might—if Shaw actually went to work so allegorically, so abstractly, so idealistically. Actually *Pygmalion: A Romance* stands related to Romance precisely as *The Devil's Disciple* stands to Melodrama or *Candida* to Domestic Drama. It is a serious parody, a translation into the language of "natural history." The primary inversion is that of Pygmalion's character. The Pygmalion of Romance turns a statue into a human being. The Pygmalion of "natural history" tries to turn a human being into a statue, tries to make of Eliza Doolittle a mechanical doll in the role of a duchess. Or rather he tries to make from one kind of doll—a flower girl who cannot afford the luxury of being human—another kind of doll—a duchess to whom manners are an adequate substitute for morals.

There is a character named Pygmalion in *Back to Methuselah*. He is a sort of Frankenstein or Pavlov. He thinks that you can put together a man by assembling mechanical parts. Henry Higgins also thinks he has made a person—or at least an amenable slave—when he has "assembled" a duchess. But the monster turns against Frankenstein. Forces have been brought into play of which the man-maker knows nothing. And Shaw's Pygmalion has helped into being a creature even more mysterious than a monster: a human being.

If the first stage of Higgins's experiment was reached when Eliza made her *faux pas* before Mrs. Higgins's friends, and the second when she appeared in triumph at the ball, Shaw, who does not believe in endings, sees her through two more stages in the final acts of his play, leaving her still very much in flux at the end. The third stage is rebellion. Eliza's feelings are wounded because, after the reception, Higgins does not treat her kindly, but talks of her as a guinea pig. Eliza has acquired finer feelings.

While some have felt that the play should end with the reception, others have felt that it could end with the suggestion that Eliza has begun to rebel. It seems, indeed, that the creator of the role of Eliza thought this. In her memoirs Mrs. Patrick Campbell wrote:

> The last act of the play did not travel across the footlights with as clear dramatic sequence as the preceding acts—owing entirely to the fault of the author.

The sympathetic analyst of the play will more probably agree with Shaw himself who, Mrs. Campbell says, "declared I might be able to play a tune with one finger, but a full orchestral score was Greek to me." The fifth act of *Pygmalion* is far from superfluous. It is the climax. The arousing of Eliza's resentment in the fourth act was the birth of a soul. But to be born is not enough. One must also grow up. Growing up is the fourth and last stage of Eliza's evolution. This consummation is reached in the final "discussion" with Higgins—a piece of dialogue that is superb comedy not only because of its wit and content but also because it proceeds from a dramatic situation, perhaps the most dramatic of all dramatic situations: two completely articulate characters engaged in a battle of words on which both their fates depend. It is a Strindbergian battle of wills. But not of sex. Higgins will never marry. He wants to remain in the relation of God the Creator as far as Eliza is concerned. For her part Eliza will marry. But she won't marry Higgins.

The play ends with Higgins's knowingly declaring that Eliza is about to do his shopping for him despite her protestations to the contrary: a statement which actors and critics often take to mean that the pair are a Benedick and Beatrice who will marry in the end. One need not quote Shaw's own sequel to prove the contrary. The whole point of the great culminating scene is that Eliza has now become not only a person but an independent person. The climax is sharp:

> LIZA: If I can't have kindness, I'll have independence.
> HIGGINS: Independence? That's middle class blasphemy. We are all dependent on one another, every soul of us on earth.

LIZA: [*rising determinedly*] I'll let you see whether I'm dependent
    on you. If you can preach, I can teach. I'll go and be a
    teacher.
HIGGINS: What'll you teach, in heaven's name?
LIZA: What you taught me. I'll teach phonetics.
HIGGINS: Ha! ha! ha!
LIZA: I'll offer myself as an assistant to Professor Nepean.
HIGGINS: [*rising in a fury*] What! That impostor! That humbug!
    That toadying ignoramus! Teach him *my* methods! *my* dis-
    coveries! You take one step in his direction and I'll wring
    your neck. (*He lays hands on her.*) Do you hear?
LIZA: [*defiantly non-resistant*] Wring away. What do I care? I
    knew you'd strike me some day. (*He lets her go, stamping
    with rage. . . .*)

With this cry of victory (it rings in my ears in the intonation of Miss
Gertrude Lawrence who succeeded where Mrs. Patrick Campbell seems to
have failed) Eliza wins her freedom. Higgins had said: "I can do without
anybody. I have my own soul." And now Eliza can say: "Now . . . I'm not
afraid of you and can do without you." After this it does not matter whether
Eliza does the shopping or not. The situation is clear. Eliza's fate is settled
as far as Higgins is concerned. The story of the experiment is over. Otherwise her fate is as unsettled as yours or mine. This is a true naturalistic
ending—not an arbitrary break, but a conclusion which is also a beginning.

Pygmalion is a singularly elegant structure. If again we call act 1 the
prologue, the play falls into two parts of two acts apiece. Both parts are
Pygmalion myths. In the first a duchess is made out of a flower girl. In the
second a woman is made out of a duchess. Since these two parts are the
main, inner action the omission of the climax of the outer action—the
ambassador's reception—will seem particularly discreet, economical, and
dramatic. The movie version of *Pygmalion* was not the richer for its inclusion. To include a climax that is no climax only blurs the outline of the play.
Pygmalion is essentially theatrical in construction. It is built in chunks, two
by two. The fluidity of the screen is quite inappropriate to it. On the screen,
as in the novel, a development of character naturally occurs gradually and
smoothly. Natasha in *War and Peace* passes imperceptibly from girlhood to
womanhood; Eliza in *Pygmalion* proceeds in dramatically marked stages—
one, two, three, four, act by act. Perhaps we never realized before the Shaw
movies how utterly "of the theatre" the Shaw plays are.

As we might have learned to expect, *Pygmalion* follows the pattern of earlier Shavian works, not duplicating them but following up another aspect of a similar problem. We have seen how the eponymous character is often the representative of vitality and that he remains constant like a catalyst while producing change in others, especially in the antagonist whom he is educating, disillusioning, or converting. *Pygmalion* diverges from the type in that the life-giver, for all his credentials, and his title of Pygmalion, is suspect. He is not really a life-giver at all. To be sure, Eliza is even more palpably his pupil than Judith was Dick's or Brassbound Lady Cicely's. But the "education of Eliza" in acts 1 to 3 is a caricature of the true process. In the end Eliza turns the tables on Higgins, for she, finally, is the vital one, and he is the prisoner of "system," particularly of his profession.

Ironically parallel with the story of Eliza is the story of her father. Alfred Doolittle is also suddenly lifted out of slumdom by the caprice of Pygmalion-Higgins. He too has to break bread with dukes and duchesses. Unlike his daughter, however, he is not reborn. He is too far gone for that. He is the same rich as he was poor, the same or worse; for riches carry awful responsibilities, and Doolittle commits the cardinal sin on the Shavian scale—he is irresponsible. In the career of the undeserving poor suddenly become undeserving rich Shaw writes his *social* comedy, his Unpleasant Play, while in the career of his deserving daughter he writes his *human* comedy, his Pleasant Play. Those who think that *Pygmalion* is about class society are thinking of Doolittle's comedy rather than Eliza's. The two are carefully related by parallelism and contrast. One might work out an interpretation of the play by comparing their relation to the chief "artificial system" depicted in it—middle-class morality.

In short, the merit of *Pygmalion* cannot be explained by Shaw's own account of the nature of modern drama, much less by popular or academic opinion concerning Problem Plays, Discussion Drama, Drama of Ideas, and the like. It is a good play by perfectly orthodox standards and needs no theory to defend it. It is Shavian, not in being made up of political or philosophic discussions, but in being based on the standard conflict of vitality and system, in working out this conflict through an inversion of romance, in bringing matters to a head in a battle of wills and words, in having an inner psychological action in counterpoint to the outer romantic action, in existing on two contrasted levels of mentality, both of which are related to the main theme, in delighting and surprising us with a constant flow of verbal music and more than verbal wit.

FREDERICK P. W. McDOWELL

The Shavian World
of John Bull's Other Island

John Bull's Other Island, Shaw once said, is one of "a group of three plays
of exceptional weight and magnitude on which the reputation of the author
as a serious dramatist was first established, and still mainly rests." The other
two plays are *Major Barbara* and *Man and Superman. John Bull's Other
Island* was popular at the Court Theatre from 1904 to 1907 and established
Shaw as a great and popular dramatist. Since then, however, this play has
not been esteemed as much as *Man and Superman* and *Major Barbara,*
although I would argue that in humor and insight it is their equal. It has
been revived only twice in London in the last forty years—in 1938 and
1947; and it is far less known to the public or to scholarship than are the
other two plays. Opinions to the contrary notwithstanding, Shaw's estimate
of his play should, I think, be taken seriously. Some critics have seen the
play as original in method, as still pertinent to the Irish situation, and as
universal in its significance. "Shaw made out of this topical subject a masterpiece," Reuben Brower has written, "one of his purest and most sustained comedies." I believe this view can be upheld.

Some readers regard the play as dated because it explores the super-
seded Ireland of 1904 and its relation to England as a ruling power. But
Shaw was only incidentally concerned in his play with such specific matters
as the Land Purchase Act of 1903 (the Wyndham Act). He wished rather to
present the truth as he saw it about Irish culture, mentality, and politics, and
Ireland's general relationships with England. As early as 1896 he had protested the romanticizing of Irish life; and he had declared himself "quite

From *PMLA* 82 (December 1967). © 1967 by the Modern Language Association of
America.

ready to help the saving work of reducing the sham Ireland of romance to a heap of unsightly ruins." He hoped for the emergence of a dynamic Ireland which would help undermine British respectability.

Shaw did expose the Ireland of romance in *John Bull's Other Island*. Through Father Keegan and Larry Doyle he expressed the values that might animate a regenerate Ireland. In the Preface Shaw recounts how the play, commissioned by Yeats, was rejected by the directors of the Abbey Theatre, not merely because it was beyond their resources but because it rejected as false the current romanticizing of Ireland: "It was uncongenial to the whole spirit of the neo-Gaelic movement, which is bent on creating a new Ireland after its own ideal, whereas my play is a very uncompromising presentment of the real old Ireland." Shaw is here perhaps mocking the "poetic" plays of Synge, Yeats, and Lady Gregory; but by 1911 he regarded these playwrights as realists rather than as perpetuators, solely, of a legendary Ireland. For him they had become pioneers of a new and more truthful kind of Irish drama: "In a modern Irish play the hero doesn't sing that 'Ould Ireland' is his country and his name it is Molloy; he pours forth all his bitterness on it like the prophets of old." It is as though Shaw were remembering in this statement the embittered patriots of his own play, Larry Doyle and Father Keegan. In 1944 Shaw observed that drama, under the censorship of an independent Ireland, was once again false to the facts of Irish life, just as the plays of the prewar London theater (which presented a bogus Irish type as the reality) and some plays of the Celtic revival had been. Irish playwrights of the 1940s, he said, were free to write only about Irish history and only as the censor, usually an Irish hero of 1916, prescribed. There resulted "fabulous" works which failed "to provide for that element of truth to nature and critical comic relief without which romance ends in disillusion and cynicism."

This last statement reflects, in retrospect, upon Shaw's own aims and achievements in *John Bull's Other Island*. He did achieve a realistic play which would tell the truth about Ireland and he did gain perspective for his own vision by judicious use of the comic mode. Instead of peasants who gain inner strength by their closeness to the soil, we have Matthew Haffigan and Barney Doran who have been brutalized by their life as farmers. We have a parish priest, Father Dempsey, who is just as much a slave to ambition as Broadbent, the "liberal" entrepreneur from England. And in Nora Reilly we have an ethereal and charming heroine who is also phlegmatic and snobbish. She is a Kathleen ni Houlihan figure whom Shaw views sardonically: she lacks the spiritual force associated with such a female symbol of Ireland by the authors of the Celtic Revival and is, instead, a parasitic and ineffectual lady.

Without being a slave to observed fact, Shaw conveys the impression that his Ireland is an actual country, not a land of romance. The circumstances connected with Broadbent's arrival at Rosscullen in act 2, for example, illustrate some of the essentials of literary realism: a saturation with detail and then a discrimination among the facts by a responsible spokesman (Father Keegan at this point). Such matters as Keegan's condemnation of Patsy Farrell for his superstition, Keegan's consolation of Nora Reilly in her restlessness and disillusionment with Larry Doyle, the bustling approach of Broadbent with Father Dempsey and Larry's father in a motor car, and Father Dempsey's altercation with the overworked Patsy Farrell who acts as porter—all contribute to the verisimilitude of the play. The naturalness, moreover, with which the situations are evolved, the acuteness with which they are analyzed, the validity and applicability of the thought informing them, the full analysis of personality and motives, and the perfect realization of major and minor characters as both individuals and types establish the veracity of Shaw's universe.

Paradoxically, Shaw attains in this truthful depiction of the Irish scene an impression of beauty. Such beauty is, of course, one element in the real Ireland and here intermingles with the robustness of the comic episodes and the grimness of the peasants' lives to provide a contrasting framework for the characters and incidents. A more authentic beauty emerges than that the neo-Celtic playwrights and poets self-consciously strove to capture in their work. Shaw's critical sense, basic to his comic view of reality, makes firm all genuine aesthetic impressions and exposes all spurious ones. Beauty invests the Round Tower as Broadbent proposes to Nora there, even though the Round Tower is a stock property and romantic feeling is being debunked. Later in this scene the pragmatic Father Dempsey establishes the poetic aspect of such towers by seeing them as "the forefingers of the early Church, pointing us all to God." The dreaming temper of the Irish, as it broods on natural beauty or the beauties of a legendary past, fascinates Larry Doyle, and us, even while he fulminates against it. He defines it memorably in act 1 because this is the side of the Irish temper that he has had to resist.

Beauty, too, suffuses Keegan's talks with the grasshopper early in act 2, and it pervades the other visionary or prophetic sequences in the play. The very alienation of Father Keegan derives from his perception that spiritual serenity and aesthetic harmony are elements too often lacking in modern life. His longing for increased order in Irish social life makes us conscious of the fact that he esteems beauty; the very fervor of his discontent with the present also contributes to the aesthetic impressiveness of his pronouncements. He would also imply that the beauty present in Irish scenery and in the heroic Irish past exert no real force upon the oppressed men and women who were formerly his parishioners and who represent the commonest Irish social type. Both Keegan and Doyle touch prophecy at times in their ability to penetrate the social sham to a more luminous reality, the realm of the beatific spirit; and in their inspired moments they become men who would renovate the torpid existence of their average countrymen. Their fervor is one quality which at certain times allows them to reach dimensions of personality that are mythic and archetypal. The visionary Father Keegan most often attains this largeness of stature; and it is perhaps no accident that in his wanderings he had been in Jerusalem and then spent six months in a monastery on Patmos, the island where Saint John received his "Revelations."

The three central figures of the play have an ordinary, everyday aspect: Broadbent is the English "liberal" and businessman; Doyle, the moody and intelligent expatriate; and Father Keegan, the Christian man of charity and unfrocked priest. Yet Keegan and Doyle are also wise men, prophets without honor in their own country. And the largeness, generosity, and aesthetic rightness of Shaw's comic vision also extend the character of Broadbent toward the archetypal. As prototypic characters, all three men achieve a magnitude which lifts them beyond the realm of the everyday. In the process, Broadbent becomes the unreflective, conquering hero, who is also the aboriginal fool; Doyle becomes the immemorial exile or "flying Dutchman" figure whose genius is deflected by his lack of roots and well-defined loyalties; and Father Keegan becomes the privileged "madman," the spokesman of the demi-urge, the oracle of supernal wisdom, and the God-intoxicated visionary.

II

The play is less formless than some commentators have maintained. Shaw was, in fact, evolving a new dramatic method which attained its most consistent application in *Getting Married, The Apple Cart,* and *In Good King Charles's Golden Days,* and its most aesthetically compelling expression in *Heartbreak House,* the trial scene from *Saint Joan,* and *The Tragedy of an Elderly Gentleman* (*Back to Methuselah,* part 4). In all this writing discussion predominates. Shaw was moving away from the conventions that animated the popular theater of the nineteenth century and toward an intellectual theater notable for a full-scale debate of ideas. In order to accommodate such increase of discussion, the structure of *Man and Super-*

man, *John Bull's Other Island,* and *Major Barbara* becomes looser than that found in Shaw's earlier works.

Ratiocination has not yet overspread these plays. Rather, the innovation is that all elements—characters, action, ideas—point toward set discussions and reach fulfillment therein, in the lovers' duel (act 1) and the hell scene in *Man and Superman,* the last act of *Major Barbara,* and the last parts of acts 3 and 4 of *John Bull's Other Island.* The interchange in act 3 has for subject the economic and social well-being of Ireland as it relates to the land question and to Irish representation in Parliament. The interchange in act 4 has for subject nothing less than the ultimate destiny of Ireland and the Irish, indeed of all human beings to the degree that the Irish embody their burdens and aspirations. The act 3 interchange first features Irish peasants, Father Dempsey, and Larry Doyle, then the peasants, Dempsey, and Broadbent. The act 4 interchange is confined to Larry Doyle, Tom Broadbent, and Father Keegan. In these scenes, as in the conspectus of the play as a whole, Shaw adroitly interweaves characters and ideas, and then just as adroitly resolves conflicting points of view.

Action is present in *John Bull's Other Island,* but emphasis is no longer placed upon it. Just as in *Major Barbara,* action and the other elements in *John Bull's Other Island* point toward "a transcendental conversation" in the last act "which will stagger the very soul of Vedrenne and send the audience away howling." Elaborate plot is absent, perhaps because the play's scope is more inclusive than it sometimes is in a work of art. Shaw has ordered his materials through the imagination, but he has been less arbitrary in so doing than those writers who fashion elaborate plots or who select with extreme freedom from their experience. The inclusiveness of the canvas may have been a legacy from the realism of Balzac and the naturalism of Zola. In any case the ranging aspect of the play helps create and sustain an impression of amplitude. Shaw seems to have realized that his materials had more than local import and that they justified both his comprehensive vision and his relaxed, though controlled, writing. Shaw did defend himself as a conscious artist and insisted that the inclusiveness of *John Bull's Other Island* was in itself a vital aesthetic element in its structure, after Walkley and other critics called it no play but at best a mere "entertainment":

> I never achieved such a feat of construction in my life. Just consider my subject—the destiny of nations! Consider my characters—personages who stalk on the stage incarnating millions of real, living, suffering men and women. Good heavens! I have

had to get all England and Ireland into three hours and a quarter.
I have shown the Englishman to the Irishman and the Irishman
to the Englishman, the Protestant to the Catholic and the Catholic to the Protestant. I have taken that panacea for all the misery
and unrest of Ireland—your Land Purchase Bill—as to the perfect blessedness of which all your political parties and newspapers were for once unanimous; and I have shown at one stroke
its idiocy, its shallowness, its cowardice, its utter and foredoomed
futility. I have shown the Irish saint shuddering at the humour of
the Irish blackguard—only to find, I regret to say, that the average critic thought the blackguard very funny and the saint very
unpractical. I have shown that very interesting psychological
event, the wooing of an unsophisticated Irishwoman by an Englishman, and made comedy of it without one lapse from its pure
science. I have even demonstrated the Trinity to a generation
which saw nothing in it but an arithmetical absurdity.

Shaw's first purpose, apparently, was to present contrasting racial types
through the association of Broadbent and Doyle, the English and Irish
partners in a firm of civil engineers. The illusion-bound yet shrewd Englishman is the foil for the intelligent yet indecisive Irishman. Shaw's second
purpose, it seems, was to contrast a typical Englishman with the Irish background and Irish types other than Larry Doyle. In the process he would be
able to throw into relief the qualities of Ireland by setting them beside the
qualities of the invading capitalist. To achieve his first objective, Shaw had
to establish the opposing characteristics of Broadbent and Doyle in London
in act 1. To achieve his second objective, he sent both men to Ireland for the
rest of the play. Act 1 may thus be regarded as a prologue, containing in
embryo the drama which develops in the Irish setting.

If the construction is loose, it is not haphazard. Shaw, in fact, used full
economy if we think of the close relationship existing between the incidents
in act 1 and those in the remaining acts. There is nothing in act 1 that is not
used later for purposes either of contrast or elucidation. Shaw's structural
principle in the play is twofold. First, he used parallel scenes, wherein characters and situations refer back and forth to one another in the reader's or
the spectator's mind as he reflects upon them. Second, Shaw saw his play as
a stream which gathers everything within it to flow with full force into the
debates which conclude acts 3 and 4. All subsidiary currents contribute to
the dialectical motion which governs the play as a whole and which reaches
two culminating points: in the discussion of social and political Ireland (act

3) and in the discussion of Ireland's destiny seen in its universal as well as its local aspects (the close of act 4).

The main incidents and concepts in act 1 relate closely to scenes and ideas present elsewhere in the play. In act 1 Hodson, Broadbent's valet, is suspicious of the sham Irishman Tim Haffigan and arouses Tim's enmity. In act 3 Hodson has a quarrel with Haffigan's uncle and incurs his animosity over the wrongs endured by the Irish. In Hodson's (and Shaw's) view, these hardships are less severe than those the English have suffered and still continue to suffer. The episode of Broadbent's being fleeced by Tim Haffigan in act 1 prepares us for an episode in act 4 when Broadbent becomes the butt of the Irish, after a pig takes over as driver of his motor car. The last laugh is on the derisive Irish, however, for Broadbent will outplay them by mortgaging their land for more than it is worth and then foreclosing their loans. Broadbent's declaration of "Liberal" sentiments in act 1 foreshadows his proclamation of them to the Irish, who are willing to use him and his sentiments for their own purposes—to secure a Parliamentary candidate who will not interfere with the new class of small landholders. Broadbent's purpose in going to Ireland is to foreclose the estate of Nick Lestrange, a landowner whom Larry Doyle has liked. Broadbent is also going to Ireland to prospect for the Land Development Syndicate in which he is a principal stockholder. In this fashion the land question which various characters discuss at length in act 3 is broached.

Larry Doyle's speech in act 1 on the Irishman's penchant for dreaming prepares us for the Irish whom we encounter in act 2. The Irishman at his best is an individual like Father Keegan who has imaginative insight but not much capacity for mundane pursuits. If the Irishman is given over to his imagination, he is not wedded to illusion like the typical Englishman. The Irishman can also be a realist like the expatriate Doyle, all the more discerning because of the imagination he tries so hard to repress. Doyle, the realist, has similarities to the Irish peasant who is shrewd when his personal advantage is in question, however often at other times he may seem to evade the discomfiting facts and to give in to his dreaming temperament. In act 1 the interchange between Broadbent and Larry establishes Larry's indifference toward Nora Reilly and leads to the romantic interview in reverse of act 4. Alone with Nora, Larry finds that he has nothing to say to the woman who has waited eighteen years for him. In act 1 Broadbent's curiosity about Nora is aroused; there is nothing grossly improbable about his proposing to her in act 2, when he first meets her at the Round Tower. The other chief incidents and ideas in acts 2, 3, and 4 are closely intercalated with one another and look forward or backward as the case may be. A unity of conception is also notable in the play, deriving from Shaw's steady psychological vision; every character, incident, speech, and idea is genuine and forms part of a larger harmony. The threads of the play are relaxed but can be made taut at will. Far from being a play without structure, *John Bull's Other Island* is one of Shaw's most coherent and deftly articulated works. It is simply that all other elements in the play are subordinated to the presentation of the characters.

III

The chief character is Tom Broadbent, one of the best comic creations in English literature. In the Preface Shaw cites as Broadbent's "first condition of economy and concentration of force, sustained purpose, and rational conduct" his "power of taking himself seriously, and his insensibility to anything funny in danger and destruction." The result is a confidence as enormous as it is humorless. Broadbent's assumption of superiority is intensified by his belief that he is speaking for England as well as for himself. First among his principles is a conviction that "an Englishman's first duty is his duty to Ireland"; the play closes with his factitious exultation as he plans to devote his "life to the cause of Ireland."

Broadbent is invincible partly because of his deficiency in intellectual grasp. He fails to communicate with other characters because he sees their ideas or situations too superficially. In act 1, after Larry castigates the excesses to which Irish imagination leads and is in despair about Ireland, Broadbent tells him not to worry but to consider, rather, the glorious prospects in store for Ireland with Home Rule under English guidance. This is an example of one of the comic patterns which Broadbent illustrates in his rejoinders, the *non sequitur* or the observation which has only slight relevance to the given situation. Keegan's description of his visit to the dying Hindu from whom he learned "the mystery of this world" again elicits an inappropriate remark from Broadbent. He regards the incident simply as "a remarkable tribute to the liberty of conscience enjoyed by the subjects of our Indian empire." In short, Broadbent reduces the profound to the commonplace, he coarsens the perceptions of others through his ignorance and one-sided intelligence, and he thinks only in terms of ready-made ideas and prejudices.

His monumental complacency has these results: he interprets all situations in terms of their advantage to himself, and he regards himself as superior to fate and the world's evils. He assumes, for example, that Father Keegan's prophecy as to his success in Irish politics represents an endorsement of his political principles. Then again, as Larry sees, Broadbent will use the pig episode, which stirs the merriment of Barney Doran and his crowd of earthy peasants, to convince himself and others that this is "one of the most providential episodes in the history of England and Ireland," presumably because it brings him to the Irish as a political candidate.

In his personal relationships Broadbent adopts the same Olympian manner, and demonstrates the same brashness and the same unreflective strength. When he woos, "he carries Nora off her feet by mere depth of chest." He is willing, he says, to wait for Nora's answer to his proposal provided her response will be favorable. He overcomes her scruples by saying that hugging will be good for her, "plump out your muscles and make em elastic and set up your figure." The humor in this affair derives from his going so far so fast; in love, no less than in other activities, Broadbent illustrates Cromwell's observation (which Shaw once said applied to Broadbent and the English): that man goes furthest "who does not know where he is going." Moreover, by his authoritative manner, Broadbent convinces others besides Nora of the truth of his absurdities. Consciously and unconsciously, he patronizes others because he is certain he is right. After Keegan denounces Irish life as hell, Broadbent serenely muses, "What an intelligent, broadminded character, considering his cloth!" Later, he patronizes Keegan to the point of impertinence, viewing him as a picturesque adjunct to the projected hotel and golf links at Rosscullen. Broadbent, of course, has no idea that he is impertinent; he would regard himself, rather, as having been especially gracious to a man inferior to himself in wealth, worldly position, and ability.

The humor derived from mistaken illusion is abundant. As a romantic and sentimentalist, Broadbent is unable to see things quite as they are. He regards Nora Reilly as an ineffable being: her fragile beauty and beautiful voice overpower him against the Round Tower by moonlight. To Broadbent's disgust Larry maintains that Nora's ethereal mien derives from an insubstantial diet, not alone from spiritual beauty.

The inconsistency between Broadbent's behavior and his professed motives means that he is a hypocrite of sorts. Because he says that hypocrisy is the vice he most detests, we see that his hypocrisy is mostly unintentional. He is lacking in self-criticism and self-awareness. When he characterizes politicians as "the wind-bags, the carpet-baggers, the charlatans, the—the—the fools and ignoramuses who corrupt the multitude by their wealth, or seduce them spouting balderdash to them," he also characterizes himself without the slightest knowledge that he is doing so. Then again when he talks to the Irish landholders in act 4, he says that he has no right to address them on politics. He has done just that, however, in declaring how blessed the Irish would be under British liberalism. One surmises, in fact, that Broadbent sometimes knows what he is doing and is the hypocrite he disclaims being. He is undoubtedly more artful than people suspect, but it often suits his purposes to convey an impression of utter guilelessness and innocence.

Broadbent is incapable of understanding irony, since he constantly accepts at face value the speeches of Father Keegan. When in the last act Keegan comes to the Round Tower to brood over the fate of Ireland, he bitterly describes how he will be comforted by the prospect of the Rosscullen hotel and of children carrying the golf clubs of tourists. Whereupon Broadbent expansively remarks that there is poetry in everything, even in the most prosaic things, provided there is someone like Keegan to extract it. As to his plans for Ireland's future, Broadbent reveals an irresponsible energy, expecting to receive credit, for example, for destroying the beauty of the landscape. He deplores the fact that at Rosscullen a magnificent river is going to waste, but he has a remedy for this failure of the Irish to use to the full the resources of their land. He will introduce motorboats, the speed and sound of which will form a "poetic" adjunct to the landscape and be a fine accompaniment to the Angelus bell.

In the last pages there are numerous instances of Broadbent's conscious and unconscious confusion of the material with the spiritual, of personal advantage with the general welfare, of humanist idealism with capitalist competitive practice, of acquiring wealth with achieving salvation. Broadbent says, for example, that an Englishman can make or lose ten pounds from land that a holder like Matthew Haffigan could not lose or make ten shillings from. Thus he would hold that sharpness in speculation over land values is the most desirable of all attributes, and provides a purpose in life more commendable to pursue than agricultural prosperity, the welfare of the farmer and the laboring classes, and "a heart purified of hatred." Broadbent will try not only to build facilities for upper-class English tourists but to make a "garden city" out of Rosscullen. There is nothing reprehensible in such enterprise except that the profits of the Land Development Syndicate are uppermost in the promoter's mind rather than the well-being of Ireland. He confuses public institutions ["a library, a Polytechnic (undenominational, of course), a gymnasium, a cricket club, perhaps an art school"] and their potential material benefits to the Irish with the spiritual renovation which Ireland so drastically needs.

Part of the reason for Broadbent's effectiveness is the largeness of his dimensions. There is something fabulous about him, something of the primordial fool, something of Falstaffian geniality, something of the breezy innocence of Parson Adams, and something primordially creative, too, in the singleness of his energies. He is the fool who rushes in where an angel would fear to tread; but he never experiences the chastisements and reverses that would descend upon an ordinary mortal. He has the charmed life which we associate with the figures of folklore; and in Ireland, a land of romance, he seems as invincible as any epic or mythological hero might be. He is both the conquering hero and a monstrous caricature of such a hero. He is, in fact, the comic butt who is natural in that role because he lacks self-consciousness. In this respect he resembles the Burgess of *Candida* and the Roebuck Ramsden of *Man and Superman* rather than the splenetic Mangan of *Heartbreak House*. Because he never sees himself as ridiculous, he has the power deriving from undiverted energies. The consistency of his personality, his absolute imperturbability, renders him humorous.

The legendary aspects of Broadbent dilate to include aspects of his political and racial heritage. He is Britain or John Bull incarnate, "God's Englishman," as Shaw claimed he was. But Shaw regarded Broadbent also as a type who is vanishing in the wake of government control over the resources of society. He has the authority of a vanished type and of a type that will always in part remain. Broadbent in his purity could only have flourished in the late nineteenth and early twentieth centuries, before two world wars challenged the unreflective optimism of the Victorian liberal and the unregulated activities of the Victorian entrepreneur. The contemporary politician has had to recognize realities that pass Broadbent by; the contemporary capitalist has had to be a more intelligent, a more conscientious, and a more socially conscious individual than Broadbent could ever be. But Broadbent is eternal as the man in business and public life whose conduct is incongruous with his principles, whose ambitions are masked as altruism, and whose hypocrisy and opportunism are hidden from himself, sometimes even from others.

In both aspects Broadbent has been completely envisioned. In his actual character the two aspects merge; Broadbent illustrates the doctrinal facets of the nineteenth-century "liberal" as well as the qualities which such a liberal might share with politicians of all cultures. Broadbent's definition of liberalism, in fact, faces two ways. It represents the point of view both of the nineteenth-century "liberal" and of the politician of any time who advocates change while he is afraid of it. Broadbent expounds his "liberal"philosophy with relish to his credulous Irish audience, which consists mainly of the new peasant landholders. They are men interested in retaining their recently acquired acres but averse to further governmental interference and to extending ownership of the land to those beneath them in the social hierarchy. Broadbent's advocacy of the "liberal" *laissez-faire* point of view in social and economic affairs is calculated to confirm them in their complacency and to assuage their fears of change. Reform means, he says, "maintaining those reforms which have already been conferred on humanity by the Liberal Party, and trusting for future developments to the free activity of a free people on the basis of those reforms." If he is elected to Parliament, he implies, he will do nothing: he will act neither to repeal the new land laws nor to divide still further the appropriated estates. Actually, in his political ideas and behavior he is governed by impulse, whim, prejudice, and emotion rather than by any rational definition of the issues, and he suggests also the universal type of the politician who temporizes.

Like Falstaff, Broadbent is appealing even if in some respects he is a rascal. His exuberance, buoyance, and vitality counteract our reservations about his activities. He is affable and good-tempered, and he harbors no animus or malice against any individual. If he is absurd, he is energetic and vital, and his vices, while considerable, are not calculated ones. He is all the more sinister perhaps for being so likable. His ethnic snobbery is his most questionable trait, his worry lest the Old English stock be diluted by alien and foreign elements, including the Jewish. Sinister also is his refusal to face the human consequences of his business practices. He is impersonal enough when it comes to the fate of Matthew Haffigan. Once Haffigan is dispossessed of his land, Broadbent says, he will be too old even for manual labor and he will have to emigrate. For Broadbent the Land Syndicate could not be nefarious, because it is respectable and its operations are in accord with the traditions of capitalist finance. Father Keegan sees Broadbent's malevolent side and realizes that Broadbent is formidable precisely because he does not perceive the implications of his activities. "Devil," he says, is not quite the right word for Broadbent; "ass" would be a lot better. Like the ass, Broadbent is diligent and conscientious; but like the ass, he is a slave to the wishes of "his greedy masters instead of doing the will of Heaven that is in himself." With alarm Keegan views Broadbent as one who is "efficient in the service of Mammon, mighty in mischief, skilful in ruin, heroic in destruction." As Doyle asserts, Broadbent is "idiot" and "genius" both. In short-range activity he has a preternatural insight; for the long view, he reveals a monumental blindness.

IV

Father Keegan is one of Shaw's most arresting creations, and his characterization reveals Shaw's mastery in depicting the religious temperament. Although Keegan is basically Roman Catholic, he is more tolerant than his Church. For absolving a Hindu and extending such unorthodox charity to him, Keegan has been unfrocked. He has become embittered because men are not really Christian in their actions toward others and in the values they profess. Otherwise, the church would have commended his act and understood his motives. He feels alienated from a church which in practice denies the parable of the Good Samaritan and rebukes those who are the most "catholic" in sympathy. From the Hindu he also has discovered the heart-sickening truth about life as most men lead it. In a passage which echoes the ideas of both the Devil and Don Juan in *Man and Superman,* Keegan informs Larry Doyle of all that he had learned from the Hindu and from his own experience as well:

> This world, sir, is very clearly a place of torment and penance, a place where the fool flourishes and the good and wise are hated and persecuted, a place where men and women torture one another in the name of love; where children are scourged and enslaved in the name of parental duty and education; where the weak in body are poisoned and mutilated in the name of healing, and the weak in character are put to the horrible torture of imprisonment, not for hours but for years, in the name of justice. It is a place where the hardest toil is a welcome refuge from the horror and tedium of pleasure, and where charity and good works are done only for hire to ransom the souls of the spoiler and the sybarite. Now, sir, there is only one place of horror and torment known to my religion; and that place is hell.

Keegan would agree with the Devil of *Man and Superman* that the earth is a place of terror and ruin and suffering; and he would agree with Don Juan that the prime characteristic of hell is an irresponsible hedonism. The "dead heart and blinded soul of the island of the saints" oppress Keegan, and he can find no hope of something better for his land in what he sees about him. Here in Ireland is a hell where insensitive men, laughing at the death of Keegan's "brother" the pig, wring the heart of the aspiring Keegan, a saint in essence, a man whom Shaw once described as "incorporeal."

Keegan shares some of Larry Doyle's reservations about Ireland. He condemns the emotionalism of his compatriots, their opportunism, and their lack of principle; and he finds in Ireland "an island of dreamers who wake up in your jails, of critics and cowards whom you buy and tame for your own service, of bold rogues who help you to plunder us that they may plunder you afterwards." Keegan and Doyle, though temperamentally incompatible, are alike in seeing Ireland as it is and Ireland as it ought to be; they also agree that the Ireland of song and story is not the same as the Ireland of today, which Keegan sees as "a hungry land, a naked land, an ignorant and oppressed land." Keegan sees, moreover, that he and Larry Doyle are both immobilized by the horror of Ireland's situation and are unable to do anything except "sneer" at those like Broadbent who exploit the Irish. Keegan's experience, however, is deeper than Larry Doyle's, and he rejects all pressures to compromise with it. In contrast to Broadbent, Keegan does not feel "at home" in the world; in contrast to Larry, he refuses to make the best of the world as it is.

Long before the figure of Keegan was conceived, Shaw revealed that he, like Keegan, had on occasion felt "dread" of his fellow human beings and had also felt that he must be "mad" if the rest of the world were to be accounted sane. According to popular report, Keegan tells Nora Reilly, the dark-skinned man whom he had befriended placed a spell on him and made him mad. Keegan confesses that it is true in a way; like Shaw he does not see life in the way "normal" people do. He is the privileged or "pure" fool, a Parsifal or Hamlet figure, whose sense of the actuality causes him distress so great that he appears at times to be more "deranged" than he actually is. His prophetic insight derives from a vision so intense and so unusual that his utterances seem, to his more phlegmatic countrymen, to be those of a madman. Keegan, in reality, is more sane than his complacent critics. As with Hamlet, however, a suspicion obtrudes that he may in fact be slightly unbalanced— when he talks, for example, of coming to the Round Tower at night to meditate on his "madness" or when that soul of pleasant normality, Aunt Judy, mentions quite casually that at present "he has his mad fit on him."

Because he sees further than his fellows, he has an extraordinary wisdom. Though this wisdom at times reaches prophecy, he also discerns, with striking clarity, the facts about men's lives in society. By virtue of his love of truth, he can penetrate the "clothes" of social usage to the reality, whether benign or sinister, dwelling beneath them. Something of an intellectual amid a group of sentimentalists and a visionary amid a group of small-souled farmers, Keegan rejects a self-defeating despair and turns instead to a rigorous scrutiny of his experiences. The comic mode, alive to the incongruities of existence, enables him to perceive the whole truth about men and aspects of the truth that men normally overlook. For him, as for Shaw, the best way of "joking is to tell the truth. It's the funniest joke in the world." For one as perceptive as Keegan, the comic vision, responsible as it is to the disproportions of existence, often suggests possibilities different from those inherent in the present.

Thus Keegan's wisdom functions near at hand among human beings and social actualities, and at a further distance in the realm of prophetic speculation. He sees clearly the relationships among human beings, the estrangement, for example, that has developed between Larry Doyle and Nora Reilly over the years: "Aye, he's come to torment you; and youre driven already to torment him." Much to Broadbent's and Doyle's surprise, Keegan reveals an insider's knowledge of the transactions by which the Syndicate will gain control of the Rosscullen land. Bankruptcies and foreclosures will be arranged to enrich a final group of shareholders; the good of the Irish people, as a consideration, will be nowhere at all.

But Keegan takes long views as well as short ones. One can catch glimpses of heaven, he says, even if this life is hell. The reality of heaven is proved by one's glimpse of it as much as if it were in full view. However, as he tells the grasshopper in act 2, we can only look toward heaven from this earth but not reach it. Yet if the ideal is remote and shadowy, it cannot be discounted. As one who has sometimes seen heaven, he cannot be satisfied with Broadbent's "foolish dream of efficiency." Rather, he will try to relate his ideals to his experience as a man in the world. When he does so, he perceives that Ruskin was right, that "there is no wealth but life" and that "the day may come when these islands shall live by the quality of their men rather than by the abundance of their minerals."

For Keegan there are but two countries, hell and heaven, and two conditions of man, damnation and salvation. The one place and the one spiritual state do not exclude the opposite. If the Irish continue to work for their damnation, they could as easily work for their salvation by ascertaining a more just basis for individual and social life. Keegan's own vision would entail a fusion of the spiritual, the political, and the social:

> In my dreams it [heaven] is a country where the State is the Church and the Church the people; three in one and one in three. It is a commonwealth in which work is play and play is life: three in one and one in three. It is a temple in which the priest is the worshipper and the worshipper the worshipped: three in one and one in three. It is a godhead in which all life is human and all humanity divine: three in one and one in three. It is, in short, the dream of a madman.

There are here, of course, overtones of the Swinburnian and Comtian worship of humanity and of the secular idealism of the nineteenth-century prophets—Shelley, Ruskin, and Morris. There is also the romanticist desire to attain identity with a mystical, luminous entity, uniting all man's attributes and activities. A reverence for life as such pervades this speech and Keegan's character throughout the play: note especially his Franciscan sense of kinship with the animals—the grasshopper, the pig killed by the motor car, the donkey, and the ass, all of whom he calls his "brothers."

Granted that his idealism is secular as well as transcendent, still Father Keegan experiences with such intensity his vision of a transformed humanity that he is not much interested in the improvement of social conditions in the here and now. Kronenberger feels that both Keegan and Doyle fail Ireland, the one finding a refuge in irony and the other in cynicism; and there is some basis for this judgment. Nevertheless, Keegan's prophetic voice is replete with urgency, and in this respect he does not fail Ireland. The traumatic wounds he has received from the world and his disappointments with it justify, he seems to say, a retreat to irony instead of a forward advance to decisive action. Action is desirable, but he perceives that, temperamentally, he is the thinker, not the doer. He provides no example for young Ireland to follow in politics; judged by what he has accomplished, he is a failure. But as one who radiates the light that may yet regenerate Ireland and her politics, he cannot be judged a failure. His forthright views constitute an intellectual choice and a commitment. Like Shaw's Caesar, he is great by virtue of what he is, not by what he does. His candor and serenity betoken spiritual power, but a power that is now held in reserve and a power that does not yet prevail to any reassuring extent.

V

John Bull's Other Island proceeds polyphonically by a series of interwoven character studies, and anticipates in its organization avant-garde novels like Norman Douglas's *South Wind* and Aldous Huxley's *Antic Hay* and *Point Counter Point*. The characters, therefore, are implicated with one another in their development, and Shaw's third major creation, Larry Doyle, has already figured in my remarks on Broadbent and Keegan. In the dialectical pattern, Doyle operates midway between the other two characters. Like Keegan, he is critical of Broadbent and his capitalist schemes; and he is acid, for example, in his exposé of the amorality and impersonal nature of the Land Development Syndicate. Yet it is perhaps symbolic that Doyle owns stocks in the enterprise. He does not reject Broadbent and his program for Ireland, since he finds that activity of almost any sort is preferable to the inactivity of the visionary Keegan. Keegan turns his back on Broadbent, whereas Larry supports him until someone else can do better for Ireland.

He is an idealist like Keegan; and while he condemns Carlyle and Ruskin for being talkative prophets only, he is as Ruskinian at points as Keegan. Keegan might himself have described the true tragedy of Matthew Haffigan as "the tragedy of his wasted youth, his stunted mind, his drudging over his clods and pigs until he has become a clod and a pig himself—until the soul within him has smouldered into nothing but a dull temper that hurts himself and all around him." Doyle is driven by conscience and by a wish to do well by Ireland. Because he is honest with his potential constituents he loses the chance of representing them at Westminster. As Shaw was, he is suspicious of unmitigated free enterprise in agriculture as in industry. He cannot see much difference between the great landholders who have just been dispossessed by the Land Purchase Act of 1903 and the small landholders who have succeeded them. Men in both classes resent being called to account and reject the notion of social responsibility as an annoyance and an irrelevance. Nor is Doyle much impressed with the Matthew Haffigans who now own the farms. He regards them as men without honor, ability, or even capital, men who know only toil and greed.

Doyle's main criticism of Ireland concerns its provinciality and blind nationalism. He describes himself as an "internationalist," he would eliminate ethnic barriers rather than raise them, and he would wish "Ireland to be the brains and imagination of a big Commonwealth, not a Robinson Crusoe Island." A Roman Catholic like Keegan, he has the same enlarged view of a church's function. Larry describes his Catholicism as that "of Charlemagne or Dante, qualified by a great deal of modern science and folklore which Father Dempsey would call the ravings of an Atheist." Larry's progressive religious views are similar to Keegan's when the latter says, "My country is not Ireland nor England, but the whole mighty realm of my church."

Larry Doyle is the "real Irishman" Shaw had in mind in his Preface to the play. Here Shaw contrasts the Irishman's "realism" and imaginativeness with the Englishman's sentimentality as represented by Broadbent. Larry is shrewd concerning the Irish and their problems, displaying "the freedom from illusion, the power of facing facts, the nervous industry, the sharpened wits, the sensitive pride of the imaginative man who has fought his way up through social persecution and poverty." Yet he is more clearminded about his native land than he is about his own aims, ideals, and ambitions. He lives in Broadbent's "real world" in England, but his introspective temper and

fastidious intellect find as little to satisfy him there as in the escapist world
of Ireland.

As an intellectual, Larry has the sensitivity, pride, insight, and flexibility which Shaw associated with the Irishman at his best (Keegan is another kind of ideal Irishman, the visionary saint). But God's Irishman is not
popular with his own countrymen, who are either dreamers like Nora Reilly,
living in illusion, or else opportunistic peasants, coarsened by suffering and
oppression. Larry is clearheaded and free of sentimentality, but lacks imaginative boldness, strength to assert himself, patience under duress in the
service of his ideals, and the political instinct to persuade people of the truth
of his views. Nor is he free of what Shaw called "that derision which is
Dublin's staple intellectual commodity, and which more or less infects all
urban Ireland, to the great detriment of our national character, and the
mean satisfaction of everything that is envious, conceited, and ignoble in
our souls."

In spite of his tirades against romance, Larry is an idealist. But he is a
thwarted idealist and consequently a cynic. The gap between his ideals and
actuality paralyzes him for constructive action. He bleeds spiritually and
can find no anodyne for his hurt, except in a denial of those qualities of
mind which might heal his divided soul—idealism, enthusiasm, vision, mysticism. Like Keegan, he feels at home nowhere: in his native Ireland, in his
adoptive Britain, or in the realm of business. Like Keegan, he feels that this
world is hell, but Larry can find nothing to improve in it except its physical
circumstances. In spite of his testiness, he is likable; and he may eventually
conjoin the practical universe of Broadbent and the visionary one of Keegan.

Shaw's conception of Nora Reilly is challenging, and she helps define
the three main male characters. Father Keegan recognizes greater spiritual
authority in her than Doyle will admit; for Keegan she makes Ireland a
purgatory rather than a hell. For Larry she represents the frayed traditions
and escapism that have proved Ireland's undoing. As an Irish realist and a
rigorous idealist, he judges her correctly but too severely. Nora's Irish sen-
timentalism finds its true counterpart in Broadbent's English sentimental-
ism; and both sentimantalisms are, of course, antipathetic to Larry. The
rapprochement between Nora and Broadbent suggests perhaps that representative English and Irish types are similar enough for the two nations to
coexist in peace.

Like all the other characters, Nora is complex. She is weak rather than
forthright, sentimental rather than perceptive, snobbish rather than sympathetic. Yet she has her moments of strength. Her pride gives her a force in
personal relationships not unlike that of Ibsen's Nora; and insofar as Nora

Reilly represents Ireland, her pride is a genuine national characteristic. Accordingly, she rejects Larry independently of his rejection of her, and his being "brutal" in urging her to marry Broadbent on the rebound reconciles her, in fact, to Broadbent. Just as Eliza in *Pygmalion* turns from the peremptory Higgins to the appreciative Freddy, so Nora transfers affection from the indifferent Larry to the ardent Broadbent. In a sense, she also recalls Candida and has about her suggestions of the Virgin Mother. Like Candida she remains with the spiritually weaker of the two men in her life, since thereby she finds the most authentic sphere for the exercise of her protective femininity.

Shaw draws into the concluding ten-page debate the themes, the psychological nuances, the temperamental types, and the values elaborated in the play. Initially in this interchange Shaw emphasizes the similarities between Keegan and Larry, just as later he stresses their divergences. At the outset Keegan laments the changes that will come to Rosscullen under Broadbent's aegis, and he deplores Ireland's spiritual impotence. Larry similarly protests against the impoverishment of Ireland's human resources in the brutalizing of its Matthew Haffigans. Next, Broadbent briefly assumes control of the debate when he promises to take Ireland in hand. For most of the rest of the scene the spotlight is on Keegan, who condemns first Broadbent and then Larry for indifference to Ireland's spiritual well-being. Larry serves as the *agent provocateur*, inciting Keegan to his most fervent utterances. Even after Keegan's demonstration to Larry that heaven as well as hell may be about one in the present, Larry is still unreconciled to the man who often touches him most deeply. It is Broadbent, with his description of the way heaven appeared to him in a dream as a boy, who next stimulates Keegan to his luminous declaration of principles, his declaration of what heaven and the Holy Trinity mean to him. This, then, is the climax of the debate, also the moment of the revelation toward which the whole drama tends. Yet if Keegan's views represent the only desirable synthesis of religion and social fact, it is Broadbent who brings down the curtain. It is his values which, for the foreseeable future, have strength; and he will not be easily divested of his powers. If Keegan is going to do his best for Ireland, Broadbent is also going to devote himself to it in his good-humored, efficient, and destructive fashion.

Although Keegan's views are prophetically incisive, no one of the participants in this interchange emerges victorious. Shaw in his visionary aspect identified himself with the unfrocked priest, and in some ways Keegan achieves Shaw's desired fusion of reality and dream. Yet Henderson and Irvine are also right in their somewhat different view of the play. They allege that Larry Doyle's realism concerning social possibilities represents the attitude to which Shaw was increasingly drawn. Doyle's realism may be ill-defined and fumbling, and he may not as yet be capable of translating his realistically defined conclusions into decisive actions. Nevertheless, he would wish to unite Keegan's vision with Broadbent's pragmatic talents, for the benefit not only of Ireland but of mankind. Doyle's position anticipates the surer union of these forces in Andrew Undershaft in Shaw's next play, *Major Barbara*. Undershaft, his own brand of vision merged with a sure sense of fact, triumphs over the idealism of his daughter to a greater extent than Doyle triumphs over Keegan. Yet the last word is with the "saints," Keegan and Barbara, because they are the vessels of the "Holy Ghost" that enkindles them and makes them invincible. Just as Barbara sees that her work is only beginning when she takes over the spiritual renovation of Perivale St. Andrews, so Keegan in a renovated Ireland will be its spiritual leader. So also Don Juan goes off to heaven, leaving behind an eloquent devil with his counsels of despair and hedonism that are based on his cynical appraisal of things as they are.

Sean O'Casey, I believe, comes closest to approximating Shaw's elusive message in the closing debate when he asserts that "from the dream efficiency could grow, but from the efficiency no dream could ever come." Only Broadbent's energy and practical sense can contribute to a new order; otherwise, his attitudes have no relevance to a revitalized western culture because he lacks vision. Can Doyle and Keegan tame Broadbent and utilize his abilities for furthering their Ruskinian idealism? Can those who advocate the ideas of the nineteenth-century prophets, of whom Marx was the most dynamic, use creatively the techniques of industrialism as they are embodied in the programs of Broadbent? Shaw at this point proposed to use the efficiencies of capitalism in the service of a new socialism and a new religious awakening. This, I believe, is the direction of the play. This social and philosophical burden, borne lightly, accounts for the stature of *John Bull's Other Island*. Shaw adroitly combines the incidental analysis of these issues with the analysis of character. His judgment that the play contains "five separate tragedies . . . besides the Broadbent comedy" indicates the scope and depth of its purely human and psychological aspects. As a work of great breadth and authority, *John Bull's Other Island* represents one of the pinnacles of Shaw's dramaturgy.

LOUIS CROMPTON

Caesar and Cleopatra

Caesar and Cleopatra is the second panel in the triptych made up by the *Three Plays for Puritans*. Like *The Devil's Disciple* and *Captain Brassbound's Conversion*, it is a military melodrama that asks us to think more deeply than usual about violence and justice. Like them, too, it is a religious allegory dramatizing the conflict between Old Testament and New Testament morality. Even its exotic setting is part of a pattern: where the Unpleasant Plays conjure up the gloom of city slums, and the Pleasant Plays the sunshine of snow-capped peaks, park lands, and the seashore, the Plays for Puritans all take place on remote imperial frontiers where what passes for civilization clashes with what is conventionally regarded as barbarism. In *Caesar and Cleopatra*, Egypt under the Roman occupation becomes, like Revolutionary America and contemporary Morocco, a proving ground for a conflict between subhuman and superhuman elements in man's nature.

Throughout these three plays Shaw attempts to define his idea of heroism. In the second he puts on the stage an actual historical figure, Julius Caesar. This choice will inevitably seem perverse to most English-speaking people. Despite the re-evaluations of nineteenth-century historiography, the popular view of Caesar in Anglo-Saxon countries is still a hostile one. That is to say, Caesar is still regarded as a usurping tyrant who seized political power for selfish ends. To the man on the street whose knowledge of history is limited to Shakespeare and Plutarch, the pro-Caesarism of Goethe, Mommsen, and Froude is wholly unintelligible, and Dante's decision to make Brutus share with Judas the place of honor in hell in the very jaws of

From *Shaw the Dramatist*. © 1969 by the University of Nebraska Press.

Satan remains a curious vagary. If we want to understand Shaw's attitude toward Caesar, we must first understand why he rejected the common estimate of him.

The view of Caesar as the great subversive who plotted from his cradle to overthrow the Republic derives, of course, from Plutarch's and Suetonius's *Lives*. But most readers of these biographies are unaware that Plutarch writes primarily as a staunch moral conservative and Suetonius as a constitutionalist who sympathized with the Senatorial faction in the Roman Civil War. Still, for all their moral and political bias both biographers make Caesar a great man. It is not until we come to Shakespeare's play that we find a picture of Caesar that reduces him to a mere petty self-glorifier. *Julius Caesar* gives us Plutarch's Caesar diminished in stature so that he is nothing more than an Elizabethan stage-tyrant who, as Shaw complained, utters no speech even up to the level of a Tammany boss:

> It is when we turn to Julius Caesar, the most splendidly written political melodrama we possess, that we realize the apparently immortal author of Hamlet as a man, not for all time, but for an age only, and that, too, in all solidly wise and heroic aspects, the most despicable of all the ages in our history. It is impossible for even the most judicially minded critic to look without a revulsion of indignant contempt at this travestying of a great man as a silly braggart. . . . As far as sonority, imagery, wit, humor, energy of imagination, power over language, and a whimsically keen eye for idiosyncrasies can make a dramatist, Shakespear was the king of dramatists. Unfortunately, a man may have them all, and yet conceive high affairs of state exactly as Simon Tappertit did.

Instead, Shakespeare exalts Brutus at Caesar's expense. But Brutus-worship logically involves Senate-worship and the endorsement of a republicanism that was antipopular at the same time that it was antimonarchical. The Roman Republic under the Senate was a narrow oligarchy based on aristocratic privilege. The roots of its power lay in the ownership of land and slaves and in the exploitation of the overseas provinces. In these respects it had much in common, say, with eighteenth-century England or with the antebellum American South, so that John Wilkes Booth, looking at Lincoln through the eyes of another ruined oligarchy, could easily idealize himself as Brutus's successor.

Ultimately, of course, it is simply a question of what meaning we give to the word republican. A republic may be either a popular democracy or a kingless oligarchy. Throughout his life Shaw called himself a republican—

meaning by this that he preferred the American and French systems of government to the feudalism of prewar Russia, Germany, and Austria. If we keep these two meanings of the word in mind, then Caesar's remark in the play—"Were Rome a true Republic, then were Caesar the first of Republicans"—becomes perfectly intelligible, and we will be able to see how Shaw's admiration for Caesar is not at odds with his democratic socialism, but part and parcel of it. Indeed, Caesar's championing of the populace against the patricians in the Roman class war made him anathema to such writers as Lucan, Suetonius, and Shakespeare. On the other hand, nineteenth-century historiography, reacting against aristocratic feudalism, hailed Caesar as the long overdue reformer of an outmoded constitution. Hence the admiration that Caesar awakened in such men as Goethe, Niebuhr, Hegel, Mommsen, Victor Duruy, James Froude, and Warde Fowler.

Of all these it is Mommsen who sets forth the pro-Caesar side with the greatest cogency. As a German liberal of the revolution of 1848, he seems to have looked on the erudite volumes of his monumental *History of Rome* as a series of tracts for the times. He clearly associated the Roman Senatorial party with the defenders of the *ancien régime* in Europe; in his vision, Rome's Catos, Ciceros, and Pompeys are the classical counterparts of the Bourbons, Metternichs, and Castlereaghs of his own day. His Caesar is the heir of the Gracchi and Marius, and the embodiment of an impulse to social reform which had been germinating in Roman society for a hundred years. In opposition to a recalcitrant, selfish, and backward-looking Senate, Caesar made himself the leader of the democratic party which was striving to enlarge the franchise, open overseas possessions to colonists, and remodel the political, military, and financial life of the state. Thus, far from finding Caesar a tyrannical autocrat, Mommsen considered his career "so little at variance with democracy," that democracy only attained its fulfillment in it.

Shaw's play is permeated with Mommsen's antiaristocratic and anticonstitutional point of view. The soldiers' prologue ridicules the snobbish pretensions of the Royal Guard, whose class prejudices and chivalric code hopelessly limit their effectiveness as fighters. The Ra prologue, in its devastating judgment of Pompey, echoes the scorn upon scorn Mommsen pours on the legalism and political myopia of Caesar's rival. Shaw further extends this antiaristocratic criticism to Egypt's rulers, scourging the flunkeyism of the court and the playboy extravagances most spectacularly evident in the reign of Cleopatra's father Ptolemy Auletes, "the Flute-Blower." In so doing Shaw presumably had in mind the wastrelism of the nineteenth-century khedives, who set a pattern familiar to the twentieth century in the person of King Farouk.

British historians who read Mommsen were naturally keenly sensitive
to the analogies between Caesar's Rome and imperialist England. James
Anthony Froude found in the collapse of the Roman Republic an object
lesson for the British aristocracy, which had also amassed great wealth at
the expense of the proletariat and failed to take its social duties seriously.
Froude regarded Caesar not as a dangerous revolutionary, but as a man
whom an age of sham and cant forced into his role as a reconstituter of the
state. But though he read Froude's *Caesar: A Sketch* (1879), Shaw does not
mention it among the sources for the play. He does, however, refer to
another book, Warde Fowler's *Julius Caesar and the Foundation of the
Roman Imperial System,* which is in the same vein. Published four years
after Victoria's Golden Jubilee, this book extends Froude's analysis to show
how Roman capitalism had, by Caesar's day, spread from Italy to the whole
Mediterranean world. For Warde Fowler, Caesar's greatest achievement
was the replacement of a self-seeking city oligarchy by a genuine imperial
system: "Julius Caesar, personifying the principle of intelligent government
by a single man, had made it possible for the Roman dominion, then on the
point of breaking up, to grow into a great political union, and eventually to
provide a material foundation for modern civilisation." Clearly it is Warde
Fowler's reading of Roman-English parallels that lies behind the Ra prologue of 1912. The Egyptian god, who here represents the *Zeitgeist,* or spirit
of history, castigates modern Britain for following the way of Rome at home
and abroad, and hails Caesar as the one man who has risen above the level
of the exploiters to grasp the necessity for change.

Undoubtedly, part of the attraction Caesar held for Shaw lay in the role
he played in Roman history. Yet, though this is an essential element of
Shaw's play, it is not central to it. As we have indicated, *Caesar and Cleopatra*
is primarily a religious rather than a political drama. Shaw's Caesar is not
the reformer of codes, but the man who has outgrown them. He stands for
progress, not in the political or social, but in the evolutionary sense. He is
a new breed of animal born with sounder instincts than the average man.
Being biologically more advanced, he is without the burden of original sin
which finds expression in resentment and vindictiveness on the one hand
and a respect for moral systems on the other. His ethic is not the creation of
any formal ethical system, but of the developed will which has identified its
ends with those of the race; Caesar is the libertarian egoist who in doing
exactly what he wants to do serves humanity. As Shaw puts it "Having
virtue, he has no need of goodness." This is a conception Shaw discovered
first in Wagner and then in Nietzsche. In Wagner's philosophy the idea of
the triumph of the individual will over the constricting trammels of Church

and State finds its clearest expression in Siegfried, and, indeed, Shaw's remarks on the hero of the *Ring* in *The Perfect Wagnerite* can quite appropriately be applied to his own Caesar. Siegfried, Shaw declared, was "the type of the healthy man raised to a perfect confidence in his own impulses by an intense vitality which is above fear, sickliness of conscience, malice, and the make shifts and moral crutches of law and order which accompany them."

Shaw is in effect warning us against trying to apply ordinary moral standards to Caesar at all. Given any code of ethics, it is always possible to trump up a telling indictment against anyone we have a mind to vilify. Macaulay's essays, in which statesmen and generals he sympathizes with politically are praised for their lofty conduct and ones he dislikes excoriated in the same high-toned fashion, are a good example of this mechanically concocted moral rhetoric, and mutual recriminations among nations in the cold war continue the tradition *ad nauseam*. Shaw is quite aware that his Caesar might be called a brutal plunderer, a destroyer of national freedom, a tyrant, a condoner of incest, a conscienceless sensualist, a reveler, a hypocrite, a vain dandy, and (in the library-burning episode) a soldier callously indifferent to literature and history. On these grounds anyone could interpret Caesar as a type of anti-Christ. But it would be equally easy, on the basis of his paternal kindness, his freedom from resentment, his insouciance, his horror of treachery and political assassination, his devotion to his followers, and the paraphrase of the Sermon on the Mount Shaw has him deliver at the climax of the play, to make him out a type of Christ. Shaw's aim is not to establish one or the other as the true Caesar, but to show that this kind of moralizing is mere childish name-calling whose categories any clever writer can invert at will.

Shaw had developed his own moral antinomianism before reading Nietzsche, and differed from him radically by remaining all his life an ardent socialist and humanitarian. Nevertheless, his Caesar does bear a strong resemblance to the "Great Man" as Nietzsche characterizes him in *The Will to Power*. Like Nietzsche's hero, Shaw's Caesar has a "loneliness within his heart which neither praise nor blame can reach" and possesses "courage even for unholy means." The loneliness is expressed in Caesar's opening soliloquy, one of Shaw's most elaborate pieces of prose poetry. Its wistfulness is meant to come as a shock to those whose experience of Shakespeare has led them to expect a ranting Caesar. Its style is surprisingly Pateresque, and it is full of antinomian and erotic overtones. Those critics who, like MacCarthy, have accused Shaw of denying the sexual side of Caesar have missed the point. Shaw does not, as Froude does, discount the stories of

Caesar's sexual exploits as mere malicious gossip concocted by his political enemies. He accepted Suetonius's description of Caesar as "every woman's husband and every man's wife," and declared that he meant his Caesar to be as susceptible to women as Mahomet was, with one important provision:

> As to my alleged failure to present the erotic Caesar, that is a matter almost too delicate for discussion. But it seems to me that the very first consideration that must occur to any English dramatic expert in this connection is that Caesar was not Antony. Yet it is precisely because Caesar in my play is not Antony that I am told he is not Caesar. Mr. MacCarthy says that Caesar stayed too long in Alexandria for Cleopatra's sake. But the fact remains that Caesar did not think it too long, and that, as the upshot proved, he was right. Antony let Cleopatra disgrace and ruin him: when he left her he came back to her like the needle to the magnet. She influenced Caesar's affairs so little that few people know that he ever met her; and when he left her she had to go after him to Rome to get hold of him again. Antony was Cleopatra's slave: Julius was "every woman's husband."

Where the question uppermost in the mind of the man in the street will be whether or not Cleopatra has become Caesar's mistress, and where the sentimentalist will be ready to condone the sexual relation provided Caesar is in love with her, Shaw thinks that the lack of any such emotional bond is the important thing. Given this, it is to him a matter of indifference whether their relation is or is not a sexual one.

Since Shaw was not concerned primarily with Caesar the politician, we can understand why he did not write a "Caesar and Pompey" or a "Caesar and Cato." But, we may still ask, why a "Caesar and Cleopatra"? If Caesar is to be shown in conflict, not with political institutions of his day, by with the very idea of moral law itself, would it not have been more logical to have made his antagonist some representative of what Shaw frequently refers to as "the Nonconformist Conscience"? This element is not entirely lacking from the play; it is represented by Britannus, who either opposes Caesar with moral clichés when he is scandalized by him or defends him with the same clichés when he is pleased. But the tone of the play in dealing with such moralizing is simply one of good-natured amusement. Instead of opposing Caesar to Mrs. Grundy, Shaw adopts a much bolder plan, and accepts the challenge of the conventional moralist in its most trenchant form. For, asks the conventional man, if one abrogates the traditional social restraints, will not society become, as Britannus puts it, "an arena full of wild beasts tearing one another to pieces"? Shaw's reply is, in effect, to present us with human nature in its most dangerously violent form and to show us his hero facing it fearlessly without any of the common moral or judicial sanctions.

In Shaw's play, Caesar stands for humanity in its highest development, Cleopatra for untamed natural passion. To underline the distance between Caesar and those Romans and Egyptians who share the stage with him, Shaw uses an allegorial device unique to this play. He identifies the aggressive, greedy Romans with bull-like and doglike animals—a wolf-headed Roman war tuba opens the play with a "Minotaur bellow"; Rufio calls himself a dog at Caesar's heels; and the Egyptianized general, Achillas, is described as looking like a curled poodle. In contrast, the feminine and treacherous Egyptians are given catlike and snakelike qualities—Cleopatra is compared to a kitten and a serpent, Theodotus to a viper, Ftatateeta to a tiger and a crocodile. Caesar is kind to Romans and Egyptians alike; but, as Cleopatra comes to realize, the kindness he bestows on others is not the result of sentimentality, as she at first supposes, but is the sort of kindness one might show to an animal of another species, free alike from passionate attachment and moral indignation.

Shaw's Caesar and Shakespeare's are simply two different men. By contrast, their Cleopatras are recognizably the same woman. Shaw's girl-queen has the winsomeness, the grace, the impertinence, the caprice, the petulance, the cowardice, the treachery, the histrionic bent, and the cruel anger of Shakespeare's Cleopatra, together with her inability to conceive of any approach to men which is not mere imperiousness, babyish wheedling, or languorous seduction. That one is sixteen and the other forty Shaw considers an irrelevance, his point being that the Cleopatra temperament is fully formed at the earlier age, since it is in fact a kind of arrested development. Shaw admired Shakespeare's Cleopatra as an artistic achievement. Where he thought the older playwright had "made a mess of Caesar under the influence of Plutarch," he considered the role of Cleopatra "so consummate that the part reduced the best actresses to absurdity." But though their conceptions of Cleopatra's character are identical, the judgments the two playwrights render are totally different. In the end Shaw accuses Shakespeare of having lent a false glamor and "spurious heroism" to someone he regarded as embodying only "the genius of worthlessness."

Where Shaw does go significantly beyond Shakespeare is in emphasizing Cleopatra's murderous and sadistic side. This is a result of Shaw's attempt to present what might be called the dynastic view of Cleopatra. Historically, the Ptolemaic kings and queens of Egypt had shown a remarkable brutality in disposing of relatives close to the throne, evincing, in their willingness to connive at the murder of parents, children, brothers, and sisters, a ruthlessness resembling that of the later Ottoman sultans. Shaw seems to have thought of Cleopatra as very much a typical Ptolemy in this sense. He replied to Gilbert Murray's charge that he had "overdone Cleopatra's ferocity," by declaring that "if she had been an educated lady of the time," he should have "made her quite respectable and civilized," but that what he was "able to gather about her father, the convivial Flute Blower, and other members of the household, joined with considerations of the petulance of royalty" had led him to draw her as he did. Here Shaw seems to have been following the lead of the Irish historian John Pentland Mahaffy, whose book *The Empire of the Ptolemies* (1895) makes Cleopatra hereditarily fratricidal and recognizably akin in "beauty, talent, daring, and cruelty," to the six earlier Cleopatras who had preceded her on the throne of Egypt.

Half of the fascination of Shaw's play lies in the way in which we are invited to watch the Cleopatra of history and literature develop from the panic-stricken hoyden of the Sphinx scene. At first she is childishly naïve on the subject of kingship. "My father was King of Egypt; and he never worked," she tells Caesar, to which Caesar replies dryly that there may have been some connection between her father's negligence and his political and financial difficulties. Six months later, she manages to sound more sophisticated. At this point Cleopatra can mouth Caesarisms in order to impress others with what she conceives to be her new maturity: "Now that Caesar has made me wise, it is no use my liking or disliking: I do what must be done, and have no time to attend to myself. That is not happiness; but it is greatness." But in reality nothing but her external manner has changed. In a deeper sense Caesar's example has not influenced her at all, and she remains profoundly ambivalent in her feelings toward him. Part of her, the affectionate and sentimentally dependent child, wants his fatherly approval and is achingly jealous of any attention he pays to others, while the other part, the passionate woman, longs to be free of his paternal surveillance. When Pothinus accuses her of secretly desiring Caesar's death, Cleopatra, who does not understand herself at all, is thrown into a murderous fit of rage, hatred, and chagrin, all the more bitter because the eunuch has come so close to the truth. Caesar, who understands her perfectly, calls her behavior natural and makes no attempt to alter her conduct beyond providing the lessons in deportment which are the most her nature can absorb.

In his interpretation of *The Ring of the Nibelungs* Shaw divides the actors in Wagner's allegory into four categories: the predatory, lustful, greedy people; the dull, patient plodders; the "gods" or lawgivers who invent the religious, moral, and legal codes society is bound by; and finally, the heroes who free men from the rule of the "gods" when their codes become obsolescent. Clearly, Cleopatra belongs to the first of these categories as Caesar belongs to the last. Of Caesar's two servants in the play, Rufio is loyal and affectionate as a dog is loyal and affectionate, but Britannus stands on a level of development beyond Cleopatra's naïve passionateness or Rufio's simple devotion. He is a man of the third class, a moralist, a legalist, and a rhetorician, shocked when Caesar challenges the "gods" by sanctioning the incestuous royal marriage, careful to restate Caesar's blunt demand for money in legal terms, and appalled at his not bothering to punish those who are plotting against him. What makes his character comical, of course, is his trick of translating all his enthusiasms and antipathies into resounding moral imperatives. Britannus cannot conceive of a world without punishment or "justice," as he calls retaliation. To him, Caesar's anarchist vision of a society without punitive laws or deterrents is unthinkable and frightening. But to Shaw as to Wagner, it is exactly the highest developments of civilization that stand directly in the way of further advance through their moral prestige; and law and order as presently incorporated in Church and State are merely swaddling bands humanity has wrapped itself in until it is ready to burst them and proceed a stage onward.

The result is that Caesar must, like Dick Dudgeon, appear to the morally hidebound as another sort of "devil's disciple"; the embryonic superman will usually impress others as shockingly immoral. The difference is that where Dick is always attended by a faint smell of sulphur, Caesar commits his impieties with Olympian serenity. This debonair quality of its hero is one of the sources of the play's remarkable charm. Another is what we may call its "musicality." From the delicate rhythms of Caesar's prose-poem soliloquy onward, *Caesar and Cleopatra* has about it a happy air of improvisation, so that its mood reminds us of one of the freer musical forms, say a fantasia or a divertimento. In this it contrasts strongly with the more closely knit, but rather mechanical, structure of the other two Plays for Puritans.

Yet these musical and poetic qualities should not blind us to the fact that *Caesar and Cleopatra* is also a melodrama. It is, for Shaw, a remarkably violent play. Two murders actually take place in the course of the action, and we are implicitly asked to judge three others. This is an almost Shakespearean quota of deaths, but, unlike Shakespeare, Shaw is not interested in the dramatic poetry of murder either on the sensational, theatrical side or from the point of view of what Samuel Johnson would call poetic justice. Rather, Shaw wants us to think critically about the moral and social significance of killing. Hence each of the five violent deaths has a distinctly different context and meaning. First we have the cold-blooded murder of Pompey by Septimius at the behest of the Egyptians, who have ordered the death of the defenseless refugee in the hope of winning political favor with Caesar. Shaw's Caesar reacts to this cold-blooded butchery of his enemy and rival with all the horror that Plutarch and Appian ascribe to him. Then follows the discussion of the judicial murder of Vercingetorix, which Caesar now repudiates as mere terrorism parading as statecraft. In the play itself we are all but spectators at the murders of Pothinus and Ftatateeta. And finally, we learn of the impending assassination of Caesar on his return to Rome, an act which Shaw regarded as a particularly outrageous blunder on the part of well-intentioned political idealists.

As we have already seen, melodrama has its roots in certain moral religious feelings of which Shaw strongly disapproved. Though a critic as civilized as A. C. Bradley found it consoling that *Hamlet* and *King Lear* vindicated retributive justice in their gory endings, Shaw would have pointed out that this is a feature they share with any movie or television western in which the audience feels gratification when the villain gets his thrashing. Once again, as in *The Devil's Disciple,* Shaw is trying to draw our attention to the contradiction in popular Christianity, which illogically mixes Yahweh-worship with the Sermon on the Mount without any sense of their incongruity. It is exactly this endorsement of Christianity on its Tolstoyan and repudiation of it on its Pauline side that underlies the banquet scene which is the climax of *Caesar and Cleopatra.* Here Ftatateeta, goaded on by Cleopatra, vows vengeance on Pothinus for his betrayal of the queen, and shortly after, kills him.

At this point it is interesting to compare Shaw with the one other major dramatist who has dramatized Caesar's relation to Cleopatra. Corneille, in *La Mort de Pompée,* wrote a typical revenge melodrama, the theme of the play being the struggle of Pompey's widow, Cornelia, to avenge her husband's death, and its denouement the overwhelming of Pothinus, Ptolemy, and the others who had connived at it. Shaw turns Corneille's ethic upside down. Cleopatra, still smarting from Pothinus's accusation, thinks her honor has been vindicated by his death and appeals haughtily to Lucius Septimius, Britannus, and Apollodorus to justify her. Each man gives an answer in keeping with his life-philosophy: Septimius discreetly equivocates, calling the murder just but unwise (since it will not please Caesar); Britannus applauds it as a moral deterrent to others; and Apollodorus regrets that he was not allowed to kill the man in a chivalrous duel. Only Caesar disagrees:

If one man in all the world can be found, now or forever, to know that you did wrong, that man will either have to conquer the world as I have, or be crucified by it. [*The uproar in the streets again reaches them.*] Do you hear? These knockers at your gate are also believers in vengeance and in stabbing. You have slain their leader: it is right that they shall slay you. If you doubt it, ask your four counsellors here. And in the name of that right [*he emphasizes the word with great scorn*] shall I not slay them for murdering their Queen, and be slain in my turn by their countrymen as the invader of their fatherland? Can Rome do less then than slay these slayers, too, to shew the world *how Rome avenges her sons and her honor.* [Italics added.] And so, to the end of history, murder shall breed murder, always in the name of right and honor and peace, until the gods are tired of blood and create a race that can understand.

This "trial" of Cleopatra corresponds, by analogy, to the other trial scenes in Shaw's melodramas, and ends like them, not with justice triumphant, but with justice repudiated. But Caesar's speech was, of course, much more than a rebuke to Cleopatra. It was, among other things, a criticism of the English, who, having waged war in the Anglo-Egyptian Sudan to avenge their national honor and the death of Gordon, had at its conclusion dug up and mutilated the body of the dead Mahdi, an act of public policy which Shaw thought revealed how little English mentality was removed from the outlook of the barbarous tribesmen they were fighting.

At the end of the scene Cleopatra sees Ftatateeta's red blood streaming over the white altar of the god she worshiped. In response to a murder done out of spite, Rufio has added another death. What, Shaw now asks, are we to make of this new killing? It is a measure of the hardheadedness that goes with his humanitarianism that he has Caesar justify the slaughter of Ftatateeta. In his essay on prisons Shaw denounces the idea of punishment relentlessly, but argues for the social necessity of killing irremediably dangerous people as one might kill dangerous animals, without malice or any pretense of moral superiority. In reply to Desmond MacCarthy's charge that he had made Caesar overly squeamish, Shaw wrote:

To confess the truth, if there is a point in the play on which I pride myself more than another, it is the way in which I have shewn how this readiness to kill tigers, and blackguards, and obstructive idealogues (Napoleon's word) is part of the same

character that abhors waste and murder, and is, in the most
accurate sense of the word, a kind character.

Like Christ's "I came not to send peace but a sword," this is a hard saying,
but one that will bear pondering by those who, while objecting to the death
penalty, think that half a century of incarceration is a humane alternative.

It is now possible to see further into the significance of the animal
symbolism in *Caesar and Cleopatra*. Morally, Shaw's refusal to draw a line
between men and animals, which has its roots in eighteenth-century humanitarianism and nineteenth-century biological science, is fraught with all
sorts of radical consequences. If we look at the animal-human world from
Shaw's perspective, we arrive at a drastic transvaluation of values. No one
pretends to be morally superior to an animal he has decided to destroy, or
hopes that its death will encourage other animals to refrain from man-
slaughter or depredations. Nor does one speak of its crimes against society,
or ask it to pay for its deeds, or cage it as a punishment for its sins or under
the pretense that this will reform its character. Instead we accept animal
nature for what it is, and act accordingly. In so doing, Shaw would argue,
we treat animals far more sensibly and kindly than we do human beings. But
on the other hand, we do not speak of the sacredness of animal life or
hesitate to kill dangerous animals or suffering and neglected ones. Caesar,
who looks at men and women from the Shavian vantage point, regards
human beings in the same way that the keeper of the Humane Society pound
looks at its inmates. As the new animal toward which nature is evolving,
Caesar is as free of malice toward, or passionate regard for, Cleopatra and
the other people in the play as the ordinary man is toward monkeys in a zoo.
It is in a mood of profound irony that Shaw has the devil in *Man and
Superman* warn us: "Beware the pursuit of the Superhuman: it leads to an
indiscriminate contempt for the Human. To a man, horses and dogs and
cats are mere species, outside the moral world. Well, to the Superman, men
and women are a mere species too." But if Shaw disagreed with his cynical-
sentimental devil, neither did he share the philosophy of Carlyle, who regarded the finding of the ablest poundkeeper as the solution to the political
problem. Rather, Shaw counts on the race as a whole leaving Yahoodom
behind; as he puts it in the preface to his next play, he wants his mob to be
"all Caesars." Thus *Caesar and Cleopatra* is not a glorification of Caesar as
a hero we should worship, but as a goal we should strive toward.

These are the currents that run through the depths of Shaw's play. But
the surface is covered with gay ripples, and the mood of Caesar's final
leave-taking is that of a festival. So little is Caesar enamored of Cleopatra

that he forgets all about her in the press of business. When she does appear, she demonstrates that she has learned nothing since they met but poise and histrionic effectiveness. Acting the grand tragedienne, she demands vengeance for the death of Ftatateeta. But Caesar simply refuses to play the scene in this key. Napoleon once remarked that the difference between tragedy and comedy was the difference between standing up and sitting down, and told how, when the Queen of Prussia appeared before him "à la Chimène," he simply offered her a chair. Caesar similarly reduces a tragic pose to farce by stuttering over the dead nurse's name, and then coaxes Cleopatra out of her sulks by promising to send Mark Antony. The Siegfried motif swells buoyantly in the background: Caesar has subdued the Egyptians and will conquer three or four more armies on the way home. He goes lightheartedly to Rome and his death, as Cleopatra, childishly enraptured, awaits the coming of her demigod—and Shakespeare's.

MARTIN MEISEL

Shaw and Revolution: The Politics of the Plays

My subject is the relation between Shaw's plays and his politics. I am not the first to be struck by a discrepancy between them more interesting than bland congruence or mere irrelevance. Shaw's playwriting was always relevant to his politics; but there were apparent contradictions between the one and the other for nearly three decades, starting with those earliest plays, which Shaw himself describes as deliberately propagandist, and lasting through the First World War.

The discrepancy shows itself in an area I will loosely call "strategy." Shaw's politics—his Fabianism—had a strategy for achieving certain desirable social ends. Indeed, a common attack upon Fabianism was to charge that it was all strategy. His plays, like all plays, are designed to engage and manage an audience by creating and organizing a flow of response. They are, in other words, strategies for achieving certain aesthetic ends. Shaw's over-all dramatic strategy, however, was also directed towards creating a residual impact; that is, his plays are not designed merely to stimulate the audience for two hours or even to purge it of stresses in some Aristotelian fashion, leaving its members essentially unchanged. Rather they are designed to culminate in a state of feeling, often including uneasiness and unresolved stress, that will effect a permanent change in consciousness bearing on social change. With such residual impact, the plays as organizations of response are better understood as rhetorical, aimed at persuasion. But between what they seem to persuade to and the Fabian strategies aimed at social change there is an apparent discrepancy.

From *Shaw: Seven Critical Essays,* edited by Norman Rosenblood. © 1971 by Norman Rosenblood. University of Toronto Press.

The strategies and opinions of the Fabian Society changed and developed, as did its individual members; but "Fabianism" as a word and an idea took on a distinctive character in the late eighties, just in the interval of Shaw's movement from fiction to the theatre. Fabianism came to mean evolution as opposed to revolution; gradualism as opposed to catastrophism; the achievement of socialism through constitutional and parliamentary means (initially through the "permeation" of existing political parties and local government); collaboration with all progressive and meliorist forces (or "practical socialism" as opposed to purist ideological concern); and, of course, middle-class intellectualism as opposed to Marxist proletarianism. The Fabians defined themselves in relation to the more Marxist and revolutionary Social Democratic Federation on the one side and the shifting groups of left or communistic anarchists on the other. Shaw reduced the strategy of the socialist groups from which the Fabians diverged to the following terms in what should have been his dotage:

> All . . . had the same policy and program. They were to preach the Marxist description and explanation of the Capitalist system to popular audiences. These, on being convinced, would join the little society to which the preacher belonged, and subscribe a penny a week to it. They would abandon and abolish all rival proletarian combinations. When the pence and the membership had accumulated sufficiently, and recruited and united the "proletarians of all lands," Capitalism would be overwhelmed, and Communism established in its place within twenty-four hours or so.
> ("Sixty Years of Fabianism," 1948)

The Fabian alternative was "permeation"—that is, it "pressed its members to join every other association to which its members could gain admission, and infect it with constitutional Socialism"—and a propaganda deliberately aimed at the educated middle class.

It is important to register two points here. First, Shaw was not simply affected by Fabian socialism: he was one of its prime shapers, more responsible for the character and cohesion of the movement, its doctrine as well as its style, than any other individual, with the inevitable exception of Sidney Webb. Lenin's famous phrase, "a good man fallen among Fabians," is misleading. Shaw tended to dominate the meetings as Webb did the committee work; it was he who drafted the important policy statements; and he was the only Fabian to contribute two essays to the famous volume of 1889, *Fabian Essays in Socialism,* including the crucial essay on "The Transition to Social Democracy." Fabian policy for many years was Shavian policy. The other point is that while revolution can mean many things, *all* socialist sects understood and desired it as a general, all-embracing transformation of society, as opposed to a merely negative cancellation of the *status quo*. Revolution can point to means as well as ends, however, and the substitution of a new social order for the *status quo* can be imagined as convulsive and violent or gradual and peaceful, and, if peaceful, effected through either coercion or persuasion. Whether violence was a necessary or indeed even a possible means to the end of socialist revolution provided much of the argument between the Fabians and their fellow socialists. (All sides could point to the lessons of the Paris Commune.) Still, the alpha and omega of Fabianism remained revolutionary; that is, it began in an overwhelming repudiation of things as they are, and its ultimate object was a radical and comprehensive transformation of society. From the vantage of 1916, Edward Pease, the moderate, not to say prissy, secretary of the society and member from the earliest days, wrote about its beginnings in terms worth quoting at length if only because they are so very pertinent to our own current scene:

> The political parties . . . offered very little attraction to the young men of the early eighties, who, viewing our social system with the fresh eyes of youth, saw its cruelties and its absurdities and judged them, not as older men, by comparison with the worse cruelties and greater absurdities of earlier days, but by the standard of common fairness and common sense, as set out in the lessons they had learned in their schools, their universities, and their churches.
>
> It is nowadays not easy to recollect how wide was the intellectual gulf which separated the young generation of that period from their parents. . . . Our parents, who read neither Spencer nor Huxley, lived in an intellectual world which bore no relation to our own; and cut adrift as we were from the intellectual moorings of our upbringings, recognising, as we did, that the older men were useless as guides in religion, in science, in philosophy because they knew not evolution, we also felt instinctively that we could accept nothing on trust from those who still believed that the early chapters of Genesis accurately described the origin of the universe, and that we had to discover somewhere for ourselves what were the true principles of the then recently invented science of sociology.

By labouring the notion that the origins and ends of Fabianism were revolutionary, I do not wish to ignore what lies between, its living or "objective" character, especially as experienced by its radical contemporaries whom it struck as profoundly unrevolutionary. A clue to what brought about this anomaly lies in Pease's account. Evolutionary doctrine, which he makes the great divide, ran counter to that sense of revolutionary alienation, that discontinuity of the generations, energizing the Fabians in the first place. Webb's *Fabian Essay* on the historic basis of socialism, for example, is saturated with a post-Darwinian use of the idea of the "social organism." He repudiates the notion of some ideal static Utopia as a socialist objective. And he declares, "The necessity of the constant growth and development of the social organism has become axiomatic. No philosopher now looks for anything but the gradual evolution of the new order from the old, without breach of continuity or abrupt change of the entire social tissue at any point during the process. . . . history shews us no example of the sudden substitution of Utopian and revolutionary romance." Webb, incidentally, does not conceive himself to be dealing only in metaphor or analogy; rather he sees social evolution as the present path of the whole evolution of life. As strategy, or process, or means to an end—that of social justice and a better world—evolution displaces revolution. But practically and even ideologically the process seems to become the end itself.

Nevertheless, as Shaw tells us in his history of the first years of the Fabian Society, when he joined in 1884 it was as "insurrectionary" and anarchistic as any rival group, and Shaw very nearly joined the Democratic (later Social Democratic) Federation instead. Even after the Society had defined its policy as permeative, piecemeal, and evolutionary, and Shaw had taken to stigmatizing his revolutionary opponents as catastrophists (a term borrowed from discredited positions in geological and evolutionary controversy), his ambivalence about the strategy he helped to create would occasionally appear in the perorations of his political writings and speeches. In "The Transition to Social Democracy," in which he argues the impossibility of a "catastrophic" transition if only because the modern economic and industrial order is so complex, Shaw ends by saying:

> Let me, in conclusion, disavow all admiration for this inevitable, but sordid, slow, reluctant, cowardly path to justice. I venture to claim your respect for those enthusiasts who still refuse to believe that millions of their fellow creatures must be left to sweat and suffer in hopeless toil and degradation, whilst parliaments and vestries grudgingly muddle and grope towards paltry instal-

ments of betterment. The right is so clear, the wrong so intolerable, the gospel so convincing, that it seems to them that it *must* be possible to enlist the whole body of workers—soldiers, policemen, and all—under the banner of brotherhood and equality; and at one great stroke to set Justice on her rightful throne. Unfortunately, such an army of light is no more to be gathered from the human product of nineteenth century civilization than grapes are to be gathered from thistles. But if we feel glad of that impossibility; if we feel relieved that the change is to be slow enough to avert personal risk to ourselves; if we feel anything less than acute disappointment and bitter humiliation at the discovery that there is yet between us and the promised land a wilderness in which many must perish miserably of want and despair: then I submit to you that our institutions have corrupted us to the most dastardly degree of selfishness.

I give this particular passage at length because it is the most frequently cited by writers who wish to show that in Shaw there was also the storm. Be that as it may, there is no uncertainty here as to the realism and indeed necessity of the Fabian course to social justice. It is true that the last word of the address declares that the catastrophist's program "still remains as the only finally possible alternative to the Social Democratic program which I have sketched today"; but the logic of the whole *including* the impassioned peroration demonstrates the impossibility of achieving the ends desired by all through a sudden and convulsive change, through a classical revolution.

The truth is that the vast bulk of Shaw's political writing and speaking from about 1885 to World War I argued or presupposed the necessity of an evolutionary as opposed to a catastrophic transition to socialism, whereas his plays, beginning with the one he started in 1884 and finished in 1892, did nothing of the sort. In 1888, a month before he delivered "The Transition to Social Democracy" as a lecture to the Economics Section of the British Association, he amused and annoyed his fellow socialists with a sketch in the socialist magazine *To-Day*, radically different in mood and manner but arguing through a fiction the same point of view. The sketch may be regarded as a half-way house between the two modes of expression, discursive and dramatic. "My Friend Fitzthunder, the Unpractical Socialist," by "Redbarn Wash" is the exasperated character-sketch of a catastrophist and "Impossibilist"—one who rejects available political and parliamentary avenues as contaminating—by a young socialist who was once his admirer. Fitzthunder insists on socialism (defined as "placing in the hands of the people the land, capital and industrial organization of the country") at once and entire, and dismisses anything less, including especially democratic political reform, as "a mere palliative." The result is the exclusion of socialists from most progressive enterprises, and effective support of the *status quo*. Of Fitzthunder's excuse for this anomaly, Wash writes, "Usually he takes a hint from Mr. Micawber, and explains that he is collecting himself for a spring. The workers, he says, are not yet organized for revolution— and Fitzthunder insists on revolution. The achievement of Socialism without it would be to him as flat as a pantomime without a transformation scene." Wash connects Fizthunder's revolutionary heroics with "the refuse of sensational novels, epic poems, and Italian opera." He connects it also (as in his essay of 1896, "The Illusions of Socialism") with popular religion, a tendency "to conceive the evolution of Socialism as a miraculous catastrophe, with alarums, excursions, and red fire." In the next issue of *To-Day* there appeared "Fitzthunder on Himself—A Defence," by Robespierre Marat Fitzthunder, also Shaw. The persona this time is pious, dull, humourless, passionate, and self-righteous. He charges Wash with holding up to the "scorn and ridicule of the common foe" socialism's great leaders including H. M. Hyndman (leader of the S.D.F.) and William Morris, whose pronouncements Fitzthunder has been merely echoing. The effect, of course, is to embellish the point of the first sketch, to rub in the irony through a further irony.

Despite Fitzthunder's outrageous stupidity, there is a hint of some ambivalence in Shaw's assumption of both personae, a hint made broad in the beginning of Wash's last paragraph, where he apologizes for having to assassinate "my poor friend—my other self, and the best fellow in the world." Wash's objection is specifically "to have anything to do with him in his public capacity," an objection shared by others "who are among the ablest Socialists we have got." Clearly, Shaw's "ambivalence," his own Fitzthunderism, was not likely to break out unawares. (He subjects such ambivalence to a lucid and sustained analysis in his chief essay on the psychology of the socialist, "The Illusions of Socialism," to be discussed further on.) Moreover, his objection to Fitzthunder, to having anything to do with him "in his public capacity," would seem to cover the persuasive plays that Shaw soon began writing, plays that were as public as he could make them and the unregenerate state of the theatre would allow. Consequently, I am not content to take what seem to be important elements of catastrophism and impossibilism in the plays as the "real" Shaw, or even as the suppressed Shaw breaking out in the irresponsible dreamwork of art as personal expression. If it is true that, although he is in remarkably little evidence in Shaw's political writings and speeches except as straw man or scarecrow, Fitzthunder's spirit seems to hover over the ultimate statement of some of the plays, then one must assume that he is there with the full consciousness of the author and to serve some strategic intent.

PLAYS AND AUDIENCES: FIRST STRATEGY

When Shaw later decided to call his first three plays Unpleasant Plays, he was advertising in that title a strategy that included audience revulsion, an assault on audience sensibilities. The name no longer strikes us as paradoxical, since aggression against the audience is a convention of the modern theatre, but it was not of the theatre of the nineties. By Shaw's own account of these plays, their strategy was, while entertaining the audience, to make its members uncomfortable, aware of their complicity in the social crime. "The didactic object of my play," he wrote of *Widowers' Houses,* soon after its performance in 1892, "is to bring conviction of sin."

Widowers' Houses, however, was an experiment, and the "didactic object" was initially complicated by another. According to Shaw, the play was also designed "to induce people to vote on the Progressive side at the next County Council election in London." Although it demonstrates with the logic of a paradigm the complicity of the *whole* of society in slum landlordism, the play suggests that the County Council and the vestries could at least alleviate the worst of the abuses; could provide, in other words, one of those "paltry instalments of betterment." But this strategy conflicts with others in the play, and is—as Shaw seems to have realized— about as adequate to the scale of the demonstration of universal complicity as a proposal by the Duke of Albany to endow public storm shelters might be at the end of *King Lear.* Consequently when Shaw revised *Widowers' Houses* he markedly reduced the availability of such easy ways out for the entangled conscience; and no such piecemeal alleviation is suggested in either of the other two plays he called "unpleasant." In *Widowers' Houses* (in its final version), municipal reform and the fact that (as the landlord says) "We live in a progressive age" simply provides the opportunity for a financial killing through fraudulent compensation.

The emotional logic of the play proceeds through the demonstration of the integrity of the social fabric in which all are implicated—slum-dwellers, rentiers, and aristocrats, as well as landlords and rent collectors—and its necessary corollary is the futility of piecemeal tinkering and private action. When the dazed young protagonist asks, "Do you mean to say that I am just as bad as you are?" the slum landlord rejoins, "If . . . you mean that you are just as powerless to alter the state of society, then you are unfortunately quite right." And Harry Trench is forthwith *"morally beggared."* To bring "conviction of sin" effectively the logic of the play can admit no relief in "paltry measures," nor can it allow an escape for the spectator through blaming individual villainy. Revulsion is deliberately displaced from the parts to the whole, from the slumlord (or the prostitute) to the System; and the issue for the audience, as for its once-innocent surrogate, becomes what it was for Fitzthunder: All or Nothing.

The end of the play narrows and enforces a "residual impact." The alternatives offered or implied are in fact not two but three: to acquiesce in the reality of one's complicity and make the best of it; to flee into private worlds of feeling and imagination; or to will the overthrow of the whole. The end of the play illustrates the first alternative in all its disagreeableness, and explodes the second alternative as illusory, leaving the third as the unstated terminus of the emotional dialectic. Trench accepts the first alternative: he "stands in" at the end with the others, to make the best of his threatened resources. His action undermines the second alternative, subjective withdrawal and private fulfillment; for the romance of the play, Trench's alliance with the slumlord's daughter, is now consummated (whether Trench admits it or not) only as part of the compact between land, capital, and enterprise. The audience is left, then, with the third unstated alternative: a revulsion from the whole in which all are so thoroughly implicated that the only release can be in the will to transform the whole.

The constituent nature of that audience ought not to be left vague, since an artistic strategy that is ultimately persuasive must take account of special qualities; and, moreover, Shaw in every public performance played directly to what he thought to be the special character of his audience. Shaw wrote his first three plays for an essentially coterie audience, self-consciously "advanced" and intellectual, though middle class in its habits of thought and standards of life; the same people in other words who provided the membership of the Fabians, except less philistine and more art-oriented than the Fabians, and as a group uncommitted to socialism. In February 1885—a time when some Fabians still contemplated revolutionary means—Shaw delivered a lecture called "Proprietors and Slaves" to a non-socialist middle-class audience with similar qualities of high-mindedness and a relative openness to advanced thought. He addresses his audience from "the Liberal and Social Union" as "a body of ladies and gentlemen of more than ordinary culture"; and accuses them (and himself) from a socialist point of view of being "cannibals of the most dangerous description." "Bad as we are," Shaw continues, "I believe that, if we all understood how we are living, and what we are doing daily, we should make a revolution before the end of the week. But . . . we do not know, and . . . many of us, foreseeing unpleasant revelations, do not want to know."

But while confronting the audience with some of these "unpleasant" truths, the lecture proceeds to use revolution chiefly as a threat. Revolutionary violence may be generated by the despair of the poor, or (more likely) by the proprietors' attempts at coercion and intimidation. For that reason Shaw's audience—presented to themselves as a temperate, responsible "middle class"—should educate themselves in socialism, "to fortify whatever is just in Socialism, and to crush whatever is dangerous in it." They especially are capable of disinterestedly "interfering on behalf of justice," and the presence of large numbers of the middle class in a socialist movement would "raise the Socialists above the danger of Coercion." Moreover, "When a Revolution approaches, those who are within the Revolutionary party can do something to avert bloodshed; those who hold aloof can only provoke it. A party informed at all points by men of gentle habits and trained reasoning powers may achieve a complete Revolution without a single act of violence." Making "unpleasant revelations" and demonstrating complicity was in the essential strategy of *Widowers' Houses* and the other Unpleasant Plays; but beyond disposing an audience to "make a revolution before the end of the week" *Widowers' Houses* does not go. Revolution as whole-cloth transformation is the end to which the argument of the play leads; in the speech, violent revolution is a means of persuasion to rational change, although the unconverted audiences for play and speech are in many essential respects of class and culture the same. The theatre setting makes a difference, of course. Accordingly, the speech seems to subordinate the logic of feeling to rational and prudential considerations, whereas the play makes rational argument part of the structure of feeling. The play has its own firm logic. The most rational characters, however, those with the plausible arguments, serve to dispel a number of flattering illusions, but are there in the end to have their reason rejected, to energize the reaction towards an alternative. *Widowers' Houses* aims to prepare and capture the will, not the reason; and (as we shall see) the will is conceived as revolutionary and catastrophic in its changes, concerned with ends rather than means, and with justice rather than prudence.

The better-known *Mrs Warren's Profession* has a very similar strategy. It is a demonstration, using an audience surrogate, of general complicity in what was conceived to be the social crime *par excellence*, prostitution. What is demonstrated is not only the inextricable involvement of all in prostitution, but prostitution's inextricable involvement in the whole economic and social fabric. Prostitution works as a metaphor for capitalist arrangements that leave no innocence untainted; but the demonstration is literal and logical as well as analogical. Since real prostitution is so inextricably involved with the entire social fabric, piecemeal reformism on this favourite ground is invalidated as a solution; only total transformation will serve.

Mrs Warren's Profession makes a particular point of the futility and inadequacy of the second alternative in the series described above, escape into the realm of the private emotions and the imagination. Poetry, art, and "love's young dream" are thoroughly undermined in the romantic illusionist Praed, and through the ironic context that prostitution supplies for an innocent young love. But this strategy of disillusionment, promoting "realism," is not the whole strategic use of the idea of subjective fulfilment. In the end Vivie Warren, Mrs Warren's daughter and Trench's counterpart, is formidable but seared and maimed in her horror of love and all that involves feeling, her now resolute philistinism, her plunge into work—actuarial and statistical—which as yet has no ethical object. Her strength is offered as a model; but her spiritual crippling, more than anything, creates that residual sense of unpleasantness, that sense of the inadequacy of the available alternatives short of the unnamed one, general revolutionary transformation.

The Philanderer forecloses the alternative of escape into private fulfilment and anarchistic individualism even more directly. It puts on the stage the Independent Theater audience itself, as a coterie of liberated intellect and advanced sensibility. The play, set among Ibsenites and Shavians, demonstrates the inadequacy of both conventional sexual arrangements and individual attempts to transcend them. Merely to be liberated and free to follow one's bent and rationalize it produces as much unhappiness and absurdity as the prevailing system. Salvation will not come through an expanded individualistic liberalism and the pursuit of private fulfilment any more than through a piecemeal reform and refinement of the *status quo*.

ALTERNATIVE STRATEGIES

That the plays I have been discussing, and am chiefly concerned with, point implicitly to revolution as an end is not in itself surprising or anti-Fabian. What seems anti-Fabian is that the Unpleasant Plays (and some of Shaw's Edwardian "Discussion Plays," such as *Getting Married*) should, as part of their strategy, demonstrate the futility of gradualism or piecemeal reform in insisting on the integrity of all social and economic arrangements. Shaw's Pleasant Plays and Plays for Puritans (which succeeded the Unpleasant Plays chronologically) do not follow this strategy, although they have a relation to it and also have their own discrepancies with Fabianism. Their focus is the private imagination of the audience, truth and illusion, the interplay between private and public ideals. All in the end present a radical criticism of the theoretical value structure, the sustaining ideals, of contemporary—that is, bourgeois—society. This is nearly self-evident: *Arms and the Man* undermines ideals of military glory and romantic love; *You Never Can Tell,* liberal rationalism and individualism as they flowered in Mill and Herbert Spencer; *Candida,* domesticity in its philistine and idealist versions; *The Devil's Disciple,* virtue, romantic love, and gentility; *Captain Brassbound,* justice and the romance of empire; *Caesar and Cleopatra,* romantic heroism and political liberalism. What is remarkable and discrepant is that, whereas many Fabians were critical of many aspects of contemporary middle-class values and ideals, the Fabian Society as a self-consciously middle-class grouping sought an extension of these values and ideals, their realization not in one class but in all. The Fabians insisted on not merely the suffering but the demoralization of the poor under capitalism, and concluded that, whereas violence might come from the poor, socialism would not. If the poor were indeed the repository of virtue—Shaw often argued— any attempt to tamper with their condition should be strenuously put down. Their virtues in a transformed society however, where of course they would not be The Poor, would be middle-class virtues: sobriety, respectability, responsibility, a sense of fair play, even class solidarity. As Snobby Price says in *Major Barbara,* "In a proper state of society I am sober, industrious and honest; in Rome, so to speak, I do as the Romans do." Fabian strategy made large use of this prospect of universal respectability, in making its respectable recruits. As Shaw wrote in a 1908 preface to *Fabian Essays,* when the Society turned its back to the barricades, "We set ourselves two definite tasks: first, to provide a parliamentary program for a Prime Minister converted to Socialism as Peel was converted to Free Trade; and second, to make it as easy and matter-of-course for the ordinary respectable Englishman to be a Socialist as to be a Liberal or a Conservative." (The Fabian view of the part to be played by the working classes in bringing about socialism was not as consistently non-Marxist as is often assumed. In 1892, in the light of considerable gains being made by the "New Unionism" and the reluctance of the Liberals to make room for more progressive candidates in the upcoming election, the Society issued Shaw's *Fabian Election Manifesto* as Tract 40. With a great deal of hedging on immediate tactics, the manifesto argues the need for a "genuine Working Class party" and the immediate desirability of working-class candidates on grounds and with a rhetoric that assume the class conflict. Aimed at the working classes, it argues against their prejudice for middle-class spokesmen, "ambitious young lawyers and journalists who have no other way of compelling the political parties to recognize their talents," and holds up as a model the propertied classes, who organize themselves behind routine class representatives as a matter of course. The manifesto is intended as a goad to political activity, and neither flatters nor attempts to be fair to those it addresses: "Slavery is popular in England provided the wages are regular: Socialism is only applauded when its propagandists give free lectures, distribute free literature, and do other people's political drudgery for nothing. The average British working man is a political pauper: he will neither do his own political work, nor pay anyone else to do it for him; and the result is that he is also an economic pauper, the mere tool and drudge of a class which leaves no stone unturned, and spares no expense, to secure the control of the State for itself." On the other hand, the Tract makes any sort of progress seem wholly unlikely without organized working-class pressure.

In contrast, the 1896 *Report on Fabian Policy* [Tract 70, also Shaw's handiwork and the *locus classicus* of Fabian principles] appeared after the apparent dead failure of the new Independent Labour Party to make headway with the unions or at the polls. The section called "Fabians and the Middle Class" says in part: "In view of the fact that the Socialist movement has been hitherto inspired, instructed, and led by members of the middle class or 'bourgeoisie,' the Fabian Society, though not at all surprised to find these middle class leaders attacking with much bitterness the narrow social ideals current in their own class, protests against the absurdity of Socialists denouncing the very class from which Socialism has sprung as specially hostile to it. The Fabian Society has no romantic illusions as to the freedom of the proletariat from these same narrow ideals. Like every other Socialist society, it can only educate the people in Socialism by making them conversant with the conclusions of the most enlightened members of all classes.")

The problem arose, as Shaw was to argue critically, when middle-class values were embodied in ideals and ideals took precedence over reality. The reality was that the system of social theft was destructive of middle-class values and virtues in the life of the masses, and indeed in the life of society as a whole. And the confusion of those values with the institutions that purported to embody them—of Justice with the Judge's trappings, of sociability with marriage and the family—and the substitution of the Ideal for the deplorable reality in middle-class thought and imagination, prevented rather than assisted remedial transformation. The strategy of the Pleasant Plays, then, was to revolutionize the mind and imagination by disintegrating conventional ideals, and making attractive an unilluded imaginative realism; that of the Plays for Puritans was to detach the sustaining ideals and protective illusions of the *status quo* from a core of genuine values.

A dominant dramatic and thematic element in the Plays for Puritans is conversion. From the moments of disillusioning illumination, which educate the protagonists of the Unpleasant and Pleasant Plays, to the idea of conversion is only a step, but a clarifying step; for conversion is, in effect, a revolution of the will. Conversion and the question of revolutionary violence are already linked in *The Devil's Disciple* and *Captain Brassbound;* the association will continue in *Major Barbara, Androcles and the Lion,* and *On the Rocks.*

THE RHETORIC OF THE APOCALYPSE

Twenty years after Shaw's first piece of work for the Fabians, the 1884 *Manifesto,* which became Tract 2, the likelihood of violence and indeed the necessity of being prepared to commit violence came back into his political speeches and writings. (Tract 2, written before the Society had repudiated catastrophism, resolved "That we had rather face a Civil War than such another century of suffering as the present one has been." Even so, Shaw had to assure the future general secretary of the organization "that it was all right since in fact no such alternative would ever be offered.") The reasons for this change are not clear, though the divisions over the Boer War and an increasing restlessness and militancy of all groups except the Fabians may have had something to do with it. More likely it was simply a sense, after twenty years, a new century, and middle age, of being farther from the goal than ever. At any rate, from about 1904, Shaw in speaking to socialists would tend increasingly to strike the note of Undershaft's master, who wrote up, "NOTHING IS EVER DONE IN THIS WORLD UNTIL MEN ARE PREPARED TO KILL ONE ANOTHER IF IT IS NOT DONE." In Shaw's political utterances, however, the violence was thrust to the farther end of the revolutionary process, whose proper road remained parliamentary action; and the responsibility for releasing the violence was laid upon the forces of counter-revolution. In October 1904, about the time he was contemplating *Major Barbara,* Shaw declared to his fellow parliamentary socialists, "Parliamentary action is usually the first stage of civil war. . . . It is of course possible that Capitalism will go under without a fight; but I confess I should regard any statesman who calculated on that as an extremely sanguine man." In his 1908 preface to *Fabian Essays,* Shaw wrote, "The Fabian knows that property does not hesitate to shoot, and that now, as always, the

unsuccessful revolutionist may expect calumny, perjury, cruelty, judicial
and military massacre without mercy. And the Fabian does not intend to get
thus handled if he can help it. If there is to be any shooting, he intends to be
at the State end of the gun. And he knows that it will take him a good many
years to get there." (At about this time [February 27, 1909] Shaw wrote a
letter to the organizing secretary of the Fabian Society which shows him
more the Fabian than ever with regard to Fitzthunderism. The pertinent
passage rejects precisely that strategy Shaw employed in the Unpleasant
Plays [short of producing the rabbit of socialism]. Shaw wrote: "We must
discredit this futile business of beginning with a crushing indictment of the
Government and of society at large, and then fizzling out into a perfectly
useless platitude to the effect that the only real remedy is Socialism. I think
I shall make an adaptation of Comte's law of the three stages, and teach the
movement that the revolutionary stage of Socialism in which the patient
breaks away from all his moorings, and sets up a vague but fierce revolt
against every human institution from his father to the Prime Minister, is the
stage in which he is no use even as an agitator, except to the Individualists."
It is worth noting that Shaw does not claim that the useless "revolutionary
stage" can be altogether omitted from the evolution of the movement or of
its individual adherents, nor does he here reflect at all on the likelihood of
ultimate revolutionary violence.)

The prospect of apocalyptic revolutionary violence as an answer to
inclusive institutionalized disorder becomes explicit in the plays for the first
time in *Major Barbara*. *Major Barbara* begins where the Unpleasant Plays
left off—with a demonstration of complicity as young Stephen learns the
source, in Undershaft's Death and Destruction factory, of the good things he
has taken for granted in his mother's house. This motif, slight and comic in
the opening, becomes central and tragic in the body of the play as Barbara
suffers Undershaft's demonstration of the grotesque complicity between
religion and active charity on the one hand and the profitable manufacture
of whisky and weaponry on the other. Barbara, like her audience-surrogate
predecessors, is "beggared"—robbed of spiritual assurance and ethical object, of a vocation. But the play does not end with Barbara at this painful
point; the dialectic continues, and the unstated third alternative of the earlier plays is now stated.

The end of the play, where Barbara finds her vocation again through
Cusins and Undershaft, points directly to revolution not as the piecemeal
achievement of a permeated socialist parliament nor even as the last stage of
the erosion of private property, but as the only avenue of transformation. It
is dominated by Undershaft, who, in his role as Industrial Capitalism, is

given his devilish due for creating a private model of state capitalism, organized and welfarized and prosperous enough to be nearly revolution proof. But Undershaft, who has made the best of his chances in the present order, is by no means committed to its permanence or desirability; and he tempts Cusins, now the focus of action, with catastrophist propositions. These are *dramatically* validated in that the new audience-surrogate, poet, classical scholar, and lover, delicate of health and archetypal man of peace, finds he must assent to them in spite of himself. Undershaft proclaims the folly of a world that "won't scrap its old prejudices and its old moralities and its old religions and its old political constitutions"—hardly an evolutionist point of view. He declares that killing is "the only lever strong enough to overturn a social system." "Whatever can blow men up can blow society up. The history of the world is the history of those who had courage enough to embrace this truth." He dares Cusins to "make war on war." This is the challenge that "beats" Cusins, who reveals his desire to arm the common man with "a democratic power strong enough to force the intellectual oligarchy to use its genius for the general good or else perish." Cusins ultimately yields to the temptation of Undershaft—who has shown him the kingdoms of the world—because it appears, in his own questioning phrase, that "the way of life lies through the factory of death." "Yes," Barbara declares; "through the raising of hell to heaven and of man to God, through the unveiling of an eternal light in the Valley of The Shadow."

The words, from Barbara's final rhapsodic aria, recall a final crescendo in Shaw's immediately preceding and exceptionally successful play, *John Bull's Other Island*. Peter Keegan's vision of heaven is of a millennial New Jerusalem, to contrast with the present reality which to Keegan is hell. ("In my dreams [heaven] is a country where the State is the Church and the Church the people: three in one and one in three. It is a commonwealth in which work is play and play is life: three in one and one in three. It is a temple in which the priest is the worshipper and the worshipper the worshipped: three in one and one in three. It is a godhead in which all life is human and all humanity divine: three in one and one in three. It is, in short, the dream of a madman.") The earlier play presents the dichotomy of action (Broadbent) and intellect, including imagination (Doyle), both divorced from spirit (Keegan) or from an informing ethical object. The union of the three in a mighty redeeming trinity is not possible in the anarchic and exploitative society of the play, the present reality; and is only projected, as a madman's dream, in Father Keegan's vision. In *Major Barbara,* however, the whole play moves to the union of the three: of Undershaft, who makes power for the world to use as it will or must; of Cusins, the man of intellect and imagination who can envisage alternative realities and channel the energy accordingly; and of Barbara, the woman of spirit and redemptive purpose, who can rescue both energy and intellect from pointlessness. The end of the play—the residual impression—is pleasant rather than unpleasant, although the union has such a clear parallel with the end of *Widowers' Houses*. The difference is between a depersonalizing ratification of the exploitative relations of the present in which all are bound and implicated and a compact for the future, a union of gifts and qualities rather than of economic interests, which is to transform society. And because one member of this union—the power and efficiency which are the fruits of capitalism—is rendered as the factory of Death, as the power to destroy, there is no room for a hope of evolutionary gradualism in the emotional logic of the play. In its residual impression is the sense that the weapons of destruction must be turned to good ends quickly, or they will continue to ravage mindlessly and pointlessly, out of the sheer momentum of anarchic capitalism. They exist to destroy and coerce, will not cease to exist of themselves, cannot exist without functioning, and therefore must be used to make the revolution.

Apocalypse—the raising of hell to heaven by high explosives—does come at last in *Heartbreak House;* and thereafter a Day of Wrath, a Day of Judgment, and embodied millennial visions recur time and again, dramatized as a literal rising of the masses (*On the Rocks*), as the descent of a more than literal angel with trumpet from the flies (*The Simpleton of the Unexpected Isles*), as a reported quantum leap to the next orbit (*Geneva*), or a biological leap to a life span of 300 years. Unquestionably it was the First World War that released or demanded such dramatic correlatives; but there were sufficient earlier intimations, as in *Major Barbara, Androcles,* and even *Misalliance* with its successful descent of the gods from the machine.

The emergent image of apocalypse, like that of conversion earlier, requires a glance at one of Shaw's most extraordinary essays, written just as he began the first of his Plays for Puritans. "The Illusions of Socialism" (1896) divided "the chief means by which Socialism has laid hold of its disciples" into two kinds of illusion: dramatic and religious. The dramatic illusion dealt in capitalist villains and worker heroes; the religious illusion "presents Socialism as consummating itself by a great day of wrath, called 'The Revolution,' in which capitalism, commercialism, competition, and all the lusts of the Exchange, shall be brought to judgment and cast out, leaving the earth free for the kingdom of heaven on earth, all of which is revealed in an infallible book by a great prophet and leader. In this illusion the capitalist is not a stage villain, but the devil; Socialism is not the happy ending of a drama, but heaven; and Karl Marx's 'Das Kapital' is 'the Bible of the working-classes.' "

Also an essential part of the religion of socialism were "salvational regenerations" and edifying conversions; and though Shaw in this essay shows himself suspicious of the most spectacular converts, "the suddenly and fervently impressionable," yet he recognizes that it is the will, shaped by feeling and imagination, that is the motor, not the reason, and that conversion has to precede rationalization. So it is that Shaw's plays, however antipathetic to illusion, however reductive their tactics, however much they depend as comedy and drama on the play of intellect, nevertheless are aimed at altering the condition of the will. It is no accident that conversion became an important idea and event in his plays, or that—despite his dramatic attack on the melodramatic and diabolic view of capitalism—he wrote plays at all. There is such a thing, Shaw declares, as a "necessary illusion"— defined as "the guise in which reality must be presented before it can rouse a man's interest, or hold his attention, or even be consciously apprehended by him at all."

In *Heartbreak House,* however, the intention is not to invoke apocalypse as part of a "necessary illusion," but rather to recognize it, and record it, and proclaim it. The strategy is still salvationist, although salvation is stripped to its barest essential, to the grace that is prior to finding a vocation and a cause. Ellie identifies it as the immanence of "life with a blessing."

The strategy is directed at a new generation, the children of Pease's restless generation of the eighties and nineties. Ellie is the audience-surrogate, the character who learns and the focus of concern, an outsider to Heartbreak House, which is in the hands of the generation of England before the War. On Shaw's part, then—and this helps account for the remarkable, complicated mood of the play—there is something that amounts to a rejection of his own generation. Ellie is to be saved from it and its members, however remarkable their virtues—from their futility, their snobbery, their cultivation of sensibility and the private emotions, from their liberal tolerance of greed and incompetence, from the paralyzing fastidiousness of the humane as well as the wooden insensibility of the capable. But liberation from the generation that had allowed the blind drift to a senseless disaster is not enough. The break with the past is not to achieve a greater anarchy; and so Ellie's new realism, after her disillusioning, is put in communion with Shotover, with the spirit (or reminder) of a remoter, more heroic, demonic, and apocalyptic past.

When Shaw teases his audience about the play coming to an end, Mazzini Dunn, who has outlived his revolutionary heritage, assures everyone that "It wont end . . . Life doesnt end: it goes on." Ellie however rejects this view: "Oh, it cant go on for ever . . . life must come to a point sometime." Since there is no conventional plot to predetermine an ending in audience expectation, there is no reason for the play not to imitate life in just going on for as long as an audience can stand it, or in coming unexpectedly to a point.

It comes to a point, of course, to our relief, in an apocalypse; but the moment itself is complicated. On the one hand the bombing—as Captain Shotover twice declares—is the judgment. It is the war, come as a judgment to the generation before the flood; for the play begins when Shaw says he began the writing, in the atmosphere of the years before. There is, terribly enough, a great joy and release in the danger and destruction, a joy which had its analogy in the war fever, and is the other face of the weariness, boredom, and heartbreak of the interminable grinding muddle "in which nothing ever does happen." The audience is implicated in this terrible joy, both through its pleasure in the spectacle of courage and in its natural desire for an ending.

On the other hand, the judgment, this ending, may be a beginning. Life does come to a point; but *also* life goes on. The characters allegorize the events in a hopeful way, though the allegory is much overweighed by the literal truth of their joy in destruction. There is revolutionary optimism in the purging of Boss Mangan and Billy Dunn "the two burglars . . . the two practical men of business" who lose their lives in trying to save them, and in the fact that "the poor clergyman will have to get a new house." The recollection of Proudhon's "property is theft" in the equation of the burglar and the capitalist (the two thieves of contemporary civilization between whom the heart is crucified [in documenting "The Illusions of Socialism," Shaw observed that "Labour is commonly described by them as crucified between two thieves, a fancy picture which implies, not only the villainy of the landlord and capitalist, but the martyred sinlessness of the Socialist"]) reinforces the hope of what can come when destruction has cleared the ground. But the final joy is, unhappily, at the prospect of further release in destruction.

The prime source of apocalyptic expectation in the gospels is directly relevant to Shaw's secular apocalypse. In *Heartbreak House* as in the gospels, the Judgment is only the last act of a drama of salvation. The salvation motif pervades the play: in Captain Shotover's transactions with the Devil in Zanzibar, in Ellie's account of the poverty that damns by inches and money as a means to salvation, in Shotover's Calvinist reckoning of the saved and the damned, the two degrees of humanity and "the enmity between our seed and their seed"; in the Burglar's dodge for extortion by claiming a call to salvation; in Mangan's canvas of who besides himself is going to "save the country"; and of course in Ellie's quest for "life with a blessing." The Judgment itself recalls the accounts in both Matthew and Luke. (Shaw later uses the former as the explicit basis of the action in *The Simpleton*.) Matthew incorporates an allusion to Noah (and, it would seem, to the world of *Getting Married, Misalliance,* and *Heartbreak House* before the war):

> For as in the days that were before the flood they were eating and drinking, marrying and giving in marriage, until the day that Noe entered into the ark,
>
> And he knew not until the flood came, and took them all away; so shall also the coming of the Son of man be.
>
> Then shall two be in the field; the one shall be taken, and the other left.
>
> Two women shall be grinding at the mill; the one shall be taken, and the other left.
>
> Watch therefore; for ye know not what hour your Lord doth come.
>
> But know this, that if the goodman of the house had known in what watch the thief would come, he would have watched, and would not have suffered his house to be broken up.
>
> (Matt. 24:38–43)

The house in the play—appearing to the audience at first in the guise of *"an old-fashioned high-pooped ship"*—is also an ark of Society, a "soul's ship" and a ship of state threatened by the rocks. The two in the field, the two women, the goodman of the house and the thief, those taken and those left, all have their echoes in the play.

Luke follows the Flood comparison with a further reminder of Lot and Sodom, where "they did eat, they drank, they bought, they sold" until "it rained fire and brimstone from heaven, and destroyed them all." It continues with some advice on reactionary impulses respecting the *status quo ante* (advice Hector seems to make a point of following during the airship attack):

> In that day, he which shall be upon the housetop, and his stuff in the house, let him not come down to take it away . . .
>
> Remember Lot's wife.
>
> Whosoever shall seek to save his life shall lose it; and whosoever shall lose his life shall preserve it.
>
> (Luke 17:28–33)

The advice on conduct in those last days is literally borne out in the instructive fates of those who try to hide in the gravel pit as opposed to those who present themselves to the thunder. But the idea of saving loss is also embodied in what Ellie earlier experiences as "heartbreak."

Heartbreak House is by no means the end of Shaw's anti-Fabianism in the drama, but it is the point of full emergence of what is most essentially antithetical to Fabianism: apocalyptic catastrophism; not as a warning to the enlightened and unenlightened to take another route, but as an acknowledgment of the failure of the enlightened and of the alternative route.

Fabianism of course had been changing too, especially under the impact of the war, which led even the Webbs into designing an at least partly revolutionary Constitution for the Socialist Commonwealth of Great Britain (1920). The practical program of the Society, however, became all the more democratic and parliamentary with the permeation and formal conversion of the Labour Party to socialism; while Shaw, even in his straightforward political writings and speeches, grew more and more savage over the hopelessness of parliamentary democracy. Webb's famous "inevitability of gradualism" Shaw maintained as an inexorable fact, vindicated by Soviet Russia's return from instant collectivism to Lenin's New Economic Policy. But political and economic catastrophism were no longer identical in Shaw's thinking, and gradualism was much discredited in his eyes as a means of achieving control, of effecting a revolutionary transfer of political power. In 1888 Shaw spoke of "a gradual transition to Social Democracy" through "the gradual extension of the franchise; and the transfer of rent and interest to the State, not in one lump sum, but by instalments." In 1928, in the chapter on Revolutions in his *Intelligent Woman's Guide to Socialism,* he still argues that the transfer of political power *need* not be bloody, but on the analogy of the nullification of Irish Home Rule and the French and Russian experience, he makes the peaceful acceptance of the parliamentary way to socialism seem exceedingly unlikely. His pessimism is acute here; for while the necessity for transformation remains absolute, the probable violence to come he sees as dead loss, as the destruction of the necessary capital and industrial base for socialism. By 1932, however, this dilemma has been resolved by economic collapse and the enormous dissipation of resources and accumulated capital even in the absence of revolution; so that Shaw can speak "In Praise of Guy Fawkes" on a Fabian platform because: "Guy Fawkes wanted the Government to do something, and saw that the first thing to enable the Government to do anything was to blow up Parliament. I think it is very much to be regretted on the whole that he failed, because . . . the whole history of Parliament has been a triumphant vindication of his grasp of the situation." In that same lecture he declares, "I do not want the catastrophe to be deferred. I am impatient for the catastrophe. I should be jolly glad if the catastrophe occurred tomorrow. But being an average coward . . . I would rather that the catastrophe were settled without violence."

From *Heartbreak House* on, Shaw's plays embody an ambivalence in feeling about revolutionary violence and coercion which is not, however, an ambivalence in expectation. Nor is there now a discrepancy between Shaw's plays and his politics. The earlier discrepancy, which I have been trying to understand and put in some perspective, grew out of a conviction, based on Shaw's private experience, about the roots of action; and out of a perception of a "contradiction" in the Fabian program itself. This perception appears in the 1896 essay on "The Illusions of Socialism." The dramatic and religious illusions of socialism are necessary to enlist and energize the will; yet they have it in them to destroy or at least nullify the socialism they instill—to prevent the realization of socialism. The superiority of socialist illusion to the "flattering" sorts that merely sustain the *status quo* lies, says Shaw, in its contact with fact and "its power of bringing happiness and heaven from dreamland . . . down into living, breathing reach." Yet "when the reality at last comes to the men who have been nursed on dramatizations of it, they do not recognize it. Its prosaic aspect revolts them." They are offended by its coming in "penurious installments, each maimed in the inevitable compromise with powerful hostile interests. . . . Hence they either pass it by contemptuously or join the forces of reaction by opposing it vehemently." Alternatively they became impossibilists.

Illusion—which is necessary—automatically generates disillusion. The "contradiction" was not soluble, but to be lived with apparently, and dealt with by applying Jevonian questions as to the degree of utility; that is, by regulating the creation of religious and dramatic enthusiasm to secure an optimum utility. This Fabian strategy, however, is simpler than that of Shaw's plays, which instead of seeking a judicious mean, put the extremes in tension. The plays use a double strategy: on the one hand of disillusion, urging the *acceptance* of reality and the attractions of a clear-seeing realism in the course of exploding various "flattering" illusions; on the other hand, of conversion, revolutionizing the will by conducting it to a *rejection* of reality—that is, of the present pernicious impasse. The necessity of living with contradiction and holding in tension fact and desire was central in Shaw's brand of Fabianism and is apparent in his dramatic method. Consequently, in his earlier plays, the idea of a transforming apocalypse could exist only as an emotion to which the logic of a rejection of the present reality led. It could exist in his plays as a real event when apocalypse—the religious illusion—had entered reality and become the common experience.

MARGERY M. MORGAN

The Virgin Mother

Though written close in time to *Arms and the Man*, *Candida* follows the naturalistic lines of *Mrs Warren's Profession* but with a more limited admixture of farce than operates in the earlier play. In some ways *Candida* is a bad play, with excruciatingly written passages. Yet its reputation as an important work in the Shavian canon is deserved. It nags at the reader's mind with the urgency of its author's deep involvement in his material and the elaborate strategy he adopted to stand free of it and get it under control. (The selective emphases of production may make it appear simpler than it does to the mind wrestling with its complexities in the study.) Finally it stands as a coherent structure that makes a rich, disturbing and wide-ranging communication. But the record of the author's struggle to explore, understand and objectively present the drama in his personal consciousness, involving the image of Woman and the idea of public responsibility, is built into the play.

The preface to *Plays Pleasant* indicates Shaw's later recognition of what had taken place. The stress it lays on pre-conscious elements in the artistic process provides ground for questioning the common opinion that Shavian drama is an art of open statement, a rationally conceived and controlled didactic drama without any intimate, subjective resonance. Immediately, we are confronted by the perplexing and insufficiently discussed claim that *Candida* is in some sense a Pre-Raphaelite play:

From *The Shavian Playground: An Exploration of the Art of George Bernard Shaw*. © 1972 by Margery M. Morgan and by the Trustees of the British Museum, Governors and Guardians of the National Gallery of Ireland and the Royal Academy of Dramatic Art. Methuen, 1972.

121

> To distil the quintessential drama from pre-Raphaelitism, medieval or modern, it must be shewn at its best in conflict with the first broken, nervous, stumbling attempts to formulate its own revolt against itself as it develops into something higher. A coherent explanation of any such revolt, addressed intelligibly and prosaically to the intellect, can only come when the word is done, and indeed *done with:* that is to say, when the development, accomplished, admitted, and assimilated, is a story of yesterday.
>
> (Author's italics)

So far, this sets in perspective the conflict presented in the play between the middle-aged Christian Socialist parson, James Mavor Morell, and the young poet, Eugene Marchbanks. The phrase, "its own revolt against itself," focuses attention on the close symbolic relation between the antagonists. Shaw goes on to write of art more generally in relation to the evolving consciousness of mankind:

> Long before any such understanding can be reached, the eyes of men begin to turn towards the distant light of the new age. Discernible at first only by the eyes of the man of genius, it must be focussed by him on the speculum of a work of art, and flashed back from that into the eyes of the common man. Nay, *the artist himself has no other way of making himself conscious of the ray: it is by a blind instinct that he keeps on building up his masterpieces.* . . . He cannot explain it: he can only shew it to you as a vision in the magic glass of his artwork; so that you may catch his *presentiment* and make what you can of it.
>
> (My italics)

The preface then slides back from this consideration of the artist as maker of the play (the truncated quotation omits a mention of Ibsen) to the portrait of the artist *in* the play. The shift is a reminder that the relative degree of self-projection to ironic distancing in Shaw's presentation of the young poet is one critical question that must be raised in any discussion of *Candida*. But more immediately to the point is the implication that this play was written out of a "presentiment" by "a blind instinct," and that the truth it had to tell was only fully evident to the author himself at the end of the task.

Over three quarters of a century later, the conventionality of *Candida* is more striking than the "revolt" it contains. It is a domestic play, and its audacities are such in reference to the respectable manners and values of everyday life in late Victorian England. The plot reflects the popularity of such social intrigue drama as Sardou's *Divorçons*. The action is centrally devoted to a love triangle: a young intruder into a happy marriage presents his challenge and departs, leaving husband and wife to take up their relationship on a new basis of understanding. Instead of playing up the titillating possibilities of the adultery motif, Shaw has chosen to develop the thesis-character of the play in an analysis of the actual role of woman in contemporary English society. As he himself later pointed out, *Candida* presents a view antithetical to that of Ibsen's *Doll's House:* instead of woman as the immature plaything of man, Shaw emphasizes her maternal aspect, her influence over men and their dependence on her strength. "The hand that rocks the cradle rules the world" was hardly a revolutionary conclusion in itself, or any reason to support the cause of female emancipation—as long as the question of how well or ill the world was ruled was kept obscure.

It is raised quite plainly in *Candida* between Morell and his father-in-law, Burgess, but then seems to be thrust aside and forgotten. The preface explains how the dramatist rejected the idea of a straight conflict between Christian Socialism and "vulgar Unsocialism": "In such cheap wares I do not deal," he protested. Yet the character of Burgess, the petty capitalist, is retained in the play, unnecessary as he seems to the development of the action. Not only is he there as an element in the idea-plot; a fact largely ignored by commentators on the play is that Candida is Burgess's daughter, as well as Morell's wife. And, while similarities and contrasts to *A Doll's House* are in mind, it should be remarked that one character, though not here the wife, does leave the home for the world at the close of the play: the young poet, Eugene, whose heroics emphasize the importance of the moment, though they have a less impressive effect than the quiet decision of Nora's going:

> MARCHBANKS (*rising with a fierce gesture of disgust*): Ah, never. Out, then, into the night with me!
> . . . (*with the ring of a man's voice—no longer a boy's—in the words*) I know the hour when it strikes. I am impatient to do what must be done . . .
>
> I no longer desire happiness: life is nobler than that. Parson James: I give you my happiness with both hands: I love you because you have filled the heart of the woman I loved. Goodbye. . . . Let me go now. The night outside grows impatient.

At this point one is inclined to assent to the criticism Edward Carpenter made when Shaw first read the play to a group of friends at Henry Salt's: that it wouldn't do, that the central characters and the whole play rang false. Certainly the conventional idiom of late nineteenth-century drama is not a sufficiently authentic language to disperse the falsities of late nineteenth-century attitudes and sentiments. Earlier in the play Shaw has used the young poet's jibes to expose the unreal or inflated sentiment in Morell's rhetoric; but at the end his burlesque impulses were inhibited with the result that Marchbanks as hero is less convincing than he has been in his previous roles of innocent fool and mischievous imp. *Candida* here seems a less mature play artistically than *Mrs Warren's Profession,* possibly because the objectivity Shaw there preserved through the medium of Frank Gardner had to be given up for a confrontation of the forces limiting his personal maturity.

Candida has given Eugene the opportunity to play out his dismissal as his own rejection of what he is denied. The ambiguousness of his relation to her and what she represents is shown visually when, at her call, he kneels to receive her kiss, before leaving the stage to the final tableau: the embrace of husband and wife, alone together in their home. A modern actor can carry off Eugene's final lines without alienating a present-day audience, if he underplays them, perhaps half-humorously. But such a technique can hardly blend with the ritualistic effect in which naturalism is transcended, that Shaw seems to have been aiming at here: a weighted acknowledgment of the power of Candida over the youth in "revolt" ("the higher but vaguer and timider vision, the incoherent, mischievous and even ridiculous unpractical-ness" recognized in the preface) as well as over the middle-aged man, ac-knowledging his weakness before her strength. The conflicts in which the play is rooted are not resolved in this ending, only distanced and stilled in an aesthetic transformation. The commonsense view of Candida expressed by Morell's secretary, Prossy, has no place here:

> She's very nice, very good-hearted: I'm very fond of her, and can
> appreciate her real qualities far better than any man can.

Realism has been abandoned for the iconography of a subjective truth.

The text of *Candida* as it originally appeared in *Plays Pleasant,* dated 1895, has the descriptive subtitle, "A Mystery," in place of the more straightforward designation, "A Domestic Play in Three Acts," found in the autograph longhand version begun on October 2, 1894, and completed on December 7 of the same year. To match this substitution Shaw added the allusion, in Eugene's final speech, to the "better secret" in his heart and the final authorial comment on Morell and Candida: *"But they do not know the secret in the poet's heart."* So he emphasized the enigmatic nature of his play and, punningly in that subtitle, the sacred character of the enigma.

He carefully and consistently cultivated uncertainties and ambiguous effects by other means. Simple stylistic devices do some of the work: the suspended sentence is an actor's tool for suggesting a more complex response than statement can convey (e.g. "MARCHBANKS. Nothing. I—"; "CANDIDA. Oh, James: did you—"), or raising questions in the spectator's mind which perhaps could be, but are not, simply answered (e.g. "MORELL [*excitedly*]. And she refused. Shall I tell you why she refused? I can tell you, on her own authority. It was because of—"). Walter King, in "The Rhetoric of *Candida*" in *Modern Drama* 2 (1959), 71–83, has noted Shaw's extensive use of verbal reiteration in this play. Among the single words that occur over and over again, in counterpoint, "understand" is very prominent. Understanding each other and the situation is a task the characters set themselves and often fail in. Their bafflement challenges the audience to do better, and the addition of a line spoken by Lexy to Morell to the first draft of act 1, as the first link in the chain of repetition, directs attention early to the central perplexity:

> LEXY (*smiling uneasily*): It's so hard to understand you about Mrs Morell—

The words "lie" and "truth," "shy," "dumb," "secret" contribute similarly to the verbal patterning of the dialogue and sometimes make a thematic pattern with variant, synonymous expressions (e.g. "cannot speak," "cannot utter a word," "talk about indifferent things," "hold your tongue"). Such details fall into place against a background of Ibsenite naturalism in the European theatre, as they evoke the already conventional view (even if it was still an *avant-garde* convention) of a hypocritical society brazenly defiant of what men in their hearts know to be true and their own individual authenticity. In the first moments of the play, Morell exposes a conventional form of doublethink that keeps truth at bay by not taking words seriously:

> MORELL: . . . You see theyre near relatives of mine.
> PROSERPINE (*staring at him*): Relatives of yours!
> MORELL: Yes: we have the same father—in Heaven.
> PROSERPINE (*relieved*): Oh, is that all?
> MORELL (*with a sadness which is a luxury to a man whose voice expresses it so finely*): Ah, you dont believe it. Everybody says it: nobody believes it: nobody.

The staple technique of verbal counterpoint presents us with a dialogue that is notably a game with words, a patterned fabric rather than a transparent medium of communication. Words may conceal more than they reveal. What characters say may be at odds with what they think; and indeed nothing that is said can be accepted without question. The method is appropriate to naturalistic characterization as it implies that the *dramatis personae* have insides, that they are not just appearances; and the drama is borne on the current of their private thoughts and motives, and even on the interplay between conscious realization and unconscious self-betrayal. The discontinuity of Eugene's response to Candida's sybilline verdict ("CANDIDA [*significantly*]: I give myself to the weaker of the two.") is as deliberately enigmatic: "Oh, I feel I'm lost. He cannot bear the burden." The subtle pair are communicating over Morell's unenlightened head. But within such a general use of dialogue even simplicities of statement invite the actor to add an emotional emphasis, or an ironic intonation, that reveals further possibilities of meaning.

Significantly, the two principal male characters are professional men of words, a preacher and a poet. Marchbank's charge against Morell is that he is "a moralist and windbag" who has lost his sense of reality in the practice of his "gift of the gab." Morell is vulnerable to self-doubt and responds quickly to the young man's insinuations that he has deceived himself with the same powers as have served him to hypnotize others, especially as his wife reinforces this view:

> James dear, you preach so splendidly that it's as good as a play
> for them. Why do you think the women are so enthusiastic? . . .
> Theyre all in love with you. And you are in love with preaching
> because you do it so beautifully. And you think it's all enthusi-
> asm for the kingdom of Heaven on earth; and so do they.

The impressions of Marchbank's poetry that are offered as indications of his particular talent can hardly be taken more seriously than the other characters take them. Morell is impatient with the irresponsibility of such dreams; Candida, who admits to a limited appetite for poetry, calls them "moonshine"; Burgess's sentimental opinion, "very pretty," is the kindest remark they elicit; and Eugene's "poetic horror" is regarded in much the same way as Morell's metaphoric Christianity—with faint indulgence, the most superficial kind of respect. What delights Candida at least as much as his talent is the unworldliness and incompetence that she associates with poets:

Well, dear me, just look at you going out into the street in that state! You are a poet certainly.

Such defects are transformed into attractions in the nephew of a "real live earl." (For Candida is a snob.) Though her remark to her father, "Poor Eugene hates politics," did not survive the 1894 draft of the play, it fits in with such a general view of the poet as Shaw was to attack satirically in Octavius of *Man and Superman*. Flatteringly, such negative qualities could be summed up as "innocence," and the action of the play carries Eugene out of such a condition, as it shatters Morell's rather different innocence.

Shaw has exploited the relativism of drama to keep sceptical enquiry alive: no view and no character has entire authoritative endorsement, and none is consistently perceptive or imperceptive. With a twist of irony, the Voltairean title of his play directs attention on the woman, not the *ingénu*. Eugene is certainly a version of Candide: innocent in the ways of the world, he progresses quickly from being the unconsciousness through which truth is revealed until he is in great part identifiable with the sophisticated consciousness of the author; and Morell, in the days of his self-confidence, orates with Panglossian optimism and unction:

> You will be married; and you will be working with all your might and valor to make every spot on earth as happy as your own home. You will be one of the makers of the Kingdom of Heaven on earth; and—who knows?—you may be a master builder where I am only a humble journeyman . . . I know well that it is in the poet that the holy spirit of man—the god within him—is most godlike . . .

But Candida, apart from her name, is Shaw's own and the focal point of his evasive technique of presentation. True to her name, she is certainly radiant and a figure of Victorian domestic purity above suspicion; but as a character she is anything but open and candid to the enquiring view, and anything but a satisfactory personification of honesty. The love, praise and comradely familiarity of Morell towards her, the worship of Eugene, the level-headed assessment Prossy makes, and the indulgent irreverence of Burgess, combine to obscure and confuse the direct view the audience, or reader, has of her. In fact, as a character she has a double identity, partly realistic woman, partly idealization; and she retains an opacity that neither of the principal male characters approaches.

The objective views of her that we receive are not balanced and supplemented by an intimate subjective view: the woman sees only her own mask and is not made to question it searchingly. To her husband she ponders aloud:

> Suppose he only discovers the value of love when he has thrown
> it away and degraded himself in his ignorance! Will he forgive
> me then, do you think? . . . will he forgive me for not teaching
> him myself? For abandoning him to the bad women for the sake
> of my goodness, of my purity, as you call it?

It is significant that the question with which she has started off is: "I wonder what he will think of me then." The touch is softer than Ibsen's, when he made Hjalmar Ekdal cry out on the death of Hedvig: "Why hast thou done this thing to me," but the question is equally self-absorbed. This is a woman who dresses herself in the gazes of others and is incapable of catching herself out with a humorous perception; she laughs only at others. Though Marchbanks exalts Candida's divine insight, Shaw—wiser than his puppet—pointedly exposes the failures of her ordinary human insight. Eugene has already spoken out to Morell, when Candida says to the latter: "Do you know, James, that though he [Eugene] has not the least suspicion of it himself, he is ready to fall madly in love with me?" Throughout the conversation that follows, she is totally unobservant of Morell's perturbation, until Shaw with a final satiric touch gives her the line: "you, darling, you understand nothing." Far from feeling any burden of responsibility for an actual situation, she enjoys what is to her a hypothetical situation.

Throughout the play, she belittles the ability of others to manage without her. The curate Lexy Mill, parroting Morell himself near the beginning of the play, unconsciously supplies a critical caption for the portrait of Candida:

> Ah, if you women only had the same clue to Man's strength that
> you have to his weakness . . . there would be no Woman Question.

The "Woman Question" the play presents may well be interpreted as the enigma an ambivalent attitude creates. Eugene Marchbanks comes to distinguish between the actual woman and the ideal to which he still does homage at the close of the play. For the audience the two are represented by the same figure, and the rational, objective distinction is still subject to blurring and confusion. If it were not so—if the dramatist had separated out cleanly and completely those warring elements which make up the total emotional response to a person—the play would lose its peculiar force and cogency.

Shaw wrote in his blarneying way to Ellen Terry (April 6, 1896):

> You have the wisdom of the heart which makes it possible to say
> deep things to you. You say I'd be sick of you in a week . . . But
> one does not get tired of adoring the Virgin Mother. Bless me!
> you will say, the man is a Roman Catholic. Not at all: the man
> is the author of Candida; and Candida, between you and me, is
> the Virgin Mother and nobody else.
>
> (*Collected Letters*, I)

He certainly had Ellen Terry's personal situation in mind: happiest, as he
saw her, with her children about her in a household without a male head.
But he was not just giving his play a gloss that would make it more enticing
to a famous actress; the 1894 longhand text of the play introduces the
heroine forthrightly:

> *A beautiful woman, with the double charm of youth and mater-*
> *nity. A true Virgin Mother.*

In the elaboration of this which appears in this published version, some less
flattering hints have intruded—Candida is *"well-nourished, likely . . . to*
become matronly later . . . a woman who has found that she can always
manage people, etc.," but the allusion to her as a *"Virgin Mother"* has been
suppressed. It looks as though Shaw might have been avoiding direct of-
fence to the pious; more probably he wanted the symbolism to remain
entirely implicit in the naturalistic character, unselfconsciously acted. To
James Huneker he wrote of his heroine in far less lyrical terms than were
appropriate for Ellen Terry:

> Candida is as unscrupulous as Siegfried: Morell himself sees that
> "no law will bind her." She seduces Eugene just exactly as far as
> it is worth her while to seduce him. She is a woman without
> "character" in the conventional sense. Without brains and
> strength of mind she would be a wretched slattern or voluptuary.

Siegfried, of course, is a superman, so that the comparison sets Candida still
beyond the range of ordinary human moral judgement. The rest of the
account is as shrewd as Beatrice Webb's verdict on the character: "a sentimental prostitute"; and one wonders if Shaw himself, in some moods,
might not have applied that phrase to his character. As a variant for the
"Virgin Mother" it is startling, but not irreconcilable with the blasphemous
humour indulged in by the male members of the Shaw household in Dublin.

The attraction to religious themes and imagery and the impulse to deface them are evident in Shaw's juvenile and uncompleted Passion Play in verse (dated February 1878 in B.M. Addit. MS. 50593) which "naturalizes" the Virgin Mary and presents her as the shrewish wife of a drunken ne'er-do-well and a capricious mother. (The adolescent misogyny that may be detected in this portrait comes out as more direct criticism in another unpublished play, *The Cassone* [B.M. Addit. MS. 50595A, B], when a character named Teddy rounds on the respectable women in his life:

> You know as much about a man's wants and feelings as that cat does . . . Between the lot of you I had come to think that I had no right to consideration and no chance of affection; and for two mortal years after we were married I was sneak enough to think her better than myself, and be cowed by her airs, and when I wanted a kiss go dodging and hankering after her like a cur putting in for a bone that he's afraid to steal. And she knew that I felt small.)

A superbly comic chapter of *The Irrational Knot* presents the Rev George Lind's reactions to an encounter with the actress Lalage Virtue:

> What interested him in her was her novel and bold moral attitude, her self-respect in the midst of her sin . . . there was a soul to be saved there, if only Heaven would raise her up a friend in some man absolutely proof against the vulgar fascination of her prettiness . . .
>
> It is not necessary to follow the wild goose chase which the Rev George's imagination ran from this starting-point to the moment when he was suddenly awakened, by an unmistakable symptom, to the fact that he was being outwitted and beglamored, like the utter novice he was, by a power which he believed to be the devil. He rushed to the little oratory he had arranged . . . and prayed aloud, long and earnestly. But the hypnotizing process did not tranquillize him as usual. It excited him, and led him finally to a passionate appeal for pardon and intercession to a statuette of the Virgin Mother, of whom he was a very devout adorer. He had always regarded himself as her especial champion in the Church of England; and now he had been faithless to her, and indelicate into the bargain.

The Virgin Mother is featured here as a protective figure, inhibiting to crude masculinity, and antithetically balanced against the "novel and bold moral attitude," the "self-respect" of the actress. Now Shaw consistently represents the heroes he approves of as "original moralists," self-justified. The Virgin Mother seems to be on the other side.

Virgin mothers, in another sense than the specifically Christian, abound in Shaw's drama and range from Mrs Warren to Lilith, in *Back to Methuselah*. "She's so determined to keep the child all to herself that she would deny that it ever had a father if she could," says Sir George Crofts of Fanny Warren. "No man alive shall father me" is Philip Clandon's comically defiant boast; Brassbound's claim, "I had a mother: that was all," is a variant on it, familiar in conventional melodrama, which reappears with the Gunner of *Misalliance*, who tries to assassinate his putative father. Mrs Morell, of course, acknowledges a husband, but by the end of the play he seems more like one of her children than her consort, her equal in power (though she exacts from others a public respect for his dignity). In view of our biographical knowledge of Shaw's mother-fixation and the lack of respect which seems to have been accorded to his father in the Dublin household, it would be easy to trace the recurrence of the mother-dominated family group in his work to private obsession. But what he made of this, in objectifying it, is possibly more interesting; and the expansion of its significance seems to account for most of the elaboration in the composition of *Candida*. By linking the sway of the central female figure with a sacred Christian image on the one hand and, on the other, with associations outside the Christian tradition, the dramatist has transformed a private symbol into an emblem of a whole society and the psychological pattern which he sees determining its character.

The leitmotifs embedded in the dialogue communicate the two kinds of association, Christian and non-Christian. Among the key words which recur, and are developed in variant expressions of the same ideas, we find the cluster, *heaven, hell, divine, prayer;* another group includes *mad, drunk, (not) contain oneself* (cf. *giddy, laugh, hysterics*), words connoting a dionysiac irrationality. The device is more significant, and probably more effective, when repetition is given the deliberate formality of ritual. Eugene, anticipating a physical attack from Morell in act 1, cries "Dont touch me"; "Dont touch me" is Morell's own frantic protest against Candida's consoling embrace after the kiss she gives him in act 2, which he judges to be treacherous; in the first part of the next act, Eugene blissfully anticipates, "I shall feel her hands touch me," and immediately explains to Morell "why I shrank from your touch"—so that that previous incident and the present variation on the idea are closely linked; "I did not mean to touch you" is Candida's cold response when her husband tries to assert his dignity and independence in the "auction" episode; in culmination, the kiss she gives to the kneeling Eugene—and, perhaps, her embrace of Morell as the curtain falls—has the solemnity of a religious laying on of hands. Again, "I shall stagger you if you have a heart in your breast," Eugene warns Morell in act 1; early in the next act, he "staggers" Prossy with his talk of her heart's crying hunger, so that she rises *"with her hand pressed on her heart"*; the gesture recurs when Eugene himself *"presses his hand on his heart, as if some pain had shot through it,"* at Candida's mockery of her husband, and his words follow—"I feel his pain in my own heart"; Morell's physical reaction to the kiss, just before, may not involve the same gesture—*"He recoils as if stabbed"*—but in a less mechanical way his words ("I had rather you had plunged a grappling iron into my heart than given me that kiss") bring it to mind with intensified impact. In the ecclesiastical context of St Dominic's Parsonage with its High Church pictures, the prophecy of Simeon to Mary may be remembered—and its later association with the lance of the Passion, when the kiss is the kiss of Judas—

> (Yea, a sword shall pierce through thy own soul also,) that the thoughts of many hearts may be revealed.
>
> (Luke 2:34)

Sitting with Eugene beside the fire, in act 3, Candida holds the brass poker— *"upright,"* Shaw added to his original directions so that the audience might see the comic symbol—*"looking intently at the point of it."* Marchbanks makes a romantic image of knightly chastity out of it: "my drawn sword between us." The firelight is beyond it, and the sword becomes angelic, "a flaming sword that turned every way, so that I couldn't go in." The domestic hearth and the fire they are playing with turn to unquenchable flame, paradisial or infernal, as the image of exile from Eden is inverted: "for I saw that that gate was really the gate of Hell . . . I was in Heaven already."

Shaw's wish to emphasize Candida's symbolic elevation to divine status continued to be operative after his original composition of the play was completed. In the 1894 longhand text, the last lines of act 1 run:

> MARCHBANKS: . . . I am the happiest of men.
> MORELL: So was I—an hour ago.

In the published text, the word "men" is replaced by "mortals."

Dominating the set and overlooking Morell's desk with its typewriter ("type" is another key word, punningly relevant to the play's symbolic figures) is the picture hanging above the hearth like an icon above the altar. It is supposed to have been Marchbank's gift to the Morells, a compliment to Candida through a discernible likeness. Shaw originally instructed that this picture should be a *"Large photograph of the Madonna di San Sisto";* when he completed his revised version in 1895 the instruction had changed to: *"a large autotype of the chief figure in Titian's Assumption of the Virgin."* The gift of the picture is matched by the young poet's verbal description of Candida as he idealistically sees her:

> her shawl, her wings, the wreath of stars on her head, the lilies
> in her hand, the crescent moon beneath her feet.

At this point Shaw's classification of his play as "Pre-Raphaelite" seems apt, inasmuch as the young man's attitude to his benefactress is informed with just such a blend of erotic with religious emotion as Rossetti's pictures frequently communicate.

As an occasional visitor to Newton Hall, meeting-place of Frederic Harrison's group of Positivists, Shaw would have been familiar with the reproduction of the Sistine Madonna hanging there as emblem of the Humanity on which Comte's Positive Religion centred. Comte's *System of Positive Polity* (trans. R. Congreve, 1877) proposed a Festival of the Virgin Mother "to lay a foundation for the adoration, the collective adoration, of the representatives of Humanity, by instituting the abstract worship of woman" (vol. 4, chap. 5). "A satisfactory institution of the worship of woman is out of the question so long as the idea of maternity is incompatible with purity," Comte argued, and he fantastically prophesied the Utopia of the Virgin Mother when woman would perfect herself by becoming self-fecundating. Meanwhile, "the feminine Utopia becomes an inseparable part of the Positive religion, for all whose heart enables them to use it subjectively, without waiting till it is an objective fact."

It is hard to believe that Shaw would not have agreed with John Stuart Mill that Comte's precise notion of addressing lengthy prayers three times daily to the idealization of some actual woman, living or dead, was "ineffably ludicrous" as a means of working up the feelings for the service of humanity. *Candida* adopts Comte's notion of an idealization of the affective nature of humanity taking the place of supernatural religion, but the absurdity of worship projected on an actual woman is focused by Prossy and acknowledged in the presentation of Morell and Marchbanks as variant kinds of fool. The ambivalence determining the portrait of the heroine becomes the vehicle of Shaw's critical scepticism regarding the effect of Comte's prescription, and of his uneasy recognition that such a feminine ideal may work conservatively, even regressively, on society.

The replacement of the Sistine Madonna image by Titian's *Assumption of the Virgin* is a shift towards a more powerfully beneficent concept. The Titian was described by Berenson in his essay on "Venetian Painters," which first appeared in 1894—a likely text for Shaw, who had been an art critic, to have read:

> the Virgin soars heavenward, not helpless in the arms of angels, but borne up by the fullness of life within her, and by the feeling that the universe is naturally her own and that nothing can check her course.

This sounds more to the taste of the playwright, naturalist and vitalist, than of the sickly Eugene, who cannot bear to think of a lovely woman in connection with boots that need blacking, onions to be peeled, or even paraffin lamps. (The fact that the picture is an Assumption also emphasizes the distance between symbol and actuality.) Berenson continues in Nietzschean terms, identifying qualities in the *Assumption* with those of Titian's pictures on classical subjects, *The Bacchanals* and *Bacchus and Ariadne:*

> They are truly Dionysiac, Bacchanalian triumphs—the triumph of life over the ghosts that love the gloom and chill and hate the sun.

The metaphor used recalls Ibsen, and the whole view corresponds to Nietzsche's philosophical programme as stated in the preface to *The Birth of Tragedy:* of countering the Christian ethical view with an aesthetic view that should be less life-denying. Morell is associated by name and profession with the ethical approach, Eugene, the poet, with the aesthetic. Whatever we make of Candida as a naturalistic character, Shaw's association of her with the Titian suggests that, after his first completion of the play, he conceived her as also being a personification of the Life Force, transcending both morality and art.

Candida's maid in the kitchen, who never appears on stage, is called Maria; the counterpart who does appear on stage is Morell's secretary, Proserpine Garnett. (The surname, etymologically associated with "pomegranate," reinforces the classical reference.) Classical mythology had been employed by Swinburne in the sixties, within the Pre-Raphaelite tradition, as a weapon against Christianity. In his "Hymn to Proserpine" he invokes the goddess of natural death, powerful over Christianity as over the rest of creation, destined to triumph over the Virgin Mother as the latter had once usurped the place of Aphrodite:

> thy kingdom shall pass, Galilean, thy dead shall go down to thee dead.

> Of the maiden thy mother men sing as a goddess with grace clad
>   around;
>
> Not as thine, not as thine was our mother, a blossom of
>   flowering seas,
> Clothed round with the word's desire as with raiment.

Proserpine, the poem acknowledges, is daughter of Demeter, the earth mother; in her symbolic identity as Demeter in eclipse, she still testifies to the splendour of physical life.

The blending of the Demeter figure with that of the Virgin Mother distinguishes *Candida* from Swinburne's vision; it smacks more of the anthropologist's and comparative religionist's view. "There is only one religion though there are a hundred versions of it," Shaw's preface asserts; and the famous first chapter of *The Golden Bough* (first edition published 1891), entitled "The King of the Wood," is essential background to the play. It is here that Frazer identifies Diana of Nemi with Diana of Ephesus and Asiatic goddesses of fertility and relates to them the Christian celebration of a Virgin Mother. Candida, whose image presides over the hearth while she occupies herself in trimming the lamps, is also Vesta; the room, though it serves Morell as a study, is essentially a temple of the domestic virtues. The typist (a spinster who has replaced a younger woman) is familiarly addressed as Prossy, a nickname that underlines her inferior relationship to Candida: not just Proserpine as the sacrificial aspect of Demeter, but the temple prostitute in a social and economic sense—and an emotional sense, too, as she gives the devotion from which Candida reaps the advantages:

> Why does Prossy condescend to wash up the things, and to peel
> potatoes and abase herself in all manner of ways for six shillings
> a week less than she used to get in a city office? She's in love with
> you, James.

Frazer's account of "the Ephesian Artemis with her eunuch priests and priestesses" is recalled by the grouping of devotees about the central female image in the play: Morell and Eugene being supported by the yet more foolishly enthusiastic and incorrigibly second-rate curate, Lexy Mill, whose first name in its familiar form, may be a girl's name too; with Prossy on the other hand, love-starved and compelled by her hopeless devotion to Morell to render her tribute of service to Candida.

The climax of the play's action, the show-down, when Candida makes her ceremonial choice between Morell and Marchbanks, is postponed—and gains more force from the consequent suspense—by the interruption of

what the preface intriguingly calls "the drunken scene . . . much appreciated, I believe, in Aberdeen." Eugene has already been dancing about excitedly. His conversation with Morell has scattered the latter's self-possession
("my head is spinning round. I shall begin to laugh presently"), when Lexy
Mill and Proserpine Garnett come in with Burgess from a champagne sup-
per: a chorus of revellers who attribute their ecstasy first to Morell's eloquence at the meeting and only then to the champagne Burgess has supplied.
Shaw set the action of his play on the October day when he started to write
it. It may have been no more than a happy coincidence that has left the
drama for ever associated with autumn—and the season of the Eleusinian
mysteries of Demeter: the Thesmophoria. The "drunken scene" corresponds
to the Bacchic revels associated with the abduction of Kore/Proserpine to
the Underworld, in which the worship of Demeter and the worship of
Dionysus/Iacchus were combined. We may see Burgess, in this context—if
he is the ultimate villain of the piece—as Dis/Minos, Prince of the Dead, to
whom Proserpine is subject. The "madness" leitmotif now falls into place as
a dionysiac manifestation, as does that image of Hebrew religious ecstasy,
David dancing before the ark—but despised by his wife in her heart, which
Eugene applies to Morell's public oratory.

Candida, it seems, is opposed to enthusiasm and the cries of the heart;
she now reminds the others of "our rules: total abstinence." Whether she is
thoroughly beneficent remains in doubt; the White Goddess has another
aspect. Marchbanks protests at her "cruelty" to Morell. But men suffer at
the hands of the gods without feeling them to be any the less gods.

Frazer identified some of the youthful mortals of legend who are loved
and destroyed by the Virgin Mother goddesses: Attis, Endymion, Hippolytus,
Adonis, Virbius. Of the last he wrote: "this mythical Virbius was represented in historical times by a line of priests known as Kings of the Wood,
who regularly perished by the swords of their successors." His chapter ends
with a description of a double-headed bust found at Nemi which, he suggests, represents "the priest of Nemi, the King of the Wood, in possession"
and "his youthful adversary and possible successor." The one head is young,
beardless, and with a steadfast expression; "the other is a man of middle life
with a tossed and matted beard, wrinkled brows, a wild and anxious look
in the eyes, and an open grinning mouth." Shaw's play presents an analogous version of Man in two persons, confronted by the power of Woman.

At the end Eugene escapes—or does he only run away?—whereas Morell
is left to his "happiness," having been stripped of his pride, with his capacity
for effective public action at least temporarily shaken. Yet the younger man,
too, pays homage on his knees and receives Candida's kiss before he de-

parts. Is she not the Life Force personified? But the dangerousness of submitting to her seductive blandness has been shown, and Lexy Mill's silly quip, "How can I watch and pray when I am asleep?," now seems an apt cry from a society unconscious of the extent to which Candida governs it. The system allows art its place, as Burgess explains:

> BURGESS (*sentimentally*): He talks very pretty. I awlus had a turn
> for a bit of poetry. Candy takes arter me that-a-way. Huseter
> makes me tell er fairy stories when she was only a little
> kiddy not that igh

With an equally mischievous blandness, Shaw himself offers *Candida* as a pretty fairy story of Victorian domesticity—and its anti-revolutionary ideals.

"The gods," in Jane Harrison's words, "reflect not only man's human form but also his human relations." Shaw's recognition of this enabled him to incorporate a dialectic of cultural change in a drama originally motivated by his personal difficulties in relating to women. By the time he came to write his preface to *Plays Pleasant* he had kicked away the ladder that started in his private world—so determinedly that the heroine is not even mentioned there. But the material in Stephen Winsten's book, *Henry Salt and His Circle,* prefaced by a document from G. B. Shaw near the end of his life, enables us to look back at the growth of *Candida* out of a particular situation that exemplified a more constant psychological patterning.

In the days before his marriage, Shaw had been a frequent visitor to the Salts with his friend, Edward Carpenter. Archibald Henderson long ago supplied the information that the triangle aspect of *Candida* was based on the playful rivalry between the two visitors to be considered the "Sunday husband" of Kate Salt. In his account, included in Winsten's book, Shaw comments on Mrs Salt's lesbianism:

> She was a queer hybrid. I never met anyone in the least like her,
> though another friend of mine, the Christian Socialist parson
> Stewart Headlam, also had a wife who was a homo.

(Headlam, of course, was the most obvious model for James Mavor Morell.) It emerges that Edward Carpenter, himself a homosexual, encouraged Kate to regard herself as an Urnung, or hermaphrodite, as a superior type of humanity. The theory fits in with Comte's view of hermaphroditism, actual or metaphysical, as the utopian form of perfected womanhood. It was Kate's own fanciful view of herself as a mother to all helpless creatures (so that she needed no particular child of her own) that gave Shaw the bridge in actu-

ality from Carpenter's *anima*-figure to his own; for Candida is certainly no
Urnung (and the writing of *Saint Joan* was many years off). But still he
wanted a figure of Woman entire. Kate Salt had another function in his life:
she typed his manuscripts for him. It was an easy step to present Woman in
two persons: as the dominant, maternal Candida and as the servant of the
successful man, Prossy Garnett. Perhaps his uncertain, fluctuating view of
himself is projected doubly too: on Morell, the able socialist preacher who
is weaker than he suspects; and on the timid and gauche Marchbanks, who
proves stronger than the world knows. In this connection the aged dramatist's reminiscent words, "Kate [Mrs Salt] loved me as far as she could love
any male creature," clash rather pathetically with a quotation from Kate
herself on the subject of Shaw:

> He is always trying to show how advanced he is about women,
> but all the time he is conscious that he has to be nice because you
> are a woman. If he were not so amusing and clever I would not
> put up with him. I do it for Henry's sake. Henry is so sorry for
> him.

We cannot now tell which was the more self-deceiving. Yet *Candida,* from
one point of view, is certainly comprehensible as a fantasy defensive of the
frail *amour propre* of the ambitious young man who had as yet tasted little
recognition from women or the general public for which he wrote. (Eugene
Marchbanks, an Orpheus in rags, has been sleeping on the Embankment
with a seven-day bill for £55 in his pocket.) Its complex machinery of ideas
and symbols conceals the author's fears of inadequacy; its hint that the
woman-dominated male is defeated by regressive social elements in the
service of capitalism may even have satisfied a vengeful impulse alternatively
expressed in the poet's Shelleyan rejection of marriage and domesticity.

   Candida stands finally as a critique of Victorian society focused, like
Samuel Butler's, on the home. It works subversively—if it still needs to work
in these days—through the touches of unease and revulsion with which it
continually affects us. Only by such means, in such a society, can the process
of revolt begin. The fact that the heroine herself stands clear of burlesque
humour and checks the ranging comedy of the play is a tribute to the
contained power of the opposition, as the author sensed it, and also to the
strength of the inhibitions he faced in his subjective knowledge of what he
was writing about.

CHARLES A. BERST

Heartbreak House: *Shavian Expressionism*

Heartbreak House has the distinction among Shaw's major plays of being the one he was in many ways most proud of yet least inclined to discuss. Indeed, he was uncharacteristically reticent and evasive about the play, remarking that "I am not an explicable phenomenon; neither is *Heartbreak House*. . . . These things are not to be explained, and I am no more responsible for them than the audience." This confession is especially remarkable considering the fact that he had subtitled his work "A Fantasia in the Russian Manner on English Themes," and had begun his long preface by explicating Heartbreak House as "cultured, leisured Europe before the war." Apparently Shaw felt that in this case especially there was an artistic substance which transcended prefacing, a quality which was essentially more intuitive than rational. This quality has, not surprisingly, evoked dissension and confusion among the play's observers. While numerous critics have echoed Shaw's own high appraisal of the play, many of these are almost as vague as he in defining its greatness, and there is a notable handful of dissenters. Clearly, *Heartbreak House* calls for both diligent and imaginative critical sensibilities.

Grasping at the obvious, critics have taken Shaw's prefatory reference to Chekhov as a touchstone to explain *Heartbreak House* as a standard against which to judge the play's special poetry. This approach is deceptively easy—so easy as to hint that Shaw must have been perverse not to merely point to the preface when he was asked to explain his work. The

From *Bernard Shaw and the Art of Drama.* © 1973 by the Board of Trustees of the University of Illinois. University of Illinois Press, 1973.

kinship of *Heartbreak House* and Chekhov's four major plays, particularly *The Cherry Orchard,* is obvious: the society is a decadent one, facing extinction because it cannot come to terms with modern social realities; the setting is a country house; the characters are upper middle class, sophisticated but aimless, listless, and frustrated; the dialogue is disconnected, dissonant, self-centered; the atmosphere is one of pathos, dreaming, heartbreak, and disillusionment; the technique is one of seeming plotlessness, small incident, and minor tones; the philosophic attitude is fatalistic; and the genre is tragicomedy, the wry comedy of life's minutiae being caught in multifold ironies and tragic ramifications. In both playwrights these microcosmic elements suggest macrocosmic counterparts, the poetry of detail evoking an epic awareness of ineptitude, waste, and futility. The greater world lurks as an all-too-real ghost just offstage and in the fringes of consciousness.

As obvious as these similarities, however, are basic differences between Chekhov and Shaw, and it is largely in terms of these differences that certain critics have found Shaw wanting. Chekhov's idiom of understatement, subtle implication, and deep inner emotions appears to be at odds with the Shavian mode. The surge of Shaw's mind, the flow of his rhetoric, and the assertiveness of his ego would seem to be inimical to quiet effects. The fact that they are not, and that he maintains many of Chekhov's qualities in spite of his more vigorous artistry, speaks for the versatility and flexibility of his talents. As one might expect, his pace is more rapid, his tone more robust, his characters more abstract and self-conscious, his intellect more didactic, and his presence more overt. However, these are qualities which impinge his particular genius on Chekhov's, giving *Heartbreak House* distinction more through uniqueness than imitation. The aesthetic direction in Shaw is away from a sad tone poem of nostalgia toward a cacophonous fantasia which forebodes apocalypse. Shaw's adoption of many of the Chekhovian qualities assures that a sense of the tone poem survives poignantly in *Heartbreak House,* but he counterpoints Chekhov's muted cadences with a toccata of doom which is distinctly Shavian, and which rises in a crescendo as the play evolves.

This counterpoint shifts the entire emphasis of *Heartbreak House,* evoking a dramatic idiom more complex, as dark, and nearly as subtle as Chekhov's. A sense of dreams, frustration, and illusions prevails in both, but while Chekhov represents a dreamy society through the distractions, traditions, obsessions, and impracticality of his characters, Shaw compounds illusion by placing this society in the context of an all-encompassing dream. Only in a limited aspect is his play about cultured, leisured Europe. Far

more profoundly it is about the anguish and despair of a sensitive consciousness facing the vanity, stupidity, vileness, and insanity of social and
historical realities. As the microcosm of the situation in *Heartbreak House*
symbolically represents the macrocosm of Europe, the microcosm of the
heartbroken impresses us as a fragmented, frustrated outpouring of a
macrocosmic dspair. This despair gains primary, almost tangible reality
through the numerous individual disillusionments, misanthropies, and trau-
mas which coalesce aesthetically with the pervasive disenchanted, nihilistic
movement of the entire play. The surface farce and trivia sustain the action,
but in the end their amusement wanes, transmuted into the grim fascination
of a dreamlike, apocalyptic harlequinade.

The basic mode of *Heartbreak House,* consequently, is as much
Strindbergian as Chekhovian. The subtle reproduction of detail through
which Chekhov raises his theater of modern realism to poetic heights is
complemented by the consciousness of a single agonizing oversoul, through
which arises the poetry of expressionism. While the power of Chekhov lies
in the keen fidelity and typicality of his portrayals of individuals, the greatest power of *Heartbreak House* lies in a central, inner psychology which
evokes a tension of reference between fact, symbol, and self. The differing
bases of reality in realism and expressionism clarify the distinction. In
Chekhov the characters, though highly foibled, are the fulcrum of reality,
and their emotional attachments, depths, capacities, and incapacities are the
realities which on one hand give them meaning and on another set them
helplessly adrift on society and life. In Shaw, the fulcrum of reality is implicit in the oversoul or dreamer, and against this consciousness the characters are set. The characters manifest fragments of this consciousness in
their un-Chekhovian self-awareness, the tearing away of masks; the oversoul
manifests itself as it sits in judgment. The mindlessness of many is thus
coalesced and reacted upon in the mind of one, and while the many are
subject to a determinism as relentless as that in Chekhov, the one has an
independence which provides a hopeful element of free will. Most important aesthetically, the emotional base which in Chekhov resides in the individuals moves in Shaw toward the oversoul. In either case it is profound,
but the former stresses variety while the latter produces concentration.

The dream atmosphere of *Heartbreak House* prevails from beginning
to end through dreamlike structuring, cumulative references to sleep, fanciful images and connotations, a strongly subjective point of view, and the
probing spirit which constantly seeks realities beneath masks. Although this
atmosphere is less obvious than in act 3 of *Man and Superman,* where
abstraction reigns supreme, it is more natural through being far less overtly

dialectical. In a conversation with Henderson, Shaw remarked that *Heartbreak House* "began with an atmosphere and does not contain a word that was foreseen before it was written." Indeed, its development is impressively episodic, following as it were the wandering progress of a dream. Entrances and exits, wanderings back and forth and in and out, recurrent references to forgetfulness in act 1, bizarre coincidences, movements, and surprises provide a sense of disconnected impressions drifting in and out of the mind of a dreamer. The episodes are tied together as much by common associations as by a string of plot, and they seem to develop more by accretion than by logic. The relative focus of the total action furthers the mood of drifting in and out of a dream by being far more fragmentary in acts 1 and 3 than in act 2. Characters and situations accumulate and fluctuate rapidly in act 1, with an air of hectic intrusion, while in act 2 they stabilize in terms of more prolonged and developed encounters, with characterization becoming deepened as differing levels of reality become apparent. Act 3 returns to fluctuation, but this time in greater serenity, with a modulation toward the grimness of fatalism. Two acts begin with characters sleeping, and all three have a ceremonial, unrealistic conclusion, with a ritualistic chant at the end of the first and nihilistic invocations at the ends of the second and third.

These dreamlike actions and structuring are reinforced by the nearly thematic recurrence of sleeping and dreaming throughout the play. The sleeping and dreaming are of many varieties, furthering an otherworldly atmosphere and suggesting an indolent society, while in their shades of consciousness bringing into question the very nature of reality. On the most mundane level Ellie dozes onstage as Hesione dozes offstage. Their sleep and drowsiness set the tone of the play in the first act. Slightly more complex are the conscious illusions of daydreaming, engaged in by Ellie regarding Othello and by Hector in his pantomime heroics. In Ellie's case the daydreaming results from youthful naïveté. For Hector daydreams seem to be the compensation of a man who finds himself at a dead end, one which Captain Shotover makes explicit: "[Hesione] has used you up, and left you nothing but dreams." On another plane is Shotover's forgetfulness, which may or may not be real, but perhaps is half so, and at any rate serves him as a great convenience. If it is not real, it is ironically a manifestation more of mind than of senility, as is his sleep in act 3, which he turns on and off at will. More complex is the matter of Mangan's hypnotic trance, a curious and authentic combination of consciousness and sleep. In the trance Mangan can hear reality but not participate in it, and as those present assume he is not conscious, he hears the truth. For once he can align his personal reality with an objective view—this latter being so disillusioning, so improper, so inconvenient that Hesione insists he is obliged to forget all he heard as though he were asleep: "You dreamt it all, Mr. Mangan." Thus social, factual, and personal views are set at odds. Dreams functioning in this manner float all life on illusion. Ellie's dreams of Othello and Marcus Darnley, which unfit her for reality, are matched by Hector's dream of heroism, Hesione's dream of culture and femininity, Ariadne's dream of homecoming, Mangan's dream of dignity, Mazzini's dream of Mangan's beneficence, and Randall's dream of Ariadne—all social, cultural, and bogus. Insofar as the characters act upon them, however, their dreams attain deformed, paradoxical reality.

The urge to disrupt and penetrate such fraudulent reality is behind the unmasking theme of the play. Being so rudely antisocial and recurrent, the game of unmasking in itself furthers the total dreamlike impression, as though it were the obsession of a single consciousness. As Hummel in Strindberg's *Ghost Sonata* peels away the social image of the Colonel, the characters in Heartbreak Hotel peel away at one another with a singular compulsion to discover the man beneath the image, and, more deeply, the subconscious beneath the conscious. The fact that the characters are ultimately ineffectual in dealing with the fundamental realities of survival produces the irony that their very sense of honesty and civilization is in substance a dream, inadequate to save them. Mangan's dignity and wealth may be fraudulent, but his bombs are real. Ellie's search for a spiritual direction, Hesione's sense of fair play, and Hector's iconoclastic cynicism are thrusts toward truth, but they prove to be romantic and ineffectual because they are devoid of objective power.

The dream atmosphere, engendered in part by the unmasking games, shortcuts prolonged psychological probes in favor of symbolic truths, and it is the *pattern* of these truths unfolding which suggests the psyche of the play. Realistically, certain portrayals may be faulted for inconsistency: Ellie suddenly shifts from the romance of Marcus to pragmatism and then to spirituality. Hector turns from pet lapdog into bitter misanthrope. Mangan falls from Napoleonic self-assurance to infantile tears. Randall degenerates from man-about-town to a pettishly jealous small boy. The mutations of these characters are consistent with the mode of the action, which is not realism, but an intuitive penetration of fraud in search for the essential factors of life and survival. Thus Ellie's transformation, the most sudden and startling of all, is executed through a psychological shorthand. It could well be logical and natural in an extended context, but here it is highly condensed in a manner of the prevailing patterns of a dream. Her change, and that of the others, is toward a greater sense of reality, a symbolic movement toward truth which serves the function of the dream. By contrast, the characters who have the greatest normal consistency—Hesione and Ariadne—are the ones who are not severely shaken in their delusions and who consequently show the least growth. As education through heartbreak is the central motif of the play, Hesione and Ariadne are not truly schooled, and to be "normal" is to be uneducated. Consistency may be a fault if one is attached to dreams which impose false images on the flux of life.

Once heartbreak shatters the most romantic illusions, each character finds a portion of a new reality. Ellie finds that materialistic motives are more prudent than romantic ones, but both are ignominious when compared to spiritual aspiration. Hector finds that he has wasted himself in romance and domesticity, and that only in danger and daring can he realize true life. Mazzini recalls that in the past he had joined socialist societies, but that the societies, long on talk and short on action, brought about no change. All three express aspects of a disillusionment which should enable them to move in a new, more purposeful direction. But Ellie and Hector's resolutions that the world is vile, and Mazzini's resolution that there must be a Providence, while partially true, are sterile, and the insights the characters achieve through disillusionment are fragmentary. As individuals they contribute substantially to the ethos of the play. Their cumulative self-discovery and despair takes on intellectual and emotional power which fuses, and aesthetically they become agonizing aspects of a greater consciousness. But the individuals in themselves are futile; their means are naïve, and their ends point toward nihilism. A focal point aiming toward a genuine resolution is needed.

The ostensible focal point of moral vision in the play is in Shotover. As a focal point he is deliberately flawed, a grotesque exaggeration whose "madness" furthers both the atmosphere of the dream and its sense, the meaning of the play being caught in both. Through him the dreamer's intellectual presence is best sensed and defined, since in all of the mask-stripping he is nearest to the crux of reality, most clearly perceiving the inefficacy and powerlessness of the others' dreams, and in his despair he concentrates emotionally the frustrations of the others. Obviously, with beard and manner, here is an aged counterpart of Shaw. Ironically, this is another mask, but one which achieves lively, poignant dimension through being recognized as a mask and not being torn off. In the sense of conventional characterization Shotover attains remarkable life, but as a projection of Shaw he has an extra magnetism which provides a kinetic effect. Regarding Shotover, Mazzini comments: "He is so fearfully magnetic: I feel vibrations whenever he comes close to me." This is bizarre, but poetically appropriate to the mythical associations of a man who is seeking the seventh degree of concentration, and dramatically appropriate to a character *sui generis*. Dramatically, Mazzini expresses what is dramaturgically a tour de force: as Shotover exists both in his own right and as a projection of Shaw, he takes on a double reality—that of fiction and that of authorial self-caricature, a character whose capriciousness is matched by earnestness and whose "madness" becomes a testament. In this sense he is, among the other players, quite supernatural, with a powerful symbolic presence which tends to confirm the sense of a dream and to make the dream Shaw's.

In this world where life is founded on illusions, Shotover, with his steady vision, ironically feels that he is dreaming. However, his particular "madness" is akin to Shaw's professed madness of seeing life with 20–20 vision while all others suffer ocular defects. This vision becomes the touchstone of the play as Shotover curses "the happiness of yielding and dreaming instead of resisting and doing, the sweetness of the fruit that is going rotten." His inner conflict is between the slothful dreams which flesh is heir to, especially in age, and the dynamic ethic of action with a moral purpose—which itself becomes a dream when set in a world of immorality and inaction. In all life, dreams of escape are repeatedly in conflict with the dreams of creative imagination, since the latter complement action rather than avoid it. Shotover's particular, prolonged heartbreak lies in the frustration of one type of dream debilitating the other, partially in himself but especially in his society.

A lively network of fantasy reinforces Shaw's Strindbergian mode, contributing to the effect of the action being dreamed, as distinct from the Chekhovian mode in which the action is dreamy. As the play progresses, the audience becomes conditioned more to the unusual, à la Strindberg, than to the usual, à la Chekhov. Physically, the country house is like a ship; metaphorically, the ship is a country. In either case the setting is incongruous—a ship on land or a country at sea—and the people in it dislocated. These people are strange, to say the very least. The captain, who is no longer truly a captain of this ship that is not a ship, is "a wild-looking old gentleman," the "Ancient Mariner," emitting "vibrations" and seeking supernatural powers. He was formerly married to a "black witch," reputedly sold his soul to the devil, and his mystical progeny are two "demon daughters," Hesione and Ariadne. One has so much heart that she emasculates men; the other has so little heart that she enslaves them. Emasculated husband Hector has a T. E. Lawrence complex, dressing like an Arab sheik, a true hero who is a liar pretending he is a hero. Absent husband Hastings is a numskull, appropriately resembling a ship's figurehead with a skull which is presumably wooden. The industrial Napoleon, Mangan, is more bossed than boss; the Italian revolutionary Mazzini has reincarnated as an apologist of the status quo. Even burglars cannot behave naturally. Billy Dunn, by chance a former husband of the housekeeper, distant cousin to Mazzini, pirate in China, and boatswain to the Captain—possessing a confusion of relationships which Strindberg would glory in—feigns burglary so that he can be caught to extort money and avoid prison by finding religion and pleading for imprisonment. He preys at the same time on social consciousness and the lack of it, both of which come to the same conclusion. Classical names add a mythical flavor to this fantasia, but, similar to Milton's Latinisms in *Paradise Lost*, they are more for mood than matter. Hesione and Ariadne are hardly even ironic reflections of their mythical counterparts, and Hector is just remotely the hero of another Troy. More apropos to this topsy-turvy world is an allusion to *Alice in Wonderland*, whose spirit is caught especially in act 1. Ellie falls asleep over her book and awakens to a grotesque tea conducted by a strange old man who is "as mad as a hatter." The adventures of Ellie in this dreamlike wonderland could hardly have a more appropriate connotation and commencement. Madness is the order of the day, and one might guess that sanity lies only in the Captain's rum.

The deciphering of this madness and the implicit search for sanity introduces still another dimension into *Heartbreak House*. The intuitive sensibilities of Strindberg and Chekhov are counterpointed by the impression of a highly active mind which is seeking a direction out of the morass, though it is profoundly thwarted by clouds of illusion. Most obviously, this is the Shavian intellect asserting itself in the semi-tangibles of this elusive, seemingly spontaneous dramatic medium. But more profoundly, the intellect takes on the caste of the medium itself by probing away at infinite layers of masks, reminiscent of the complex mode of Pirandello. The bizarre setting, functioning in part as a psychological state made visible, and presided over by a sane old man who is thought to be mad, is a haunting precursor of Pirandello's *Henry IV*, and the concern about levels of reality, with the authorial presence being one of those levels, anticipates *Six Characters in Search of an Author*. The sacrosanctness of objective fact is severely shaken, since so few characters appear to have a true grasp of it, and those who are most confident that they do are also most suspect. As fact is interpreted through the subjective consciousness, it is frequently so transmuted that the subjective consciousness may be said to create fact, which then takes on reality only in terms of consensus and may or may not have an objective correlative. Since the nature of genius is to run at cross purposes or to reach beyond consensus, geniuses may therefore be admired as transcendent or derided as mad. Frequently, of course, they are a little of both, and it is difficult for mundane standards to properly discriminate between transcendence and madness. Such is the case regarding Captain Shotover.

The greatest subjective consciousness of *Heartbreak House* is clearly that of the dreamer, whose presence is sensed most forcefully in Shotover but also less purely in Hector and Ellie, and finally in fragments of insight, emotion, and tone throughout the play. As this consciousness moves both mode and mood, its sense of reality is pervasive, even in madness. The incoherence of the action reflects that of a dream and depicts the aimlessness of society, providing a psychological complement to the erratic behavior of Shotover. More hauntingly, it reflects a feeling of frustration in the play's oversoul as the oversoul seeks to inform intransigent materials. In terms of this greater consciousness the most influential reality of facts exists more in their symbolic significance than in their objective details. Most revealing about *Heartbreak House*, therefore, are not the grim fragments of political and social incompetence which historically led up to World War I but the interpretation of those fragments via individual characters who serve as vital indicators of man's nature, a nature whose limitations portend man's future. These characters have a treble reality, personal, social, and symbolic. Aesthetically, their personal realities, flawed and diverse, contribute to a more complete sense of the symbolic reality of the play, since through their microcosmic world of pettiness and delusions the macrocosm of society, normally an inaccessible abstraction but a powerful reality in its own right, is laid bare in its all-too-human weaknesses. The tragedy of the situation thus revealed is that a myriad of mores, conceits, and illusions take on a social reality as these finite minds project themselves onto society in terms which are tangible and influential. The dynamics of assertion tend to create the realities—or illusions—by which men live. The despair of *Heartbreak House* lies in the fear that those of noble and cultured sensibilities have lost their dynamism, and that the vacuum has been filled by ignoble, self-centered, materialistic seekers of power or by guardians of a mindless status quo. Reality itself has shifted in a dangerous direction, because in Yeats's words: "The best lack all conviction, while the worst/Are full of passionate intensity."

This is starkly objectified in the play by Ariadne's pungent oversimplification: "There are only two classes in good society in England: the equestrian classes and the neurotic classes." The comment is an example of symbolic assertion which gains strength in the irony that, though it is outrageous, it approximates truth graphically and becomes definitive through being memorable. Limited to "good society," the two classes represent the sophisticated, educated pool from which leadership should arise. In this lies a crux of the play: Heartbreak House has no stables because its inhabitants appreciate personal values over horsey ones. Blessed with imagination, culture, and leisure, the Shotover demesne has indeed incorporated as its highest values the cultivation, charm, advancement, humanity, democracy, and free thought which are praised by Mazzini in the last act. By all signs its bohemianism is the outgrowth of a sensitive touch with the greatest realities of life, those involving individual freedom and conscience which abhor fraud, cant, and hypocrisy. From these ranks one might expect the most benevolent, open-minded, qualified leadership.

Juxtaposed to Heartbreak House is the horsey set, dubbed "Horseback Hall" in the preface. This group, concerned more with animals and sport than with humans and ideas, gravitates toward answers which make life simple and accommodating. Its realities involve order, ceremony, authority, and rules which lift the complexities of life from the shoulders of the individual. Thus Ariadne at the beginning of act 1 recalls her early dislike of the "disorder in ideas, in talk, in feeling" of Heartbreak House, and her desire "to be respectable, to be a lady, to live as others did, not to have to think of everything for myself." And near the end of act 3 she reemphasizes this in a reference to Mazzini's pyjamas—life is *simplified* by rules of propriety. In a similar vein, far more pathetic and telling, is Mangan's desperate question: "How are we to have any self-respect if we dont keep it up that we're better than we really are?" A life of well-regulated appearance leaves time for a life of easy escape in well-regulated pleasure. Life with such order is life with balance; life without it is, naturally, neurotic.

What Shaw has symbolically and sharply (albeit oversimply) defined is archetypal: his distinction is as old as the one between the ideals of Athens and the ideals of Rome, and as modern as that between college intellectuals and college athletes, humanists and scientists, or professors and businessmen. He has given the distinction of a new idiom and place, but, more important, he has attached to it the question of the world's physical and spiritual survival. As such, idiom and locale symbolically transcend the characters, England, and even the play's dreamer in terms of a universal schism confronting a universal imperative. As might be expected, the outward simplicity of the problem is belied by myriad complexities, complexities involving not only values but basic, contradictory assumptions regarding reality. The realities of Heartbreak House are illusions to Horseback Hall, and vice versa. The contradictory assumptions of the two houses are dramatized in conflicting views of man and society, order and disorder, social masks and social games. In prizing human values and culture, Heartbreak House assumes that society must above all be honest and free, allowing each man's genius to express itself openly and without intimidation. The assumption is philosophically romantic, stressing that the greatest reality is in being true to oneself, and that disorder is a healthy reflection of human differences. Social masks and abstractions, consequently, are fair game to the iconoclast, since they conceal and pervert personal reality. Horseback Hall, on the other hand, is philosophically closer to Hobbes, though its inhabitants would probably never bother to read him. From its viewpoint the individual is untrustworthy, and true reality lies in society because society fosters order. The individual realizes himself in terms of social standards, and his greatest reality is tied to his respectability in performing his social role well.

The play is partly structured on the personal reality, disorder, and games of Heartbreak House tearing away at the social illusions, order, and masks of Horseback Hall. We might expect a dramatization of Shaw's distinction regarding the reformer-realist as the great unmasker, which he drew in *The Quintessence of Ibsenism.* But other forces are at work in the play which reveal a vision far more sensitive and complex. The gospels of both houses are apocryphal. While the personal realism of the heartbreakers—Hesione, Hector, and Shotover—enables them to strip away social masks through devastating games, the disorder of their house debilitates them. Instead of moving society, they are playing with it. Their games are ring-around-the-rosy, dizzying but leading nowhere because they do not affect the center of power. These people chastize hypocrisy but do not reform it. Indeed, their greatest reality is that their bohemianism incapacitates them, setting them adrift from meaningful affairs. Thus their personal reality, lacking pragmatic power, renders them irrelevant, almost illusory, in terms of the great social machine which is grinding toward man's destruction. Conversely, the horsebackers—Ariadne, Hastings, Randall, and their bourgeois cousin Mangan—with all of their illusions of propriety, are nearer to the reality that counts. Their order, though artificial, equips them for action, and their thick-headed insularity removes fear of the consequences. They may be personally humiliated by the heartbreakers, but their creations, their institutions and machinery, will not be. In a curious way their pragmatic skepticism regarding individual human nature has brought about monsters far greater than man, Frankenstein terrors beyond their control. But they dance the social dance nonetheless, insensitive to fate, in an odd sort of romance with their abstractions. Romancing with life is ultimately the failing of both houses. One romances on its own little island of culture, sophistication, and intellectual games; the other, between intervals with horses and social chatter, romances with business, church, politics, and war.

The dichotomy takes on intriguing qualifications in terms of the individual characters. The temporal ruler of Heartbreak House is, notably, neither Shotover, who has faded from vigorous manhood into petulant eccentricity, nor Hector, who is debilitated by frustration between heroic aspirations and ignominious realities. Rather, the real monarch is Hesione, with an infirm daddy and a princeling regent. Appropriately, Hesione remarks, "Oh, *I* say it matters very little which of you governs the country so long as we govern you.... The devil's granddaughters ... The lovely women." With her beauty, charm, intelligence, and ability to adapt herself admirably to whomever she is speaking to, Hesione is the ideal hostess and the real power of her society. In this fact lies the fatal weakness of Heartbreak House, for the essence of Hesione's capacities is derived from congenial, entrancing femininity. As a delightful portrayal of womanhood, she is superb. With her uncorseted figure naturally asserting her beauty, she exudes a natural frankness with women, an intuitive tact with men, a warm and lucid love for her husband, and even an attractive feminine absentmindedness, revealed in her confusion about introductions. But because of these very qualities Hesione's house is in trouble. Ariadne senses the problem in observing that Heartbreak House is "only a very ill-regulated and rather untidy villa," and Mazzini unwittingly pins it down as he exclaims, "Bless you, dear Mrs Hushabye, what romantic ideas of business you have!" For although Hesione may be practical about money to keep the household going and sensitive to the realities of Ellie's young love, her intuitions above all reflect her womanhood, reacting more than acting, feeling more than thinking. Her obsession with the domestic domain of loves, fancies, and heartbreaks indicates the obliqueness of her touch with the real world outside of Heartbreak House. Thus she at first misappraises Mangan and looks upon Mazzini as the selfish father of a melodrama. Despite all her good intentions, Hesione's house is not in order because of her supremacy in it. Woman's intuition, valuable as it may be at a tea party or a weekend social, is not likely to guide a ship into port, to govern a country well, or to save the world.

Hector's mind, vision, and capacities indicate that he is probably the one who should be the new captain of this ship. Rather, he is its self-conscious, tormented gigolo. Hector's character unfolds in dreamlike fashion as the play progresses, becoming deeper, richer, and more tragic. He gains greater self-awareness and disgust as the full implications of his impotence become apparent. In the face of demands on his psychic virility, he evolves from his position as Hesione's household pet and Ellie's romantic fiction to absurd Byronic escapism ("Let us all go out into the night"), to a despairing sense of unreality ("We do not live in this house: we haunt it"), to the sensational nihilism of tearing down the curtains at the end. Ironically, it is Hector, the man of masks, daydreams, tall tales, and costumes who objectifies the sport of Heartbreak House: "In this house we know all the poses: our game is to find out the man under the pose." The fact that all the while he has the greatest potential of all suggests his confusion of spirit. He is perhaps more aware than anyone else of the elusiveness of reality and the reality of illusion as he advises Randall, "Never waste jealousy on a real man: it is the imaginary hero that supplants us all in the long run."

Hector's greatest problem is that at one time in his life he surrendered to romance, and ever since he has been unable to extricate himself. The fact that his heroics are more counterparts than surrogates of a genuine heroism indicates his potential, yet at the same time it hints at a psychological incapacity to live up to reality. The particular poignancy of Hector's frustration lies not in a lack of ability, but in a failure to make his ability meaningful. The crux of his problem is Hesione, whose feminine, marital, and maternal powers have prevailed over her husband, destroying his independence and affecting an insidious emasculation. Hesione, well-meaning but perverse, has turned their original deep love into a projection of her ideal society, a society which is essentially matriarchal. With cutting disparagement Ellie inveighs against Hesione, "I should have made a man of Marcus, not a household pet," and later Hector rants, "Is there any slavery on earth viler than this slavery of men to women?" His threat to choke Ariadne is but a desperate, pathetic attempt to recover his lost masculinity—an admission, in its violence, of his defeat and despair. The twentieth-century matriarchy prevails. The female principle of the Life Force has asserted itself in a cancerous way, sapping the noble, creative, affirmative impulses of the male by petty romance, social games, and domesticity. The result, naturally, is no sort of superman, but proper, conventional children who are scarcely worth mentioning. And thus we have a Lear-like Hector at the end of act 2 exclaiming, "Oh women! women! women! [*He lifts his fists in invocation to heaven*]. Fall. Fall and crush."

In this light we may see once again in Shaw the type of subtle irony between action and setting which he employs so well in *Arms and the Man, Caesar and Cleopatra,* and *Major Barbara.* Except for a small teak table, the setting is strikingly, assertively masculine. But as this ship is displaced in space, it is also displaced in time. Clearly it is an anachronism, a relic and symbol of bygone days when the exploring, adventuresome spirit of men *did* rule the world. As an aesthetic device the setting makes immanent and subtly, quietly pervasive the sense of passing time, of nostalgia, and of social evolution in which entirely new and less dynamic principles of life have come into being. The captain of this ship, Shotover, personifies this sense, giving the impression of a ghost flitting in and out. As the setting is anachronistic and not quite real, neither is he. Similarly, his convictions echo upon the scene as assertions of the past, and, as they are counterpointed with impressions of the present, the tones are those of a weird, nightmarish cacophony. A sense of the universal gap between generations is thus given highly poetic expression. What is vital and real to one age is abstraction and illusion to the next.

Except for Ellie, youthful exuberance plays very little role in *Heartbreak House,* since this is the middle-aged society on whom the country's fate depends. Once again, however, Shaw sets up a youth-age dichotomy, this time primarily between the middle-aged and ancient. And once again, as in *Caesar and Cleopatra* and *Major Barbara,* he inverts usual patterns of vital insight and reveals in age the more dynamic spirit. When Shotover expresses his abhorrence of yielding and dreaming instead of resisting and doing, a yielding which he depicts as his own senility, he is with cutting accuracy describing the mode of Hesione and Hector's bohemian existence. His grip on fatal realities is all too clear, and his senility proves to be more game than fact: his observation that Ariadne is no longer the daughter that left home twenty-three years before reveals a natural sensibility to a reality devoid of sentiment, and his mixing of the two Dunns is proven by Ellie to be conscious play. Similarly, he is lucid on ethical grounds, perceiving the debilitating sterility, disorder, and inaction which are subjecting Heartbreak House to the danger of Horseback Hall's inhumanity. His realistic answer to the problem is twofold: first, he appeals to eternal verities—the kindness and charity of "God's way," which he mentions to Ariadne, and the spiritual quality of selflessness, which he approves of in Ellie. Second, he urges a specific combination of the virtues of both houses—the culture and vital individualism of Heartbreak House must be given relevance to life through the sense of order and action possessed by Horseback Hall. Thus Shotover's reality is a sensitive synthesis which combines eternal values of charity with modern humanism and vitalism. The fact that with these views he is considered "mad" reveals the desperate spiritual plight of his society.

Mazzini Dunn is poised between the two houses. As an employee of Mangan he is physically subservient to the Establishment. But his sense of social propriety, which makes him "safe" with Hesione, is subordinate to an instinctive kindliness and understanding, which make him appreciate the informality and honesty of Heartbreak House over the social façades of Horseback Hall. It is clear whose side he is naturally on when at the first he comments, "The great question is, not who we are, but what we are." The statement, which would be commonplace were it to come from a more sophisticated source, is so typical of the humility and sincerity of Mazzini that it comes through with quiet effectiveness and depth. Mazzini combines naïveté with a sharp sense of reality, both originating from a good heart, and the subtlety of his portrayal results in large part from the humanizing mixture of both. Shaw manages to capture a rounded sense of a truly sweet soul without becoming saccharine—a rather rare feat in literature. With great naturalness Mazzini is engaged by the charms of Hesione, but unlike Mangan he maintains his integrity. He may be deluded about the personal villainy of Mangan toward himself, but his delusion rises from an instinctively charitable and trusting spirit. On the other hand, his vision is amazingly clear regarding Mangan's weaknesses, Ellie's strengths, and the nature of poverty. His suggestion that the burglar become a locksmith is incidental, but it pinpoints his practical coalescence of naïve simplicity, charity, and a practical mind. Obviously, saintly simpletons who work for industrial Napoleons, who admire the humanity, charm, and freedom of the Heartbreak House society and who trust in Providence (like Shotover's drunken skipper), are most unlikely to save the world and are most likely to be taken advantage of. However, with economy and purity of statement, Mazzini's sensitive innocence is poignantly portrayed. He has the unreal reality of an ideal that is seldom realized, prompting Ellie to remark, "There seems to be nothing real in the world except my father and Shakespear."

As Hesione rules over Heartbreak House, Ariadne is the queen of Horseback Hall. It is she who articulates the distinction between the two in terms of the "wrong" people, the neurotic heartbreakers, and her type, the "right" people, the "natural, wholesome, contented, and really nice English people," i.e., the equestrians. But before the issue is articulated, Shaw presents it dramatically and thereby achieves an implicit dialectical effect. At the very first he juxtaposes Ariadne's sense of social propriety and order to the bohemianism and disorder of her sister's house. Ariadne, as fully corseted as Hesione is not, returns home after twenty-three years expecting a warm and joyous reunion, only to be met by casual indifference. The situation would be shocking to any conventional sensibility, and humor is at first evoked at what seems to be the unconventional response of her sister and father. The base of humor switches very quickly, however, and Ariadne begins to appear foolish as she insists on her prerogatives. The prevailing logic, in short, assumes some of the "madness" of the house as the repre-

sentation of reality shifts slightly. Obviously, Ariadne is no longer "little
Paddy Patkins," and her desire for The Kiss takes on absurdity as it seems
more social than familial. She is in one aspect an anachronism, a memory,
an illusion the family dismissed long ago, which returns not as the nineteen-
year-old girl of memory but as a forty-two-year-old apparition, demanding
a better room in proper regard for her age and position. In this respect she
is a silly, pompous, sentimental ghost. As an apologist of society, her views
are compromised when she admits to Hector that a woman may do as she
pleases as long as she is socially respectable, and she becomes ridiculous
when she defends social masks in the last act: "I know by experience that
men and women are delicate plants and must be cultivated under glass. Our
family habit of throwing stones in all directions and letting the air in is not
only unbearably rude, but positively dangerous." Such a defense of the
façades which seem desirable to Horseback Hall echoes the more epigram-
matic observation of Lady Bracknell in *The Importance of Being Earnest*:
"Ignorance is like a delicate exotic fruit; touch it and the bloom is gone."
The weight of the simile is not likely to be to the advantage of the society
which supports it.

   The role of Ariadne in Horseback Hall offers a ready gauge with which
to compare the two houses. Like Hesione, she is the devil's granddaughter
with a beauty and fascination for men, but unlike Hesione, the king is not
emasculated—he is merely not present. Ariadne may have an emasculating
influence as she leaves lovers strewn about the Empire, but she does not
surrender her propriety, nor does she respect weak men. Randall is a rotter
because he is lazy, and she cites Napoleon's opinion that "women are the
occupation of the idle man." Hector is a handsome diversion, possessing
gallantry and a degree of dash, but he is part of a social game akin to the one
she is playing with Randall, since she has no intention of paying off. The
absent Hastings, on the other hand, is her lord in a very well-regulated
world, and the manner in which she cites him reveals that she never forgets
it. Randall remarks disparagingly that Hastings "has the gift of being able
to work sixteen hours a day at the dullest detail, and actually likes it."
Obviously, this is part of what qualifies Hastings as governor and husband,
and what disqualifies Randall and Hector. Hastings may be pedantic, he
may be a numskull, but he has power not only because he can ride horses,
but because he *works*. Thus Ariadne can make her assertion, "The man is
worth all of you rolled into one." The dangerous irony is that men of so
little imagination have climbed to the top while greater, lazier men play
games in their wives' parlors. Hastings could save the country with auto-

cratic power and enough whips, but would a country thus saved be worth living in?

Mangan may not belong in Horseback Hall in terms of family, but according to position, temperament, and values he does. He overdresses, which a man of good family would consider in poor taste, but he reveals thereby a consciousness of image which is the mystique of Horseback Hall society. In defiance of Mazzini's sententiousness, he asserts that who we are is a fair measure of what we are. He is in many ways a parallel of Hastings— both are pedantic drudges, both are ruthless, and both have power. Sadly, worldly respect and influence come to them on an ascending scale according to these qualities, and as they are not imaginative men they assume that the world is right, and that order, aggressiveness, and power are virtues in themselves. The facts that Mangan is a money-grubber, afraid of his men, unsure of himself, and not personally wealthy are less real to the world than his image. As Mazzini remarks, "People believe in him and are always giving him money, whereas they dont believe in me and never give me any." This well-ordered, rational society thus exists on an irony which inverts reality and illusion: what counts is who we are, not what we are, since belief is more important than fact. As might be expected, society is double-crossed, getting the worst, which it deserves. While Ariadne has her games of love, and Heartbreak House has its games of truth, Mangan has his games of business and government, which naturally reflect his ignoble character: "Achievements? Well, I dont know what you call achievements; but Ive jolly well put a stop to the games of the other fellows in the other departments. Every man of them thought he was going to save the country all by himself, and do me out of the credit and out of my chance of a title. I took good care that if they wouldnt let me do it they shouldnt do it themselves either. I may not know anything about my own machinery; but I know how to stick a ramrod into the other fellow's." Thus, in a devilish game of one-downmanship, the country is incidentally sabotaged. For anyone acquainted with the civil service, probably of any country at any time, this fearful exaggeration of a certain sort of debased mentality has symbolic power.

Strangely, Mangan is more credible in his mask of an industrial Napoleon than as the psychically stripped man of act 3 who desperately feels he may as well be physically stripped also. In his extreme incapacitation he is bizarre, almost surrealistically dream-like, partaking of and contributing to the undercurrent of despair. But there can be no question that he has gone through a most unnerving wringer: the absolute truth. With irony, humor, and drama Shaw presents the symbolic tableau of two women standing over a prostrate, defenseless, hypnotized man, discussing with complete candor, even ruthlessness, his vices and inadequacies and how they plan to use him for their own ends. Social amenities are discarded; female stars are absolutely in the ascendant; the image is smashed. Doubly poignant is the afterview that all the time the poor male was helplessly conscious, hearing reality, as it were, in a dream. Within minutes the shock treatment of Mangan effects the emasculation that Hesione took years to produce in Hector. As in Ellie's case, psychological evolution is dramatically short-circuited, effecting dreamlike economy and sharp symbolic emphasis.

Similarly symbolic, though also as capricious as a dream, is the burglar incident. The Heartbreak House society may bare the man beneath the monster in Mangan, but on practical grounds it is incapable of controlling the monster, and this incapacity is manifested simply in its reaction to Billy Dunn, a less sophisticated thief and fraud than Mangan. The incident with Billy pointedly objectifies vague abstractions of law and order by thrusting them into the parlor, and the sum of the characters' reactions is a desire for disinvolvement, Hesione on humane grounds, Ariadne on grounds of privacy and inconvenience. In its one chance to assert itself in terms of the greater world, Heartbreak House finds its civic responsibility distasteful or too troublesome. Typically, Mazzini manifests the social-worker consciousness in suggesting that the burglar turn to an honest trade, but, most telling, it is the horsebacker Ariadne who finally loses patience and urges prosecution. While the bohemians allow themselves to be run over, the law-and-order temperament takes initiative by default because it will not be pushed too far. The social analogy is poignant—since Mangan is a gangster boss on the side of law and order, the bohemians are in a sorry plight indeed. Not being able to handle microcosmic realities, they are desperately inadequate regarding macrocosmic ones. Surrounded by their upper-middle-class milieu, they are insulated from the total social environment, and their base of conceptualization is pathetically finite. To some degree they are like the average Yahoo that Shaw describes in the preface, for whom World War I existed not as the giant catastrophe it was, which he could not imagine, but as many little catastrophes of a size befitting his limited sensibilities. The immense realities do not exist for these people because they do not have the greatness of consciousness to comprehend them.

Apparently a new order of consciousness is needed, and as Ellie evolves toward this she becomes the play's aesthetic focal point, complementing the moral focal point in Shotover. The degrees of self-knowledge that others achieve through heartbreak are but variants and complementary motifs of her movement toward understanding. She progresses through the major options of the play, each with its particular set of realities, clarifying them through a single vision and frame of reference. Starting in an adolescent dream world of Othello and Marcus Darnley, where reality is bounded only by the limits of her fancy, she is jolted into the world of Heartbreak House as her dream of a hero is contradicted by mundane fact. But the realities of the house—the disorder, inaction, frustration, enjoyment of broken hearts, playing at love, sentiment, and iconoclastic games—are clearly no answer for a poor girl. In her station they offer only the most futile and fruitless of diversions, which would end not just in disillusioned, neurotic old age, but in very real penury. So with cold calculation she turns to the practical, ordered world of Horseback Hall with every indication that she can beat it at its own game. The inversion of a potential melodramatic pattern is striking. Instead of the rich, lecherous old man forcing marriage on a poor, innocent young heroine, the hard-minded, practical young woman measures the old man for his money and presses for marriage, at the same time making it perfectly clear that she intends to pursue a close relationship with a younger man. The change in Ellie from innocent young thing to hardened cynic works as a dreamlike foreshortening of very credible psychological processes. But even more, her change involves a self-assertion well motivated by obvious realities: not being a fool, she will exercise the options she has and fill her role as a woman in the individualistic, free, dominating fashion of Heartbreak House, while reaping the rewards of Horseback Hall's money and respectability. With her romantic illusions well chastized she instinctively seeks the best of both worlds, and in taking Mangan she still plans in some degree to retain her original romance with Hector. Such romance may be second hand, but it will at least be well financed.

Ellie's compromise makes excellent sense, being a prudent extraction of all she can hope for from romance and the two houses. But counterposed to this rational course is her soul, and while her response to reality is at first spirited, it lacks spirituality. Her description of heartbreak reveals her awareness of this latter, indicating that her soul is far nearer to Shotover's than to the others':

> It is a curious sensation: the sort of pain that goes mercifully beyond our powers of feeling. When your heart is broken, your boats are burned: nothing matters any more. It is the end of happiness and the beginning of peace.

The effect of disillusionment has been to propel her toward age and wisdom, rendering her susceptible to education by Shotover, whose words indicate their spiritual kinship: "Old men are dangerous: it doesnt matter to them what is going to happen to the world. . . . I tell you happiness is no good. You can be happy when you are only half alive." Heartbreak has great potential if it brings an end to the pursuit of illusion, especially illusion founded on self-interest, because only by reversing the spiritually consuming whirlpool of egocentricity can the soul awaken to the broader consciousness of life and reality. Ellie is on the right path when she remarks: "I feel now as if there was nothing I could not do, because I want nothing," which Shotover approves: "Thats the only real strength. Thats genius." This is the great spiritual leap enabled by heartbreak, far transcending the ignoble materialism which Ellie embraced in the first phase of her disillusionment. Through adopting a materialistic course, she might eat, but she would not truly live. Now, in wanting nothing, there is nothing for her to fear or to sell her soul to, and she can be spiritually honest, for, like an old man, she has nothing to lose. Thus Shotover is her spiritual husband and second father, and Ellie offers the glimmering hope of combining youth with wisdom.

However, while Ellie's evolution explores the deeper implications of heartbreak, traversing the social realities and psychological strata of the play, it reaffirms the social problem. Ellie may take to the Captain, but the fact remains that the Captain has taken to rum, and no one is at the helm. Nothing seems to be real except her father and Shakespeare, both of whom give quality to life but cannot save it. "Life with a blessing" is indeed an admirable goal, signifying the beauties and richness of an existence dedicated to humanistic values, but this is not enough. Even Ellie's spiritual marriage to Shotover, while symbolically hopeful, is a futile gesture in the face of cruel fact. All that is left at the end is a *desire* to feel life fully, and this desire reaches its ultimate form in confronting the most inexorable of realities, death. Earlier, Ariadne remarked that she had never *lived* until she rode a horse, and similarly, Shotover felt life most keenly when confronting the reality of the elements, piloting his ship in a storm. To confront danger and death is to confront life. Thus Ellie urges Hector to set fire to the house, so that they will be a better target for the bombers, hazarding, as it were, a double immolation. At this point the action comes full circle back to romance—with Ellie still calling Hector "Marcus"—but it is a romance of life, not an illusion, since it involves a danger which most meaningfully intertwines life and death. This romance loses its sense, unfortunately, as it is linked to hysteria. The tone is grotesque and macabre, the characters behaving, as Hector observes, like moths flying into a candle. Ellie's hope at the very end that the bombers will come again is an ambivalent reaction to fate. At last these people embrace their humanity, sensing life in true violence and danger, but their exuberant reaction is as practically futile as was their former indolence. Their desire for life is locked in a death wish, and the play ends in a haunting paradox.

This sensational conclusion climaxes not only the mental flux between reality and illusion in *Heartbreak House;* far more potently, it is the culmination of an apocalyptic spirit of prophecy which grows throughout the play. Surprisingly, critics have concentrated on Shaw's mention of Chekhov in the preface, and have usually neglected the nearly equal space he gives to Tolstoy, whom he mentions first. Aside from the dream play aspect, which is very compatible with the Chekhovian mode, the assertive, highly ethical and messianic voice which rises through the action has a distinct kinship to that of Tolstoy. In distinguishing between the two men, Shaw observes that, as opposed to Chekhov's gentle fatalism, aloofness, and charm, "Tolstoy did not waste any sympathy on [Heartbreak House]: it was to him the house in which Europe was stifling its soul; and he knew that our utter enervation and futilization in that overheated drawing-room atmosphere was delivering the world over to the control of ignorant and soulless cunning and energy, with the frightful consequences which have now overtaken it." One need only to substitute "Shaw" for "Tolstoy" in this quotation to capture an emphatic spirit in *Heartbreak House* which qualifies its Chekhovian tone, energizes its Strindbergian consciousness, and informs the entire context of illusion and reality with a grim sense of underlying moral and spiritual truths. In foreboding the consequences of culture and power being in separate compartments, the play assumes much of that deep seriousness about life which Tolstoy had found wanting in *Man and Superman:* "Dear Mr. Shaw, life is a great and serious affair."

Judging and judgment are recurrent motifs in the play. The characters judge one another, the authorial presence is constantly judging, and, above all, there is the impression of an eternal, immanent, inescapable Judgment presiding over the whole. The depiction of the characters is in keeping with this severe aspect. With a seeming deliberateness they are not rendered strongly sympathetic, and the audience itself assumes the role of judge through a sense of detachment. Emotional disengagement is the general mode: Ellie neutralizes sympathy, since heartbreak hardens rather than debilitates her; the pathos of Shotover is mitigated by his eccentricity, his rum, and his unwanted happiness; Hector is too much a fraud, too bizarre, and too cutting in his disillusionment; Hesione and Ariadne are too confident and self-controlled; Mangan is too ignoble as a boss and too ridiculous in heartbreak; Randall is absurd in his pettiness and childishness; and the burglar is an amusing grotesque. Most sympathetic is Mazzini, whose heart and charm are strong, but he is a motif secondary to the central action. Since the characters are more fascinating than engaging, the dramatic emphasis falls on the social situation and maintains a degree of aesthetic distance. Yet there is a profound quality of emotion which rises from the play as a whole. This results from the accretion of the many expressions of heartbreak, disillusionment, and despair which shadow the house increasingly toward the end, giving constantly greater weight to Shotover's conviction of the folly of it all. Implicit cries of "folly, folly, folly," and "beware of the day of Judgment," though very old-fashioned, seem apropos.

The moral, almost biblical fervor and sense of judgment arise fragmentarily in act 1, gain focus as Shotover lectures Ellie in act 2, and become prophetic in act 3. They exist in a double sense of allegory, Christian and social. The groundwork is laid in act 1, when all mankind is implicated in the drama, presented as a brotherhood in which none are perfect but each is responsible for the other. Man shares a common lot, and with an awareness of this should face his fellow men and his God. Notably, this assertion comes from the bohemians of Heartbreak House, not from the socially respectable horsebackers. Hesione cuts through abstractions of good and evil which, by making a melodrama of life, create false social attitudes: "People dont have their virtues and vices in sets: they have them anyhow: all mixed." Shotover, through the perspective of age, neutralizes social divisions: "Do you suppose that at my age I make distinctions between one fellowcreature and another?" Mazzini asserts the importance of the personal nature of an individual over his social station: "The great question is, not who we are, but what we are." And Hector links this concept of a common order to his personal perception of a higher order: "We are members one of another. . . . I must believe that my spark, small as it is, is divine."

On this ground of man's equality before God, Shotover later addresses Ellie in terms which are universal, Christian, and as old as the distinction between *cupiditas* and *caritas:* "It's prudent to gain the whole world and lose your own soul. But dont forget that your soul sticks to you if you stick to it; but the world has a way of slipping through your fingers." Old-fashioned this may be, as Ellie observes, but it is nonetheless true and relevant. In the manner of *Major Barbara*, Ellie feels that poverty is damning her by inches, to which Shotover responds in a messianic tone: "Riches will damn you ten times deeper"—because, as riches insulate a man from life, with its hardships and dangers, they insulate him from his intrinsic humanity, which is inextricably bound to his spiritual reality, to the spiritual realities of others, and to God. Thus it is harder for a rich man to get into heaven than for a camel to pass through the eye of a needle. The principles of Undershaft are pitted against spiritual principles and ultimately are found to be deficient. The individual who sells himself is not likely to have a soul worth salvaging.

Act 3 serves as an exemplum of Shotover's words to Ellie. The act opens in a dreamlike mood—here is the social ship drifting toward disaster on the indolence of its middle-class luxury and attitudes. Its soul, having avoided the realities of the greater world for so long, has been incapacitated by irrelevance. Over all hangs Mangan's presentiment of doom, absurd at first, but poetically reinforced by the strange drumming in the sky. The drumming, though reminiscent of the breaking harp string in *The Cherry Orchard,* is more ominous than nostalgic, and Hector sets the tone of the act by describing it with symbolic accuracy as "Heaven's threatening growl of disgust at us useless futile creatures," to which he adds, "There is no sense in us. We are useless, dangerous, and ought to be abolished." The speech has special poignancy both as an expression of Hector's personal frustration and as a general harbinger of doom which rises out of the prevailing mood of the play. After Ariadne's distinction between the equestrians and the neurotics, an obsessive question floats upon the scene, quite illogically, but with dreamlike pertinence to the underlying moral theme: Who will save the country? Mangan is talented at jamming the other fellow's efforts, Hector will not be listened to, Hastings would rule with a stick, Hesione gives women ultimate power, Ellie seeks life with a blessing, and Mazzini trusts in Providence. Implicitly, they are all judged for foolishness, ineffectuality, tyranny, or blindness. Clearly, in Shotover's prophetic terms, which keynote the strain of cosmic disgust at the end, they have not found "God's way," and the old man transcends his rum with sudden savagery and vehemence, envisioning England as a ship and this society as the drunken skipper, all about to smash on the rocks. His final exhortation, citing "the laws of God," comes like that of an exasperated prophet, or as the voice of the dreamer suddenly breaking through before awakening in a sweat: "Navigation. Learn it and live; or leave it and be damned." And, apocalyptically, the bombs explode. The Tolstoyan, Christian, Shavian judgment is upon Heartbreak House.

Augmenting this element of Christian parable and apocalyptic myth is the allegorical frame. Shaw executes the allegory on several levels, both concrete and suggestive, which give an additional poetic richness to the drama. Most obvious is the ship metaphor, expressing the central theme in terms of setting, characters, and action. As we have observed, the setting indicates England's adventuresome past, when, as Shotover remarks, England experienced true life through danger. The props are those of an England of work, creativity, and action, all also past. The characters, playing against the tradition of England's past, are the idlers or rogues of today, members of the class which would ordinarily be looked to for leadership. One group, the cultured society most fit to govern, is too bohemian and detached; the other group is too mundane, corrupt, or unimaginative. Mangan, the "captain of industry," is the pilot at home; Hastings, the petty tyrant of the colonies, is the vestigial remnant of Empire. In their hands lies the poor, honest confidence of the simple Mazzinis. Shotover, who once navigated as England once ruled the waves, selling his soul to the devil (of imperialist ambition) in Zanzibar (the Far East), is too old for power and can do nothing but despair at the corruption and idleness of the modern sailor.

Various names, in a rather haphazard manner, are puns in accord with the allegory. Shotover has overshot, and his shots are over; Hector Hushabye is the hero of Troy, asleep; Ariadne and Hesione are classically irrelevant; Mazzini Dunn is the revolutionary, done, finished; Hastings Utterword is, by inference, hasty in utterance, without thought of moral complexities, a namesake of the notorious, high-handed, authoritarian governor general of British India (the utter word in colonial assertiveness); and Mangan is a "Boss"-man, metallic, manganic—hard, brittle, not magnetic. As culture in Heartbreak House and power in Mangan are in separate compartments, youth in Ellie and wisdom in Shotover coalesce only spiritually. Their union is a sterile one. More fertile was the union of white and black, of Shotover with the "black witch" of Zanzibar (a half-echo of the *Othello* references), which produced the demon daughters and which lends a morality tone to *Heartbreak House.* References to devil, demons, damnation, and hell abound, but, like the punning, they are more suggestive than cohesive. Though Shotover's soul was redeemed by the Negress who presumably educated him in the ambiguities of life through the perspectives of another culture, his demon daughters make the world a hell for their lovers by triumphing over them in an inversion of nature. Heaven growls in disgust because this is not God's way. The old orientation involving salvation through action and understanding has begotten a disorientation involving damnation through sloth and bewilderment. Meanwhile the captain, like Adam (and Voltaire), turns ever more to the innocence of his garden, which becomes his Gethsemane.

The dramatic idiom of *Heartbreak House,* in sum, is far more complex than the realistic mode of Chekhov. It is a fantasia in a very full sense of the term, reaching back into the nineteenth century for religious and political tradition and forward to the twentieth century for dramatic expression.

Along with Strindberg it finds most intense reality in inner consciousness, and along with Pirandello it is fascinated with the myriad of illusions and realities in art and life. But mutating all of these mediums is the Shavian puritan consciousness, dealing in metaphor, parable, and morality, nearly as old-fashioned and fundamentally Christian as Tolstoy. This latter gives focus to the free movement of the expressionism, while the expressionism gives richness and artistic scope to the moral consciousness. The total effect results from intense personal conviction combining with the broadest worldly concerns in such a way that each gives life to the other. Thus the broken hearts of individual characters in the play cumulate in terms of common denominators to provide a unitive sense of a much greater heartbreak, partly in the consciousness of the dreamer, which is sensed through them, and, more broadly, in the whole society which they represent.

The quality of this heartbreak gives it profound significance. It is not primarily romantic, but anti-romantic, being destructive of illusions as the realities of life force themselves upon the individual: heartbreak, in short, is life educating man. Ellie finds peace in it, but this is atypical, perhaps a feminine reaction, since indications are that Hesione has also found a sort of peace with herself. Far more typical are Hector, Mangan, Randall, and Shotover, for whom heartbreak apparently begins in indignation and ends in despair. Only Mangan experiences the complete process on stage, but all have clearly gone through the cycle at some time and are manifesting some aspect of it, with heartbreak lingering in the despair. The universal sense of heartbreak rises from many particulars, starting in act 1 with Shotover seeking the seventh degree of concentration in order to destroy the enemies of society. His ambition, in its irrationality, seems to involve the desperation of a last step where all else has failed, the pursuit of an ideal unattainable because of ubiquitous folly and corruption. The universals of his problem and his feeling of personal inadequacy are expressed in his question, "What then is to be done? Are we to be kept for ever in the mud by these hogs to whom the universe is nothing but a machine for greasing their bristles and filling their snouts?" He reflects the philosophy of *Major Barbara* as he asserts, "We must win powers of life and death over them . . . I refuse to die until I have invented the means." But the absolute fact of death confronts Shotover's age, feeding his despair and breaking his heart because he knows it will overtake him, and he acknowledges the fact by escaping into rum. He built a house so that his daughters might marry well and produce better children, but one married a numskull and the other married a liar, neither producing progeny fit to inherit the earth.

Very likely Shaw found *Heartbreak House* difficult to discuss not only because of its intuitive nature, but also because its dilemma and heartbreak were so personal to him. As Shotover is Shaw, suspended between caricature and alter ego (an aged version of the Tanner-Juan composite), we see in his age, obsolescence, and impotence the playwright's profound agony at his own insignificance and powerlessness in the face of the brutal realities of World War I. There is a strong sense of Shaw's personal animus in Shotover's frustration and vehemence, especially as the frustration gathers force through being echoed by the other characters. Shaw himself was being educated by the world in a manner which confirmed the doubts he had held at the writing of *Man and Superman*. The power to blow up one's enemy's ammunition by a mind ray and the pursuit of a seventh degree of concentration are bizarre projections of Shaw's desire to effect social change through means primarily mental, and to achieve perfection through the will of the Life Force. All, of course, to no avail—instead, the way of the world was violence, not intellect, and the exploding ammunition was directed by capitalists who, virtually unimpeded, had propelled the world into war, a war wherein the drifting, chauvinistic, stupid masses were applauding the death of Beethoven at the hands of Bill Sikes. And instead of Creative Evolution we see the Life Force vitality being sapped by age, the Life Force woman emasculating her husband, and all optimism for a better future drying up in a sterile union of youth and wisdom, a union whose only reality is symbolic.

The moral assertions in act 2 might as well be undercut by rum, for all the good they do, and Shaw, like Shotover, may well have dreaded his dreams as the mental meanderings of one whose life was by all odds nearly over—meanderings such as those of this play. In act 3 Shaw appears briefly and pathetically in Mazzini, who "joined societies and made speeches and wrote pamphlets. . . . Every year I expected a revolution, or some frightful smashup: it seemed impossible that we could blunder and muddle on any longer. But nothing happened, except, of course, the usual poverty and crime and drink that we are used to." More tragically, he appears in Hector: "[*Fiercely*] I tell you, one of two things must happen. Either out of that darkness some new creation will come to supplant us as we have supplanted the animals, or the heavens will fall in thunder and destroy us." The image of England as a ship, a metaphor derived originally from Carlyle, stayed with Shaw for years. Don Juan had asserted that to be in hell was to drift, to be in heaven was to steer. Shotover asserts navigation. But it is too late, since, in Hector's words, again reminiscent of *Man and Superman*, "We sit here talking, and leave everything to Mangan and to chance and to the devil."

The delineation of psychological and associational patterns in *Heart-*

break House does not depend on a knowledge of Shaw's state of mind, since the patterns have independent power and evoke their own moods. They are factors in a nightmare which by inversion creates its dreamer. But as Shotover slips between eccentricity and prophetic coherence, and as Hector gives voice to the cumulative despair, extra dimension is added by sensing the dreamer as Shaw, confronted with the implacable movement of history and unable to do anything about it. Similarly, the bohemians' stripping away of masks gives them a special Strindbergian expressionistic quality, but also makes them more distinctly characteristic of Shaw than of "cultured, leisured Europe." Whether the despair rises through Shaw or an anonymous dreamer, however, it expands beyond finite consciousness toward a foreboding of general dissolution, a result of the spiritual nature of man being too weak to control his material powers. The dramatic poetry is again evocative of Yeats: "Things fall apart; the centre cannot hold; / Mere anarchy is loosed upon the world, / The blood-dimmed tide is loosed."

The ending comes with a convergence of nightmare and reality. By the time of the bombing, the play has moved sufficiently into a dreamlike atmosphere, with a basic frustration so well conveyed and a psychological pattern so well developed that the characters' abnormal, enthusiastic reception of impending catastrophe is grotesquely appropriate to the situation. The themes of the drama are met by a Beethovenesque climax, German and bombastic. In a striking physical objectification of the earlier games Hector tears down the curtains as if he were tearing off masks. Now the reality is death, the one inexorable reality of the play; with metaphorical irony, turning on the lights of the house manifests a desire to turn on the light of the soul in a confrontation with dangers which are the essence of life. Appropriately, the Life Force people want light, while the horsebackers hide or tremble. Aesthetically it takes Beethoven to revitalize the psyche and to destroy the mundane forces, such as Mangan and the Church, which plague the world. The fact that World War I did *not* destroy civilization allows Shaw's sense of anticlimax to save Heartbreak House. But the danger, clearly, is still there, for the bombers will probably come tomorrow, and unless Heartbreak House's frenzy of nihilism can be converted to energy which will steer the ship out of the storm, the ship will no doubt end up on the rocks.

Poetically, the end speaks for itself, but in his preface Shaw strikes a significant note in accord with the ending's hollowness and lack of resolution: "Heartbreak House, in short, did not know how to live, at which point all that was left to it was the boast that at least it knew how to die: a melancholy accomplishment." Lest some nobility other than that born of madness and desperation be attached to such suicidal bravery, he observes: "In truth, it is, as Byron said, 'not difficult to die,' and enormously difficult to live. . . . Does it not seem as if, after all, the glory of death were cheaper than the glory of life?" Looking ahead, Shaw speaks of the vindictiveness of England in demanding stringent reparations after the war, and he prophesies that "this thoughtless savagery will recoil on the heads of the Allies." He refers to "the next war" and remarks that, "with the usual irony of war, it remains doubtful whether Germany and Russia, the defeated, will not be the gainers." His remarks are strikingly apropos, reminding us how Shaw, though occasionally wrong, could so frequently be penetratingly right. In fruitlessly urging charity and humanity, Shaw is once again Shotover: "Alas! Hegel was right when he said that we learn from history that men never learn anything from history. . . . If men will not learn until their lessons are written in blood, why, blood they must have, their own for preference." The stage was being set for a repeat performance.

MAURICE VALENCY

Back to Methuselah:
A Tract in Epic Form

Two years after *Heartbreak House* was finished, and two years before its
first production in New York, Shaw began what he considered to be his
major work, the play that was to sum up everything he had so far written.
In this period his only other important writings were *Doctors' Delusions,*
published in installments from December 1917 to March 1918 in the *English Review,* and *Peace Conference Hints,* a brochure published in 1919,
which he later reprinted in *What I Really Wrote About the War* (1930).

The first was a carefully reasoned diatribe aimed at the abuses of
organized medicine. Both the arguments and the abuses they deal with are
curiously the same as those which in the 1970s we recognize as
contemporary. The other had to do with the management of the post-war
situation in Europe after the defeat of Germany, and the formation of a
League of Nations with sufficient police power to ensure the world order.
Neither of these estimable pieces appears to have had any influence
anywhere.

Early in 1918, directly after finishing *Doctors' Delusions,* Shaw took
up *The Gospel of the Brothers Barnabas.* He worked at the play steadily
until May of that year. By that time he had finished *The Thing Happens* and
had begun *The Tragedy of an Elderly Gentleman.* Apparently he put these
scenes aside at this point in order to write the brochure on the peace conference. When he took up his play again, he decided to extend his plan of
composition to include the story of the Garden of Eden. The two scenes of

From *The Cart and the Trumpet: The Plays of George Bernard Shaw.* © 1973, 1983
by Maurice Valency. Oxford University Press, 1973.

In the Beginning were completed in February 1919. In July 1919 he wrote to Trebitsch: "I am working at a huge tetralogy (like Wagner's Ring) called *Back to Methuselah*. First Play, Garden of Eden. Second Play the present day. Third Play, 300 years hence. Fourth Play, 1000 years hence."

About a year elapsed, however, before he took up this work again. *The Tragedy of an Elderly Gentleman* was finished in mid-March of 1920, and immediately after it Shaw began *As Far As Thought Can Reach*. The cycle of five plays was actually completed toward the end of May 1920, and the preface was written shortly after. In all, *Back to Methuselah* took a year and a half to complete. It was produced in its entirety by The Theatre Guild at the Garrick Theatre in New York beginning February 27, 1922. The play took three nights to perform, even with drastic cuts in part 4. It was presented in cycles of a week, ran nine weeks, and then closed. Its reception was extremely respectful; but it cost the Theatre Guild $20,000, a ruinous loss in the 1920s.

As Shaw had foreseen, *Back to Methuselah* was not a popular success anywhere. It was first produced in England on October 9, 1923, by Barry Jackson at the Birmingham Repertory Theatre with a cast that included Edith Evans and Cedric Hardwicke, both at that time—in Shaw's phrase—provincial nobodies. It was played there four times with great acclaim and lost £2500. The following year it was brought briefly to the Court Theatre in London and in 1927 it was recalled for some additional performances. In 1958—after Shaw's death—a condensed version was produced by the Theatre Guild in New York, with neither profit nor critical approval. On the whole, it was among the least successful of Shaw's great plays.

Shaw was awarded the Nobel Prize for literature in 1925. Nineteen years later, Oxford University Press asked him to select one of his works for publication as the 500th volume of its series of World's Classics. Shaw chose *Back to Methuselah*. In the postscript to the Oxford edition he wrote that this play was his masterpiece and, with becoming modesty, he ascribed its composition to a superior power:

> I do not regard my part in the production of my books and plays as much greater than that of an amanuensis or an organ-blower. An author is an instrument in the grip of Creative Evolution, and may find himself starting a movement to which in his own little person he is intensely opposed. When I am writing a play, I never invent a plot: I let the play write itself and shape itself, which it always does, even when up to the last moment I do not see the way out. Sometimes I do not see what the play was driving at

until quite a long time after I have finished it; and even then I
may be wrong about it just as any critical third party may.

It may be assumed that in this semimystical identification with the Life
Force Shaw had in mind a process analogous to that through which his
mother had produced some volumes of automatic writing. The difference
was that, while his mother considered her spiritual guidance to be supernatural, Shaw considered his to be supremely natural, an elemental intelligence communicating through his agency tidings of exceptional urgency.
Back to Methuselah was, he intimated, the latest effort of the Life Force to
make itself intelligible, a supreme attempt of the vital spirit to achieve
self-consciousness. As such it was holy, a work of scriptural importance
which was destined to supplement the Bible.

For a twentieth-century writer to speak seriously of an external power
as the source of his writings seems quaint, if not downright mad, but Shaw
had not only excellent literary precedents, but by this time very likely he had
complete faith in himself as an agent of the Creative Will. His was the
outstanding voice of the time, of this everything combined to assure him. In
the circumstances it was with a certain humility that he presumed to speak
with the voice of God.

Milton had called upon the Holy Spirit for inspiration in writing *Paradise Lost*. Shaw had equal reason to believe that the Life Force would take
a hand in the composition of *Back to Methuselah*. In an approving reference
to Lorenz Oken's *Nature Philosophy* (1809), Shaw assimilated the Life
Force to the Holy Ghost—with which, apparently, he associated Hegel's
Weltgeist—and thus brought his evolutionary theory into a positive relation
with acceptable Christian doctrine. Similar feats of syncretism had long ago
been achieved in the early efforts at promoting Darwin's hypothesis. Oken,
whom Weismann cited approvingly in his *History of Evolution,* had defined
natural science as "the science of the everlasting transmutations of the Holy
Ghost in the world." Shaw commented: "The man who was scientific enough
to see that the Holy Ghost is a scientific fact got easily in front of the
block-heads who could only sin against it."

The preface to *Back to Methuselah* employs, together with some very
convincing arguments, all the artifices of the hard sell, and the vehemence of
the discourse gives cause for wonder. Shaw's motives are seldom entirely
lucid. At sixty-five he was certainly in no need of money, and his position as
a literary figure was enviable. On the other hand, he was a man of boundless
ambition, and his longing for power had been cruelly thwarted. For one
who aspired to be a world leader it was hardly enough to have been elected

Vestryman of St. Pancras at the age of forty-one and nothing more. Evidently even at the last the dream of political preferment was difficult for him to relinquish. In the postscript he composed at the age of eighty-eight for the Oxford edition of *Back to Methuselah*, he wrote, only half-humorously:

> Physically, I am failing: my senses, my locomotive powers, my memory are decaying at a rate which threatens to make a Struldbrug of me if I persist in living: yet my mind still feels capable of growth; for my curiosity is keener than ever. My soul goes marching on; and if the Life Force would give me a body as durable as my mind, and I knew better how to feed and lodge and dress and behave, I might begin a political career as junior civil servant and evolve into a capable Cabinet Minister in another hundred years or so.

But while he was too old, even at sixty-five, to dream of governing a nation, he was certainly not too old to aspire to be the spiritual guide of those who governed. The age requirements for the divine apostolate have never been fixed; indeed, age is an ornament to the successful seer. Very likely, Shaw more than half believed that *Back to Methuselah* had been dictated to him as the Koran had been dictated to Mohammed, and that one day it would be appointed to be read in churches.

Regardless of the source of his inspiration, Shaw's description of the spontaneity of his method is more justly applicable to his later works than to his earlier comedies. It was in the series of "disquisitory plays" culminating *Heartbreak House* that Shaw put aside the calculated effects of the well-made play in favor of the freewheeling methods of his later compositions. Doubtless his growing faith in the creative ingenuity of the Life Force induced him to abandon himself so completely to its dictation that any preconceived plan of composition might be considered an obstacle to its influence. In these plays, accordingly, he came close to those writers who, under symbolist influence, felt that the unconscious is the surest guide to truth and that the artist's principal function is simply to describe the stream of images which are presented to his consciousness.

Accordingly, such plays as *Heartbreak House* in some ways anticipate the methods of surrealism without actually making use of surrealistic idioms. With regard to the association of ideas Shaw willingly relaxed the principle of logical sequence, the more so as he considered that any restraint was unjustified in a man of genius. Nevertheless, he never completely relinquished his rational control over the fancies that came into his mind. What he abandoned was the tight blueprint which was generally thought to be indispensable to sound dramatic construction. In his later plays the sequence of incidents often defies logical analysis, but the material itself is always under the control of the intellect.

In *Back to Methuselah* the result of this method is disappointing. It is by no means the worst of Shaw's plays. That honor must be divided among such potboilers as *Augustus Does His Bit* and the *Inca of Perusalem*. But while *Back to Methuselah* includes some of Shaw's best writing and some of his most vivid scenes, it is, on the whole, a dramatic composition so tedious as barely to support the spectator's attention in the theater. It is certain that Shaw was aware of its shortcomings as drama. Some time before the New York opening, he wrote to Granville-Barker of the contrapuntal scheme which governed the disposition of the characters in *Back to Methuselah:* "To this end I may have to disregard the boredom of the spectator who has not mastered all the motifs, as Wagner had to do; but I daresay I shall manage to make the people more amusing, some of them more poetic, and all of them more intelligible than they are now in this first draft."

Far more important, however, than the effect of the play as drama was its spiritual message, and it was this which made it, in Shaw's opinion, a great literary masterpiece. *Back to Methuselah* was not intended to amuse, but to edify. The usual sugar-coating, with which didactic comedy was made palatable, was of secondary importance in a work of such serious import. The play was intended to be a symphony, an opera, a gospel, and a prophecy. In the 1944 postscript, Shaw wrote: "The history of modern thought now teaches us that when we are forced to give up the creeds by their childishness and their conflicts with science we must either embrace Creative Evolution or fall into the bottomless pit of an utterly discouraging pessimism."

Shaw was by this time using the word "discouragement" in the sense of a heart-withering ailment. To those afflicted with it the play was to bring new hope, as *Faust* had done in its day:

> Goethe rescued us from this horror with his "Eternal Feminine that draws us forward and upward" which was the first modern manifestation of the mysterious force in creative evolution. That is what made *Faust* a world classic. If it does not do the same for this attempt of mine, throw the book into the fire; for Back to Methuselah is a world classic or it is nothing.

To the original preface of 1920, Shaw added some paragraphs in the nature of an apology, which provide a clue to his intentions both in the play and in his later work. Here he explicitly rejected the Horatian idea of a poetic work as a combination of the *utile* and the *dulce*. Such an idea was suitable, Shaw intimated, for a writer in the exuberance of youth; but one who has entered, like the ancients in his play, upon the stern disciplines of adult life, no longer has much taste for the *dulce,* nor any desire to sweeten his thought for the delectation of others. This is, he added, as true of himself as of his time, which has also achieved maturity in the theater:

> In 1901, I took the legend of Don Juan in its Mozartian form and made it a dramatic parable of Creative Evolution. . . . The effect was so vertiginous, apparently, that nobody noticed a new religion in the centre of the intellectual whirlpool. . . . Since then the sweet-shop view of the theatre has been out of countenance; and its critical exponents have been driven to take an intellectual pose which, though often more trying than their old intellectually nihilistic vulgarity, at least coincides with the dignity of the theatre. . . .
>
> I now find myself inspired to make a second legend of Creative Evolution without distractions and embellishments. My sands are running out; the exuberance of 1901 has aged into the garrulity of 1920; and the war has been a stern intimation that the matter is not one to be trifled with. I abandon the legend of Don Juan. . . . I exploit the eternal interest of the philosopher's stone which enables men to live forever.

He added, a bit wistfully: "I am doing the best I can at my age. My powers are waning; but so much the better for those who found me unbearably brilliant when I was in my prime."

He had, in fact, thirty years more to live.

As a play for the theater, *Back to Methuselah* leaves much to be desired; as an illustrated lecture on Creative Evolution it is unsurpassable. The play is a sequence of brightly colored vignettes animated chiefly by the ideas they develop, linked together by a group of recurrent type-characters, each of which is meant to be played by a single actor. Shaw did not see history, like Yeats, in terms of cycles of recurrence; but it is possible that he believed in something like reincarnation. At any rate, in *Back to Methuselah* the same types recur in generation after generation; possibly they are the same souls in successive manifestations. The characters that manifest them—Cain, Burge, Lubin, Haslam among others—are woven into the design of the play like threads in a tapestry. Each serves to represent a mode of thought. The resulting pattern is predominantly pictorial, but Shaw undoubtedly thought of it as an interweaving of Wagnerian *Leitmotiven* in a musical design.

The narrative hardly conceals the underlying tract. This is addressed to a world that has barely avoided crashing on the rocks and is once again drifting dangerously near them. In preaching this sermon, Shaw did not relinquish his customary role as socialist, economist, and statesman. He simply invested himself with his new priesthood, under which all these callings were subsumed. Without any special transition, he moved from the service of humanity into the service of God.

These were, at bottom, the same; but from this time forward, Shaw took on the guise of an evangelist preaching salvation in more or less traditional fashion, along with the threat of hell-fire for the unredeemed. His role was henceforth both saintly and prophetic. In the preface to *Saint Joan* he spoke with evangelical vehemence of "our shameless substitution of successful swindlers and scoundrels and quacks for saints as objects of worship, and our deafness and blindness to the calls and visions of the inexorable power that made us, and will destroy us if we disregard it."

This transition from political economy to theology necessarily put a different complexion on Shaw's work as a dramatist. He now proclaimed himself the "conscious iconographer of a religion" and instituted an attack on his principal literary competitors on the basis of their lack of genuine significance. As he saw it, Shakespeare had neither a religious viewpoint nor a consistent philosophic outlook. The same was true of Ibsen and Strindberg:

> The giants of the theatre of our time, Ibsen and Strindberg, had no greater comfort for the world than we: indeed much less; for they refused us even the Shakespearean-Dickensian consolation of laughter at mischief, accurately called comic relief. . . . Goethe is Olympian: the other giants are infernal in everything but their veracity and their repudiation of the irreligion of their time: that is, they are bitter and hopeless. It is not a question of mere dates. Goethe was an Evolutionist in 1830: many playwrights, even young ones, are still untouched by Creative Evolution in 1920. Ibsen was Darwinized to the extent of exploiting heredity on the stage much as the ancient Athenian playwrights exploited the Eumenides; but there is no trace in his plays of any faith in or knowledge of Creative Evolution as a modern scientific fact. True, the poetic aspiration is plain enough in his Emperor or Galilean; but it is one of Ibsen's distinctions that nothing was valid for him but science; and he left that vision of the future

which his Roman seer calls "the third Empire" behind him as a Utopian dream when he settled down to his serious grapple with realities.

If Ibsen was not able to grasp the idea of Creative Evolution, it was because the concept was not, in Shaw's judgment, a rational inference, but an intuition of which Ibsen was simply not capable. For Shaw this intuition, however, was of critical importance. Happiness was an illusion he had long since abandoned in the service of the Will; but in the absence of an understandable aim such service would be no more than slavery. Its aim, however, is evident. The Will develops intellect in order to attain self-consciousness, that is to say, in order to know itself. Consequently man is impelled to strive unceasingly for self-knowledge. Thus, while the Will remains inscrutable, its goal is clearly manifest to the elect. It is nothing less than the attainment of unlimited wisdom, and with it, unlimited power. In short, its end is godhead.

As it seemed to Shaw each age defines God in terms of its own limitations. The God of the Old Testament was once a useful concept. He is no longer serviceable in the age of science and must give way to a more accurate representation of the primal energy. Since the Will is immanent in man, the progressive intuition of truth takes place in the most intellectually advanced members of the species, for truth is nothing other than the knowledge attained by human minds, which in the aggregate are the mind of God. These elect must be heeded by the rest of humanity at its peril, for it is through them that the Will directs the course of its evolution. Since this evolution, apparently, cannot stop short of the absolute, the will to live is eternally operative as the mainspring of the cosmic process. The science of this process Shaw called metabiology:

> I had always known that civilization needs a religion as a matter of life and death; and as the conception of Creative Evolution developed, I saw that we were at least within reach of a faith that complied with the first conditions of all the religions that have ever taken hold of humanity: namely that it must be, first and fundamentally, a science of metabiology.

From the assumptions of this science it follows that evolution does not take place by chance, nor wholly through trial and error. It is through a conscious act of will that mankind transcends into higher forms of life. To this end great works are written, for all great art is fundamentally religious, and it is its high function to promote as far as is possible the impulses of the vital principle.

Metabiology is, obviously, no laughing matter, and cannot be presented in comic terms. *Back to Methuselah* is comic only in the sense that Dante's *Comedy* is comic. It exhibits Shaw for once in sober earnest, writing not in the guise of a bright and bellicose young man, but as the wise, stern, and all-seeing father, heavy with the need to admonish and to guide. It was a posture he had so far assumed chiefly in his prefaces and treatises.

The solemn nature of the preface to *Back to Methuselah,* with its show of erudition and its very plausible discussion of evolutionist theory, cannot obscure the fact that the play is essentially a work of science-fiction based on the improbable assumption that human life can be prolonged by a certain effort of the will. Underlying this assumption was Shaw's often expressed conviction that mankind, as it is presently constituted, is neither fit to govern itself, nor capable of being governed, so that any substantial advance in social conditions must await the evolution of a superior race of men. In *Man and Superman* the breeding of such a race is left to the Life Force operating through the beauty of woman. It is in this manner that the Eternal Feminine leads us upward, and from this standpoint Creative Evolution is an erotic adventure appropriately represented by the loves of John Tanner and Ann Whitefield.

In *Man and Superman,* these characters, in their universal aspect, are not depicted as being entirely in accord with the evolutionary pressures to which they are subjected. While Doña Ana is evidently eager to bring the superman into being through the usual channels, Don Juan somewhat perversely declines to lend his collaboration, and he withdraws at the first opportunity into the spiritual realm where sexuality has no meaning. In *Back to Methuselah* this disparity of purpose is further developed in the evolution of humanity, and the sexes are ultimately assimilated by the abandonment of sex as a means of reproduction. In contrast to *Man and Superman,* the amatory content of *Back to Methuselah* is minimal. For the will to live, love is a temporary expedient, which science in time supersedes.

In *Back to Methuselah,* the superman comes into being not through artificial selection, but through mutation. Genetic changes are motivated and realized in each case by an act of volition. Shaw ascribed this idea to Samuel Butler upon whose writings he had already drawn for the theoretical basis of *Man and Superman.* Butler's evolutionary hypothesis was teleological. In amplification of Lamarck's thesis, Butler had written: "I am insisting that important modifications of structure have always been purposive. A bird learns to swim . . . by trying to swim . . . but without exactly knowing what it is doing" (*Evolution Old and New*). In similar fashion, Shaw reasoned, a man would learn to live longer by desiring to live longer. It was a

conclusion which Butler had fully anticipated. Through an examination of
the workings of the racial memory passed on from parent to offspring,
Butler wrote:

> a new light is poured upon a hundred problems of the greatest
> delicacy and difficulty. Not the least interesting of these is the
> gradual evolution of human longevity—an extension, however,
> which cannot be effected till many generations as yet unborn
> have come and gone. There is nothing, however, to prevent man's
> becoming as long-lived as the oak if he will persevere for many
> generations in the steps which can alone lead to this result.

Passages of this sort provided the plan for *Back to Methuselah*. The
actual working out of the system, however, necessitated a more complex
concatenation of ideas. In formulating *The Gospel of the Brothers Barnabas*,
Shaw combined the Lamarckian theory of use and disuse with the
Schopenhauerian will to live, the Hegelian World Spirit, and the theory of
mutation recently developed by De Vries. The result was a heady "scientific" cocktail which only faith could make palatable and which, accordingly, might well be called a religion.

From a philosophic viewpoint the Life Force approximated Nietzsche's
will to power more closely than Schopenhauer's will to live; but in order to
bring Nietzsche's idea into a fruitful relationship with the Lamarckian concept, Shaw assumed that the will to power was normally expressed as the
individual's will to have power, not so much over others, as over himself—
that is to say, in self-mastery. Thus the She-Ancient of part 5 explains to the
children she is looking after, who are still involved with their dolls and
drawings and their sex, that the object of a mature art is oneself and only
oneself:

> When I discarded my dolls as he discarded his friends and his
> mountains, it was to myself I turned as to the final reality. Here,
> and here alone, I could shape and create. When my arm was
> weak and I willed it to be strong, I could create a roll of muscle
> on it; and when I understood that, I understood I could without
> any greater miracle give myself ten arms and three heads.

An ideal humanity, however, implies complete self-mastery. By the year
31,920, Shaw's ancients have not yet attained to that blissful state, but they
have made some progress toward it. They have quite freed themselves of
political concerns. Society has ceased to exist. There are only individuals

and, apparently, not many; for birth, among other things, is under effective control.

As they are constituted in our time, it is suggested, men and women are ungovernable not because they are depraved, but because their lives are short. They have hardly passed beyond childhood when death takes them. The evolution of the superman depends, therefore, upon the prolongation of life long enough for the individual to attain intellectual maturity. In *The Gospel of the Brothers Barnabas* the optimal life span is considered to be 300 years. Such an extension of life is attainable, it is thought, through an act of volition sufficiently intense to communicate the necessary impulse to the unconscious forces at the service of the will. When this occurs a change may be expected to take place in the genetic substance, as a result of which mutants will come into being which will engender a long-lived race.

These new people will have leisure to attain wisdom through experience and study; the consequence will be a society in which individuals will be able to order their lives rationally. The state will then wither away as a useless framework, and an ideal anarchy will result. This is, indeed, the political situation that Shaw depicts in the year 31,920. By this time old age has ceased to be a burden, and life is enjoyable throughout its duration. There remains the risk of accidental injury. The social problem is solved; but not the vital problem. As yet nobody lives at will. The world spirit is still some distance from the freedom toward which it strives.

Nineteenth-century literature was rich in science-fiction, but as yet nobody had ventured to put anything serious of this sort on the stage. What was performed in this genre was chiefly extravaganza of the type of W. S. Gilbert's *The Happy Land,* or *Utopia, Ltd.* Shaw was very willing to have his later utopian fantasies thought of as extravaganzas—evidently he fully intended to adapt this genre to serious purposes. *The Apple Cart* (1929), *Too True to be Good* (1931), and *Geneva* (1938–39) are all three subtitled "Political Extravaganza." *Back to Methuselah,* however, has only the vaguest affinity with this sort of play, and it has no subtitle. Shaw was certainly familiar with such classics as the *Republic, Utopia,* and *The City of the Sun.* In writing *Back to Methuselah* he had in mind, also, the utopist writings of Swift, Samuel Butler, H. G. Wells, and William Morris, and he levied specifically on Bulwer-Lytton's *The Coming Race.* But *Back to Methuselah* differs both in scope and in purpose from any of these works. In a curious way, it rather recalls *Paradise Lost.*

The Gospel of the Brothers Barnabas was written very soon after the end of the Great War, so that this play and *The Thing Happens,* which was written immediately after it, clearly reflect Shaw's wartime attitudes. Burge is a broad, but unmistakable caricature of David Lloyd George, the rough and ready Welshman who succeeded Asquith in the war ministry. Asquith is represented by the genial Lubin, elegantly educated and, aside from party intrigue, completely out of touch with political realities. Since both these statesmen were alive at the time of composition, and Lloyd George was still prime minister of England, these plays dealt polemically, and even daringly, with critical questions which now seem vital only by analogy. As social satire *Back to Methuselah* thus occupies a position somewhere between *The Acharnians* and *Gulliver's Travels,* but it is doubtful that either Aristophanes or Swift would have afforded himself the luxury of such an assault on the reader's patience as Shaw evidently felt his subject warranted.

In contrast to Burge and Lubin who, as practical men of affairs, decline to look an inch beyond their noses, the Barnabas brothers are endowed with the kind of foresight which is indispensable to political navigation. Conrad Barnabas is a biologist. Franklyn, his brother, is a statesman of clerical background. Together they typify the kind of politician that nations never entrust with the actual conduct of affairs; their work looks to the future, not to the present state of things. They are, indeed, involved not with politics but with metabiology, a science of which biology, religion, and statesmanship are necessary elements.

In the seemingly hopeless situation of contemporary Europe, it is their idea to perpetuate a race of men who will ensure the future of mankind. To this end, Conrad has published a work which suggests the possibility of achieving longevity by concentrating the will. The actual mechanics of the exercise are not entirely clear, but apparently it is enough to plant the possibility in people's minds in order to have it realized in time.

The thing happens some 250 years later, along with some other things forecast in the Fabian prospectus. At this time, mankind as a whole has not reached anything like its maturity, but social pressures have brought about some pleasant political changes. In the year of our Lord 2170 there is no longer any thought of war. In England there is communism, and the economic problem is solved. There is an equal distribution of wealth. Children are maintained and educated at the public expense up to the age of thirteen, after which they are required to work for the community for the next thirty years. The workers are retired at forty-three, with their maintenance guaranteed for the rest of their lives, and their pensions are calculated on the basis of an average life expectancy of seventy-eight years. It is through an infraction of this statistic that the actuarial authorities discover the secret presence of some unusually long-lived members in the community.

At this time communication is by television, and transportation takes

place generally by air, but the British are still incapable of governing themselves. Parliament is an assemblage of harmless lunatics. The head of state,
Burge-Lubin, is a pleasant figurehead, elected by popular vote, who hardly
differs from his ancestral prototypes of 1918. The actual management of
public affairs is in the hands of Chinese and Negro bureaucrats. The state is
efficient, but soulless; it suffers from the disadvantages pointed out by
Raznaikhin in Dostoyevski's *Crime and Punishment:* "The phalanstery is
ready, but nature is not ready for the phalanstery; it wants life; the living
process is not yet fulfilled."

In these circumstances it is suddenly discovered that the Bishop of York
and the Domestic Minister have lived quietly through several lifetimes and
are now in the third century of their age. These long-lived people are,
indeed, none other than the scatterbrained parson and the parlor maid of
part 2. Much to their own surprise, these unlikely beings have demonstrated
the validity of the gospel of the Brothers Barnabas, and to the consternation
of the short-lived ministers, once they became aware of one another's existence, they rush off together to breed the super-race.

By the year 3000 the new strain of long-lived people is firmly established in the Western Isles, and the British capital, with its short-lived inhabitants, has moved eastward to Baghdad. A deputation of these eastern
Britishers has come to Ireland to consult the oracle of the long-livers. The
delegates are accompanied by an elderly tourist of exceptional inquisitive-
ness, and also by a Napoleonic figure strongly reminiscent of Cain. The
contrast between the childishness of these visitors and the calm maturity of
the super-race so discourages the Elderly Gentleman that he wishes to die
and is mercifully killed by a glance of the Oracle's eye.

Shaw was consistent in ascribing death, as well as life, to an act of will.
In his authoritative work *The Evolutionary Theory,* August Weismann had
written that death is a device of nature to prevent the unnecessary accumu-
lation of exhausted organisms from cluttering up the earth. Weismann was
a staunch Darwinian. He considered that death was no more than a convenient method of weeding out, in the ordinary course of natural selection,
such individuals as were no longer adapted for survival.

The difficulty with this idea, from Shaw's standpoint, was its determin-
ist bias. Shaw found the sense of free will absolutely necessary to his comfort. In his view, accordingly, in the absence of accident, death also is the
result of an act of volition, a measure taken freely by man in the beginning
as a relief from the burden of everlasting existence.

In a treatise entitled "Parents and Children," prefaced to *Misalliance*
(1910), Shaw had written:

> The Life Force either will not or cannot achieve immorality except in very low organisms. . . . With all our perverse nonsense as to John Smith living for a thousand million eons and for ever after, we die voluntarily, knowing that it is time for us to be scrapped, to be remanufactured, to come back, as Wordsworth divined, trailing ever brightening clouds of glory. We must all be born again, and yet again and again. . . . There is only one belief that can rob death of its sting and the grave of its victory; and that is the belief that we can lay down the burden of our wretched little makeshift individualities for ever at each lift toward the goal of evolution.

The intimation that the time has come to die, Shaw called "discouragement." He had read travelers' accounts of the morbid despondency of primitive people who are suddenly exposed to the marvels of civilization, and he accounted on this basis for the rapid extinction of primitive races such as the Indians of North America. In *Everybody's Political What's What* (1945), he wrote of feeling something of the sort in his youth in the presence of a venerable Jew whose spiritual power made him feel insignificant:

> I was simply discouraged by him. . . . Since then, my observation, and the stories I have read about the dying out of primitive tribes at the impact of civilized invaders, have convinced me that every living person has a magnetic force of greater or less intensity which enables those in whom it is strong to dominate those in whom it is relatively weak, or whose susceptibility to its influence, called shyness, is excessive.

The idea that the mechanism of discouragement operates through magnetic pressure in all likelihood came to him through Strindberg. The experiments of Charcot with hypnosis at the Salpetrière, and Bernheim's experiments at Nancy in the 1880s, had convinced Strindberg that every meeting of individuals implied a psychic conflict to establish the mastery. This soul-conflict was the spiritual aspect, he thought, of the physical struggle for survival which Darwin had described in *The Descent of Man*. The conditions of existence were thus under constant adjustment through psychic encounters by means of which the stronger forced the weaker souls into subservience or, if need be, destroyed them. This idea of psychic murder is central in Strindberg's *Creditors*, *The Father*, and *Crime and Crime*.

Shaw readily adapted the idea of soul-murder into his system. "Discouragement" was a humiliation of the will to live which might be so intense as to extinguish it in the individual soul. "You cannot converse with persons of my age for long without bringing on a dangerous attack of discouragement," the Woman tells the Elderly Gentleman in the year 3000. "Do you realize that you are already shewing grave symptoms of that very distressing and usually fatal complaint?" The Elderly Gentleman does not realize it, but he does not feel as well as he might, either; and, in the end his discouragement becomes altogether too intense to be borne. The implication is that intellectual discrepancies of this magnitude cannot be endured for very long, and that the colonization of the short-lived by the race of supermen must end, sooner or later, in the extinction of mankind as we know it.

By the year 31,920, in part 5, this process is concluded, and the very aspect of humanity is altered. The cycle of growth has by this time been vastly accelerated. People are hatched, fully developed, from the egg. In infancy they make love, dispute, and dance. Their alimentary organs have vanished. They no longer require sustenance, and there are no longer animals, nor birds, nor fish, for the Life Force has passed beyond such fruitless biological experiments. Sexuality is now a pastime which ceases at about the age of four; at this time people lose their secondary sex characters, and the sensual life rapidly gives way to the life of the intellect. But while there is no limit to the duration of life the body is still vulnerable to injury, and accidental death is, in the course of time, a certainty. The goal of humanity at this stage of its development is therefore the complete divestiture of the spirit from its bodily vehicle.

Even at this advanced stage of evolution, such an idea is not agreeable to the young. But since the period of youth is compressed into the first three years of a life of prodigious duration, the opinions of the young do not greatly concern the ancients. The revolt of youth which was to perturb the world in the 1960s and 1970s is pleasantly anticipated in Shaw's account of the gerontocracy of the future. In part 5, there is a brief dialogue between a newly born girl and her nurse which comically foreshadows the campus dialogues of the present day:

THE NEWLY BORN: But I want power now.

THE SHE-ANCIENT: No doubt you do; so that you could play
    with the world by tearing it to pieces.

THE NEWLY BORN: Only to see how it is made. I should put it all
    together again much better than before.

THE SHE-ANCIENT: There was a time when children were given

> the world to play with because they promised to improve it.
> They did not improve it; and they would have wrecked it
> had their power been as great as that which you will wield
> when you are no longer a child.

This passage measures the distance that separated the Shaw of 1920 from the young radical of the early street-corner days. The scene is, indeed, not unduly prolonged. The She-Ancient is a patient schoolmarm, but not indefatigable:

> THE NEWLY BORN: What is being tired?
> THE SHE-ANCIENT: The penalty of attending to children. Farewell.

Shaw's disillusionment with contemporary politics, which these passages reflect, is paralleled by the disenchantment implied in the Festival of Art which follows. The children amuse themselves with an exhibition of pictures and statues, but there is a discordant note which curiously anticipates the situation in Pirandello's *Diana e la Tuda* (1927). The aging sculptor in Shaw's play, at the age of four, has smashed his statues because he is unable to give them life and is now turning his attention to more important things than dolls. He is at this point pretty well grown-up and is therefore in a position to give his junior the benefit of his experience as an artist: "In the end the intellectual conscience that tore you away from the fleeting in art to the eternal must tear you away from art altogether, because art is false and life alone is true."

It is, indeed, to life alone that the Ancients look for their creative activity, for they have discovered that ultimately one can create only oneself. This takes time. It is for this reason that death has been postponed indefinitely. The question of a convenient life span has been decided only after extensive experimentation. In part 1 of *Back to Methuselah*, Adam, in a mood of discouragement, sets his life-span at 1000 years: that is all he can bear. But while Adam, in the beginning, invents death as a precaution against boredom, he continues to be troubled by the possibility of an inopportune accident. The possibility of such a thing is brought home to him at the very beginning of his life in Eden, when his destruction would necessarily involve the annihilation of all humanity; and it is in order to obviate any such possibility that the serpent imparts to Eve the secret of reproduction. But while reproduction, which at first Eve finds distasteful, ensures the survival of the race, it does nothing to ensure the persistence of the individual. Even after the life span has been indefinitely extended by the ancients, the fragility of the body continues to be a matter of concern, and the dualism of matter and spirit remains as a principal obstacle to the progress of those who survive to the imaginable limits of human longevity. Thus, in the year 31,920, the He-Ancient tells his class:

> THE HE-ANCIENT: That, children, is the trouble of the ancients. For whilst we are tied to this tyrannous body we are subject to its death, and our destiny is not achieved.
> THE NEWLY BORN: What is your destiny?
> THE HE-ANCIENT: To be immortal.
> THE SHE-ANCIENT: The day will come when there will be no people, only thought.
> THE HE-ANCIENT: And that will be life eternal.

The idea of a bodiless existence seems both unattractive and improbable to the children of this era, but the grown-ups fervently anticipate the delights of becoming a vortex of pure energy:

> THE SHE-ANCIENT: None of us now believe that all this machinery of flesh and blood is necessary. It dies.
> THE HE-ANCIENT: It imprisons us on this petty planet and forbids us to range through the stars.
> ACIS: But even a vortex is a vortex in something. You cant have a whirlpool without water; and you cant have a vortex without gas, or molecules or atoms or ions or electrons or something, not nothing.
> THE HE-ANCIENT: No: the vortex is not the water nor the gas nor the atoms: it is a power over these things.

Shaw's ancients aspire to power, not to Nirvana. They have no desire to relinquish individuality. They desire, on the contrary, to preserve their self-consciousness and to exert their will so far as is possible. Adam found the burden of life too heavy to bear for very long. Not the ancients. The difference is that Adam knew only the life of the body, while the ancients have already gone a long way toward the pure vitality of the spirit. They represent the finite aspect of the Don Juan of *Man and Superman,* but, like him, they are engaged in an infinitely extended intellectual adventure.

There is, of course, some question as to the purpose of a spiritual enterprise which ends about where it began. In *Back to Methuselah,* the author's optimism is overshadowed by a sense of futility which no rhetoric can conceal, and, in the end, Adam thinks the whole thing a piece of foolishness in which he would as soon not have taken part. But, at the last, Eve is content. The offspring of Cain, her bad son, have vanished. Only her good children have survived. Man was never really evil. He was merely childishly aggressive; and this is a fault that time has cured. As with Schopenhauer's saints, salvation lies in "joyfully forsaking the world," and this the ancients appear to have done with all possible alacrity. In Eve's opinion, a good time has been had by all, or nearly all, and the results have amply justified the effort.

In the end, however, Lilith, who has brought life into the world out of her own being, seems as uncertain as Adam as to what the whole thing was about. She has infused life into matter and brought a semblance of order out of chaos. The experience has been interesting:

> I am Lilith: I brought life into the whirlpool of force, and com-
> pelled my enemy, Matter, to obey a living soul. But in enslaving
> Life's enemy I made him Life's master; for that is the end of all
> slavery; and now I shall see the slave set free and the enemy
> reconciled, the whirlpool become all life and no matter. And
> because these infants that call themselves ancients are reaching
> out towards that, I will have patience with them still; though I
> know well that when they attain it they shall become one with
> me and supersede me, and Lilith will be only a legend and a lay
> that has lost its meaning. Of Life only there is no end . . . and
> though its vast domain is as yet unbearably desert, my seed shall
> one day fill it and master its matter to its uttermost confines. And
> for what may be beyond, the eyesight of Lilith is too short. It is
> enough that there is a beyond.

Thus Lilith, as the source of being, remains enigmatic. She is the Life Force, but she is neither life nor force. She is the principle through which the two are combined and progressively ordered, an entity whose existence is purely inferential. Samuel Butler had written: "Von Hartmann personifies the unconscious and makes it act and think—in fact, deifies—whereas I only infer a certain history for certain of our growths and actions in consequence of observing that often repeated actions come in time to be performed unconsciously." Such an abstract conception of the Will behind evolution was perhaps suitable for the preface of Back to Methuselah, but it was obviously useless for dramatic purposes. If the Unconscious is to be represented on the stage, it must be personified. Thus, while Shaw has Lilith say that she represents the primordial Will through which life is embodied in matter, he is careful not to identify her with life itself. She is, in Shaw's conception, a phase in the development of the vital energy, but, in the light of eternity, a provisional phase, like everything else that lives.

Back to Methuselah is perhaps unduly didactic, but it displays a perspective of truly Wagnerian grandeur. As a poetic statement, obviously, it does not bear comparison with the great epic works, neither with *Faust,* nor *Paradise Lost,* nor *The Divine Comedy,* with all of which it has some affinity. These are myths completely realized as works of art, poetic entities based on a total conviction of truth, and what was once their truth is now their beauty. *Back to Methuselah* is a tract in epic form. Like Dante's *Comedy* and Milton's *Paradise Lost,* it bears the stamp of its time and country and is shaped, like both these works, in accordance with the author's political and social preconceptions. It has some fine poetic passages, but neither the universality nor the sublimity of a poetic synthesis. It belongs, therefore, not with the great masterpieces which abstract the essence of an age, but with the type of utopian literature which satirizes the unhappy present, while at the same time it affords a provocative glimpse of a more agreeable future.

Judging by his prose writings, Milton had no doubt that Adam and Eve once actually existed, and that Satan, having deprived them of the joys of Eden, was still busy in his efforts to discommode their progeny. Doubtless the sincerity of his belief has much to do with the extraordinary power which his work still exerts over the imagination. But for Shaw, Adam was no more than a convenient symbol, and the myth of the Garden was useful principally for its poetic value. In the preface to *Back to Methuselah,* it is true, the theory of Creative Evolution is advanced as scientifically valid and is accordingly bolstered up with much documentation and a great show of authority. There is no reason to doubt that at the time this preface was written Shaw believed in his facts as fervently as Dante believed in the love that moves the sun and the other stars. But by 1944 Creative Evolution appears to have taken on the guise in his mind of a myth of government, part of the necessary religious framework of an orderly state. "It is through such conceits," he noted, "that we are governed and governable." Evidently his faith in the supremacy of the Life Force was subject to change. Like everything else in an essentially mutable universe, his religion had by this time become a useful metaphor, and his fervor, however sincere, was now to be considered in the light of a promotional effort.

For these and other reasons, *Back to Methuselah* is unlikely to occupy so high a place in the estimation of posterity as Shaw bespoke for it. But the greatness of his conception cannot be denied. In spite of the chattiness of the early scenes, the perspective the play affords of the vital force developing blindly through a series of progressively complex material forms, including humanity, towards its entelechy as pure intelligence is an impressive example of nineteenth-century romantic thought.

The fact that it appears to be a tardy example of neo-Aristotelian doctrine should not obscure the glamor of the conception. In attempting to integrate, in the manner of Dante, Milton, and Goethe, the most advanced thought of his time with the philosophic tradition he found personally most congenial, Shaw accepted a challenge normally taken up only by the major poets of our culture. Unhappily, he was not of their company. He was an exceptionally gifted journalist with a genius for dramatic writing. In the circumstances, his pretensions to prophetic vision seem, like everything else about him, magnificently extravagant, but their magnificence is more impressive than their extravagance. When we compare his vision with the vision of Yeats they even seem reasonable.

Both Dante and Milton stood on secure theological ground. The science they interpreted was sanctified by authority and was, in their time, beyond controversy. On the other hand, Yeats permitted his imagination to roam luxuriously through a jungle of cabalistic imagery. He did not trouble to support his cosmology in A Vision (1937) with even a semblance of empirical testimony, and it is far from clear to what extent he himself was convinced by the universe he had created. Shaw, however, had unbounded confidence in the scientific basis of his conception and, at least for a time, complete faith in the accuracy of his intuition. He lived, however, in a skeptical age, when no dogma, theological or scientific, was sage, and he was forced to promote his views with unseemly vigor. In speaking of their gospel, the Barnabas brothers reach a height of enthusiasm more suitable to the marketing of a patent medicine than to the exposition of a philosophic system:

> CONRAD: . . . Ever since the reaction against Darwin set in at the beginning of the present century, all scientific opinion worth counting has been converging rapidly upon Creative Evolution.
> FRANKLYN: Poetry has been converging on it: philosophy has been converging on it: religion has been converging on it. It is going to be the religion of the twentieth century: a religion that has its intellectual roots in philosophy and science just as medieval Christianity had its intellectual roots in Aristotle.

In their understandable enthusiasm the brothers Barnabas seem a bit over-emphatic. Creative Evolution had no more secure basis in twentieth-century science than theosophy or anthroposophy, and scientific writers such as Julian Huxley declined to take it seriously. The evidence against the inheritance of acquired characters was at this time overwhelming. There was absolutely nothing to indicate that the course of evolution was ever directed by an act of volition, either conscious or unconscious: nothing, that is, but common sense, the conclusions of which ordinarily carry little weight in the laboratory. In the time of the brothers Barnabas, neither poetry nor philosophy nor scientific opinion could be said to converge upon anything; and least of all upon Creative Evolution. Shaw's religion, however attractive, had at no time any discernible future as a popular creed save in Shaw's imagination and, for all his urging, he was unable to will it into anything like general acceptance. If the alternative to Creative Evolution was despair, as Shaw believed, humanity evidently preferred despair. In the 1950s, existentialism emerged as a dominant influence on twentieth-century thought. It was a far cry from Shaw's optimistic faith.

Thus, from every viewpoint, save the aesthetic, Shaw's "world classic" might be judged a failure. He was, by all odds, the most important English dramatist since Shakespeare, and possibly the most influential spirit of his time, but his genius did not extend to an epic conception. If *Back to Methuselah* proves anything, it is that great ideas do not—as Shaw believed—make great drama. But great drama can make great ideas.

J. L. WISENTHAL

The Marriage of Contraries:
Major Barbara

Since Shaw's preface to *Major Barbara* is presented as an explanation of
the play, one might begin a discussion of the play by looking at it. The
opening section of the preface is entitled "First Aid to Critics," and the next
begins by saying that Shaw is driven "to help [his] critics out with Major
Barbara by telling them what to say about it." In accepting Shaw's help,
however, critics might bear in mind his own critical dictum that "the existence of a discoverable and perfectly definite thesis in a poet's work by no
means depends on the completeness of his own intellectual consciousness of
it." And what Shaw says about the play in the preface does not, in any case,
necessarily represent his whole view of it. His explanations of everything are
deliberately one-sided: he brings to his public's attention the aspects of a
question which he wishes them to consider.

The aspect of *Major Barbara* which Shaw wished his readers to consider, or which he himself saw as the essence of the play, is the economic
one. The second section of the preface is entitled, "The Gospel of St Andrew
Undershaft," and this gospel has to do with money and poverty—according
to the preface. After his statement that he will tell critics what to say about
the play, Shaw begins to do so: "In the millionaire Undershaft I have represented a man who has become intellectually and spiritually as well as
practically conscious of the irresistible natural truth which we all abhor and
repudiate: to wit, that the greatest of our evils, and the worst of our crimes
is poverty, and that our first duty, to which every other consideration should
be sacrificed, is not to be poor." In the play itself Undershaft's gospel is

From *The Marriage of Contraries: Bernard Shaw's Middle Plays.* © 1974 by the
President and Fellows of Harvard College. Harvard University Press, 1974.

189

twofold. His religion, he tells Cusins in act 2, is "that there are two things necessary to Salvation . . . money and gunpowder." In the preface the second article of Undershaft's faith is not really dealt with at all; the manufacture of weapons is referred to only in an economic context, as the profession which was his alternative to poverty: "Undershaft, the hero of Major Barbara, is simply a man who, having grasped the fact that poverty is a crime, knows that when society offered him the alternative of poverty or a lucrative trade in death and destruction, it offered him, not a choice between opulent villainy and humble virtue, but between energetic enterprise and cowardly infamy." This argument is identical with Shaw's analysis of Mrs Warren's profession (see preface to *Mrs Warren's Profession*), and Undershaft's gospel, as presented by Shaw in the preface to *Major Barbara*, is no different from Mrs Warren's in essentials.

In many ways *Major Barbara* is similar to *Mrs Warren's Profession*. According to Archibald Henderson, Shaw told him that "perhaps a more suitable title for this play [*Major Barbara*] . . . would have been *Andrew Undershaft's Profession*," if it had not been for the fact that he had already used the formula twice before, in *Mrs Warren's Profession* and *Cashel Byron's Profession* (the novel that he wrote in 1882). Both *Major Barbara* and *Mrs Warren's Profession* proclaim Shaw's instrumentalist, relativist morality: one must act, not from any absolute moral principles, but according to the practical demands of a particular set of circumstances. Both Undershaft and Mrs Warren make the more moral choice—that is, the more practical, useful one—while Mrs Warren's half-sisters and Peter Shirley illustrate the error of basing one's actions on the dictates of conventional "morality." Given a badly organized society which forces one to choose between "moral virtue" and material well-being, it is more moral to be "wicked" than to be good. In both plays a high-minded daughter learns unpleasant truths about the real world through a parent whose profession represents its most shocking features; and each daughter must decide whether to accept or reject her parent. Although Barbara and Vivie make opposite choices, they both base their choice on the desire not to be useless, and they both reject the life of the leisured middle-class lady.

Also, *Major Barbara*, like *Mrs Warren's Profession*, is much concerned in a direct way with money. In the masterly opening scene Lady Britomart has summoned Stephen to discuss the family's money problem with him; his sisters' impending marriages, she tells him, require her to find a way of increasing the family's income. It is this necessity that sets in motion the events of the play: Undershaft, the provider of money, is brought into contact with his family after a separation of many years. In this first scene

Stephen is disillusioned about the source of his wealth in a way reminiscent of Vivie's disillusionment by Crofts (and of Trench's discovery in act 2 of *Widowers' Houses*).

LADY BRITOMART: I must get the money somehow.

STEPHEN: We cannot take money from him. I had rather go and live in some cheap place like Bedford Square or even Hampstead than take a farthing of his money.

LADY BRITOMART: But after all, Stephen, our present income comes from Andrew.

STEPHEN [*shocked*]: I never knew that.

This nicely anticipates, in a minor and comic way, Barbara's shattering discovery in act 2 that because she is a member of the Salvation Army her money "comes from Andrew" and his like. Similarly, Lady Britomart's statement to Stephen that "it is not a question of taking money from him or not: it is simply a question of how much" anticipates the Salvation Army's behavior in act 2 in rejecting Bill Walker's pound while accepting Undershaft's five thousand. The question in both cases is not a moral one, but a practical, economic one. As Frank Gardner says to Praed, in a remark which sums up so much of *Mrs Warren's Profession,* "It's not the moral aspect of the case: it's the money aspect." It would be true to say that in *Major Barbara* the first act is in part concerned with the economic problems of the rich, the second with the economic problems of the poor, and that in both cases the money comes from Undershaft. The settings of all three acts draw one's attention to the importance of money. The Salvation Army shelter in act 2 is a symbol of the fruits of poverty, while the aristocratic opulence of Wilton Crescent and the bourgeois amenity of Perivale St. Andrews reveal the advantages of money. Undershaft himself points to the contrast between the cannon works and the shelter: "I see no darkness here, no dreadfulness. In your Salvation shelter I saw poverty, misery, cold and hunger." Undershaft is here justifying the superiority of his kind of salvation over that of the Salvation Army, and in the speeches of his that follow he proclaims the importance of money and the sinfulness of poverty.

But is the need for money the central concern of *Major Barbara*? In order to answer this, one must ask how important it is that Undershaft's way of making money is the manufacture of weapons. Given what Shaw says in the preface about the play, Undershaft's profession could be anything lucrative and unsavory: he could be a slum landlord like Sartorius, a brothel owner like Crofts, or a distiller like Bodger. But if he had been one of these, the play would have been profoundly different. There is a crucial distinction between Undershaft's profession and the others: weapons can be a direct instrument of social change, which slum dwellings, brothels, and whisky are obviously not. Undershaft defends gunpowder in a way in which the other immoralists could not defend their wares. He does not simply say (as Mrs Warren does) that it is better to engage in disreputable activities than to starve: he goes much further than Mrs Warren in that he offers a positive defense of his weapons as the necessary means of reforming society. The climactic debate at the end of the play is more concerned with gunpowder itself as an instrument of change than it is with its manufacture as a source of money. The debate ends with Undershaft's challenge to Cusins, "Dare you make war on war?," and Cusins is more central than Barbara in act 3 as a whole. But Cusins is mentioned only once in the preface, and then only as the "Euripidean republican" who is perfectly understood by Undershaft. The preface is prefatory mostly to act 2 and hardly at all to act 3, for it is in act 3 that the second article of Undershaft's faith is dealt with. The conflict in act 3 is not about money, except in the indirect sense that Barbara is offered well-fed men to save (and note that although they are well-fed, they still need saving: money is a means, not an end). Undershaft talks about the choice that he made as a young man not to be poor, but no party to the debate is in fact poor; neither Barbara nor Cusins joins the cannon works in order to acquire money. The play would have been more consistent with the preface (and of course a much less interesting play) if Peter Shirley's decision to join the cannon works, rather than Cusins's, had formed the basis of the final act. But as the play stands, the preface provides a very misleading introduction to it.

II

Major Barbara is not so much about money as about power. It can best be seen as an exploration of the nature of power: the possession of control or command over others. The word itself occurs twenty-eight times in the last fourteen pages of the play, and all through the play examples are to be found of different kinds of power, of which money is only one. We have seen, for example, that the power of money is made manifest in the scene between Lady Britomart and Stephen. But so is Lady Britomart's power over Stephen: the power of an authoritarian, domineering mother over an uncertain, immature son. In the course of the play she loses her power over Stephen, who is the only person she has really dominated: clearly an authoritarian personality by itself is of little use. Undershaft, who is less authoritarian and domineering than his wife, has more power; and Cusins, who is far less authoritarian than either of them, has in a sense more significant power than anyone else in the play, as we shall see later.

The Bill Walker episode in act 2 dramatizes various kinds of power. Bill's own kind of power is brute force, which is a crude and inadequate version of Undershaft's weapons. The parallel with Undershaft, in fact, extends further: both Bill Walker and Undershaft are trying to win a young woman back from the Salvation Army (and Undershaft has fallen in love with Barbara, "with a father's love"); both have determination and a touch of brutality; and both offer money to the Salvation Army. A stage direction at the end of act 2 describes Bill as *"unashamed,"* which is Undershaft's motto. I think that one of the functions of the Bill Walker episode is to demonstrate these parallels between Bill Walker and Undershaft: parallels which suggest both Bill's potential strength and Undershaft's limitations.

Also related to the major strands of the play is Bill's near-conversion. It is brought about largely by Barbara, but not entirely by her. He is subdued as well by the threat of superior physical force in the person of Todger Fairmile, the wrestler; he speaks with *"undissembled misgiving"* when he learns that it is Todger Fairmile who has taken his girl-friend from him, and his belligerence disappears. As Bill says on the point of conversion, "Aw cawnt stend aht agen music awl wrastlers and awtful tangued women." This almost successful combination of Barbara's religious power and the brute force of Todger Fairmile prefigures the union of Barbara and Undershaft at the climax of the play.

Barbara's power over Bill is itself a mixture of various kinds. The first factor to subdue him has nothing to do with her personal qualities: he is much taken aback when Peter Shirley tells him that "the major here is the Earl o Stevenage's granddaughter"; and his awe of the aristocracy is clearly one of the reasons why Barbara is able to deal with him while Jenny Hill is not. Another factor is Barbara's ladylike self-possession and calm superiority in handling Bill, as opposed to Jenny Hill's lack of self-control. That these qualities of Barbara's can be attributed to her aristocratic background is implied by what Lady Britomart says in act 1: "It is only in the middle classes, Stephen, the people get into a state of dumb helpless horror when they find that there are wicked people in the world. In our class, we have to decide what is to be done with wicked people; and nothing should disturb our self-possession." In this, as in her power to command her subordinates in the Salvation Army, Barbara is her mother's daughter.

But the principal element in her near-success with Bill is what she has inherited from her father: her religious nature. She derives personal forcefulness and the ability to sway others from her feeling that she is working

not for her own happiness but for a larger purpose. She feels herself to be
an agent of the Life Force, which she calls God. Her religion, though, is not
based (at any point in the play) on the two articles of her father's creed,
money and gunpowder. Nor is it the traditional Christianity of the Salvation
Army. As Cusins tells Undershaft, "Barbara is quite original in her religion." Barbara's religion, which is revealed mainly in her wooing of Bill
Walker's soul, has to do with making men of people.

> BARBARA [*softly: wooing his soul*]: It's not me thats getting at
>   you, Bill.
> BILL: Oo else is it?
> BARBARA: Somebody that doesnt intend you to smash women's
>   faces, I suppose. Somebody or something that wants to make
>   a man of you.
> BILL [*blustering*]: Mike a menn o me! Aint Aw a menn? eh? Oo
>   sez Aw'm not a menn?
> BARBARA: Theres a man in you somewhere, I suppose.

In the same scene she urges Bill to "come with us . . . to brave manhood on
earth and eternal glory in heaven." By the end of the play Barbara has
decided to get "rid of the bribe of heaven," but it does not seem to have
played a very significant role in her soul-saving while she was in the Salvation Army. Her desire is not so much to ensure Bill Walker's entry into
heaven as to make him behave decently on earth. This is Shaw's own concept of religious conversion, expressed, for example, in Tanner's account of
his acquisition of the "moral passion" in the first act of *Man and Superman,*
and dramatized in *The Shewing-Up of Blanco Posnet* (1909). The really
religious people, Shaw wrote to Janet Achurch in 1895, "have dignity,
conviction, sobriety and force"; religion "substitutes a profound dignity
and self-respect for the old materialistic self."

Barbara's way of converting Bill Walker to manhood is to make him
aware that he is not yet a man: to awaken a sense of sin in him. This is akin
to what Shaw considered part of his own role as an artist. "It annoys me to
see people comfortable when they ought to be uncomfortable," he says in
the Epistle Dedicatory to *Man and Superman;* "and I insist on making them
think in order to bring them to conviction of sin." According to Shaw's
Lamarckian view of evolution, life can progress only if individuals desire to
improve, and it is therefore vital that they be made aware of the need for
self-improvement. The giraffe will not make the effort to acquire a longer
neck until it feels that its present neck is too short.

This religion of Barbara's is directly contrary to what Shaw regards as a principal element in conventional Christianity: the belief that one can be saved without changing one's behavior—by atonement, forgiveness, punishment, or vicarious redemption. In the section of the preface entitled "Weaknesses of the Salvation Army," Shaw writes that he does not think that "the inexorability of the deed once done should be disguised by any ritual, whether in the confessional or on the scaffold. And here my disagreement with the Salvation Army, and with all propagandists of the Cross (which I loathe as I loathe all gibbets) becomes deep indeed. Forgiveness, absolution, atonement, are figments: punishment is only a pretence of cancelling one crime by another; and you can no more have forgiveness without vindictiveness than you can have a cure without a disease. You will never get a high morality from people who conceive that their misdeeds are revocable and pardonable, or in a society where absolution and expiation are officially provided for us all." It is when Christian redemption is unavailable that the ruffian feels obliged to cease to be a ruffian. Then, as Shaw puts it in the preface to *Androcles and the Lion,* "the drive of evolution, which we call conscience and honor, seizes on [our] slips, and shames us to the dust for being so low in the scale as to be capable of them." The awakened conscience of the thief "will not be easy until he has conquered his will to steal and changed himself into an honest man by developing that divine spark within him which Jesus insisted on as the everyday reality of what the atheist denies." It is this divine spark that Barbara refers to when she says to Bill Walker, "Theres a man in you somewhere, I suppose."

The precise position of the Salvation Army on this key question of redemption is not made plain in the play, and the preface is self-contradictory. After the passage quoted above about Shaw's deepest disagreement with the Salvation Army, Shaw says that Bill "finds the Salvation Army as inexorable as fact itself. It will not punish him: it will not take his money. It will not tolerate a redeemed ruffian: it leaves him no means of salvation except ceasing to be a ruffian." This is the way in which Barbara treats him in the play, but the Salvation Army's policy is left unclear. One does notice, however, that Jenny Hill asks Barbara whether she might take some of the money which Bill offers "for the Army," and that Bill's conversion is frustrated—or at least postponed—when he sees that the Salvation Army accepts the money of Bodger and Undershaft, thus apparently offering them automatic salvation instead of demanding a real moral conversion. Shaw also remarks in the preface that members of the Salvation Army "questioned the verisimilitude of the play, not because Mrs Baines took the money, but because Barbara refused it." The implication of both preface and play is—although neither makes this entirely explicit—that Barbara's religion is, all through the play, different from that of the Salvation Army in that she alone uncompromisingly rejects the conventional Christian concept of salvation.

III

A reading of *Major Barbara* that based itself on the preface might see Undershaft as one of the ideal heroes of Shaw's plays and as Shaw's spokesman in this play. For in the preface he is presented as if he were the *raisonneur* of the play, who demonstrates the inadequacies of the points of view of the other characters, particularly of Barbara. The preface implies that the play is about the justified triumph of Undershaft's gospel over that of Barbara and the Salvation Army. We have seen that Cusins, who is Undershaft's chief opponent in the climactic debate of the final act, is barely mentioned in the preface.

In the play itself, of course, Undershaft is by no means an unattractive character. Part of his attractiveness lies in his power, and it is important to recognize just what is the nature of this power, and what its limitations are. His power is mainly of three different kinds. There is his will to survive, the power that enabled him to say as a young man, "Thou shalt starve ere I starve." There is the religious power which he shares with Barbara—the energy, vitality, and instinctive grip over others that come from the conviction that one is serving a just and irresistible purpose. Then there is the power of weapons, of which he is the manufacturer and symbol, and the power of money, of which he is the possessor. These qualities are, for the most part, what I called in discussing *Man and Superman* [elsewhere] Philistine qualities. There are some elements of the Realist in Undershaft—his argumentative powers, his consciousness of his role, and his desire to change the world (although these last two, as we shall see, are equivocal)—but his leading characteristics are those of the Philistine, of Ann and Violet in *Man and Superman*. The principal differences between Undershaft and Ann and Violet are that he manifests these characteristics in the marketplace rather than the drawing room, and that he is more articulate than they. But while he is more articulate, what he articulates is a point of view very close to theirs. He believes, as Ann does, in the primacy of the acquisitive will. Much of his philosophy is an elaboration of Ann's remark to Octavius that "the only really simple thing is to go straight for what you want and grab it." Like Ann—and like Nietzsche's aristocrats—he is the beast of prey, stopping at nothing to get what he wants. His methods are more direct than those of Ann and Violet, as he is a man of business rather than a lady of leisure, but unscrupulous, predatory instincts dominate the behavior of all three. Buying the Salvation Army is to the marketplace as a chase across Europe or secrecy about one's marriage is to the drawing room.

Like Ann and Violet, Undershaft is able to get his own way: his overpowering of Cusins is directly comparable to Ann's overpowering of Tanner. In both cases there is the suggestion of some instinctive irresistible force. We have seen the way [elsewhere] in which Ann overcomes Tanner, in spite of his desire to escape: she is an incarnation of the Life Force. In *Major Barbara* Undershaft overcomes Cusins not only with arguments but also with a comparable energy, which is called by Cusins Dionysiac (Dionysos being his name for the Life Force). Here is part of the scene between them at the Salvation Army shelter.

> CUSINS: . . . Barbara is quite original in her religion.
>
> UNDERSHAFT [*triumphantly*]: Aha! Barbara Undershaft would be. Her inspiration comes from within herself.
>
> CUSINS: How do you suppose it got there?
>
> UNDERSHAFT [*in towering excitement*]: It is the Undershaft inheritance. I shall hand on my torch to my daughter. She shall make my converts and preach my gospel—
>
> CUSINS: What! Money and gunpowder!
>
> UNDERSHAFT: Yes, money and gunpowder. Freedom and power. Command of life and command of death.
>
> CUSINS [*urbanely: trying to bring him down to earth*]: This is extremely interesting, Mr Undershaft. Of course you know that you are mad.
>
> UNDERSHAFT [*with redoubled force*]: And you?
>
> CUSINS: Oh, mad as a hatter. You are welcome to my secret since I have discovered yours. But I am astonished. Can a madman make cannons?
>
> UNDERSHAFT: Would anyone else than a madman make them? And now [*with surging energy*] question for question. Can a sane man translate Euripides?
>
> CUSINS: No.
>
> UNDERSHAFT [*seizing him by the shoulder*]: Can a sane woman make a man of a waster or a woman of a worm?
>
> CUSINS [*reeling before the storm*]: Father Colossus—Mammoth Millionaire—

Cusins, who is never entirely overcome by Undershaft, recovers; but at the end of the act he prepares to march off with Undershaft, leaving Barbara behind, with the words "Dionysos Undershaft has descended. I am possessed." J. I. M. Stewart objects to Cusins's behavior here: "At the moment of Barbara's utmost despair he has thrown himself so irresponsibly into an ironic Dionysiac masquerade that we retain very little interest in him." But Cusins is not a fool; he *is* possessed by an irresistible power, as Pentheus is in *The Bacchae*. That this was Shaw's intention in these scenes is shown not only in the text, but also in his instructions to Louis Calvert, who created the role of Undershaft at the Court Theatre in 1905. Undershaft's speech to Mrs Baines near the end of the act about the destructiveness of his weapons is, he says, "sort of a fantasia played on the nerves of . . . [Cusins] and Barbara by Machiavelli–Mephistopheles. All that is needed to produce the effect is steady concentration, magnetic intensity." In another letter Shaw points out to Calvert that once Undershaft decides that Cusins is the man he is looking for, he "takes the lead in the conversation and dominates Cusins at once. It all goes on in a steady progression of force." This letter also tells Calvert how to play the last part of act 3: "And now for the main point, on which the fate of the play depends. If you once weaken or soften after 'Come, come, my daughter: don't make too much of your little tinpot tragedy,' we are all lost. Undershaft must go over everybody like Niagara from that moment. There must be no sparing of Barbara—no quarter for any one. His energy must be proof against everybody and everything . . . You must sweep everything before you until Lady B. knocks you off your perch for a moment; and even then you come up buoyant the next moment with your conundrum. . . . Conviction and courage: that is what he must be full of, and there is no room for anything smaller or prettier." Shaw sees Undershaft less as a debater than as a man of magnetic intensity and overwhelming energy which captivates Cusins as Ann captivates Tanner.

Like Ann and Violet, too, Undershaft represents the forces of the real world. Money is common to both plays as a symbol of the actual, physical, and immediate. The parallel in *Major Barbara* to sex, which Ann represents, is Undershaft's gunpowder. Just as sex is (along with money) the basic reality of the private, drawing room life which is the milieu of *Man and Superman,* so gunpowder (along with money) is the basic reality of the public, political life which is the milieu of *Major Barbara*. Undershaft may be a religious figure in that he possesses the Dionysiac energy I have been discussing, but this energy, like Ann's, is devoted to the immediate and the practical.

Undershaft, although he has a much stronger grasp of the world than Barbara or Cusins, is less highly evolved than either of them. His religious vision does not extend as far as Barbara's, and his political vision does not extend as far as Cusins's. In both cases, his vision does not extend to the spiritual; it does not go beyond money and gunpowder.

Like Barbara, he talks about saving souls, but what he means by this is not what Barbara means. Undershaft claims that he has saved the souls of his employees, as he has saved Barbara's soul, by giving his men adequate food, clothing, and shelter. He evidently feels that a man is saved if he has been saved from poverty. He cannot see the need for further evolution beyond material well-being, as Barbara can. Although he describes the lives of his employees with ironic detachment, he does not appear to be dissatisfied with the level of civilization that they have attained: "I dont say, mind you, that there is no ordering about and snubbing and even bullying. The men snub the boys and order them about; the carmen snub the sweepers; the artisans snub the unskilled laborers; the foremen drive and bully both the laborers and artisans; the assistant engineers find fault with the foremen; the chief engineers drop on the assistants; the departmental managers worry the chiefs; and the clerks have tall hats and hymnbooks and keep up the social tone by refusing to associate on equal terms with anybody. The result is a colossal profit, which comes to me." This society is very far from Shaw's ideal. In his essay "The Impossibilities of Anarchism" (1891), for example, he says that in our present, capitalist society snobbery flourishes at all levels except among the very poor. "The moment you rise into the higher atmosphere of a pound a week [wages at the Undershaft foundry began at thirty shillings], you find that envy, ostentation, tedious and insincere ceremony, love of petty titles, precedences and dignities, and all the detestable fruits of inequality of condition, flourish as rankly among those who lose as among those who gain by it." Undershaft is evidently not disturbed by the "detestable fruits of inequality of condition"; because his employees are not poor, he feels that they are saved.

Barbara's view—and Shaw's view—is that Undershaft has provided not salvation, but the necessary precondition of salvation. Barbara will build on the foundations which her father has provided, and try to convert the men to something beyond Philistine, bourgeois, snobbish individualism. What attracts Barbara to the cannon works are "all the human souls to be saved: not weak souls in starved bodies, sobbing with gratitude for a scrap of bread and treacle, but fullfed, quarrelsome, snobbish, uppish creatures, all standing on their little rights and dignities, and thinking that my father ought to be greatly obliged to them for making so much money for him—and so he ought. That is where salvation is really wanted." An early draft of this speech makes Barbara's concept of her new role more explicit: "I want to begin where hunger and cold and misery leave off. Anybody can convert a starving man: I want to convert prosperous ones. And I will. These souls here shall have the sulkiness and the quarrelling and the uppishness taken out of them by Major Barbara. She will teach them to live with one another, I promise you." What satisfies Undershaft clearly does not satisfy Barbara. In fact, she implies not only in act 1 but also near the end of the play, after she has heard his gospel, that he himself is in need of salvation. When Lady Britomart orders her children to come home with her because Undershaft is "wickeder than ever," Barbara replies, "It's no use running away from wicked people, mamma . . . It does not save them." Undershaft apparently does not feel in need of salvation; he seems to feel no need to develop beyond his Nietzschean individualism, with its self-seeking and its contempt for the common people ("the common mob of slaves and idolaters"). Precisely what Barbara would want Undershaft and his employees to become is not stated explicitly in the play—Shaw, as usual, is concerned more with direction than with goal—but what the play does make clear is that Undershaft's concept of salvation represents only a step on the way to salvation.

His political vision, which is closely related to his religious views, is similarly limited. His society of "saved" men, as we have seen, is a society of individualists: men who have no concept of the community as an organic whole with common goals. His own political philosophy is one of extreme individualism. He is proud of the fact that he never gives his employees orders, that the community at Perivale St. Andrews is self-regulating, without any need for external compulsion. His remedy for poverty is for individual poor men to decide to cease to be poor—to act on their own, as he has done, in demanding money from society. If every man behaved as I did, he claims (and Shaw argues in the preface), then poverty would disappear: "*I* was an east ender. I moralized and starved until one day I swore that I would be a full-fed free man at all costs; that nothing should stop me except a bullet, neither reason nor morals nor the lives of other men. I said 'Thou shalt starve ere I starve'; and with that word I became free and great. I was a dangerous man until I had my will: now I am a useful, beneficent kindly person. That is the history of most self-made millionaires, I fancy. When it is the history of every Englishman we shall have an England worth living in." It may be true that a nation of Andrew Undershafts would be superior to a nation of Peter Shirleys, but is there much point in urging every man to act as Undershaft has acted? Undershaft is a rare type: he has the enormous force of will to determine not to be poor. In *The Intelligent Woman's Guide to Socialism,* Shaw writes that "in great social questions we are dealing with the abilities of ordinary citizens: that is, the abilities we can depend on everyone except invalids and idiots possessing, and not with what one man or woman in ten thousand can do." And in *Major Barbara* Undershaft himself propounds an environmentalist view of society: economic factors determine human conduct. Poverty is in all ways debilitating; it "strikes dead the very souls of all who come within sight, sound, or smell of it." Undershaft's individualist argument that the solution to the problem of poverty is for the poor to determine, as he has done, not to be poor, is confuted by his own statements on the effects of poverty, which are illustrated in the scene in the Salvation Army shelter. It is also confuted by his own practice: he does not preach to the poor to act as he has done, but gives them jobs with adequate pay. The only person within the play who ceases to be poor is Peter Shirley, and this is not because he has declared "Thou shalt starve ere I starve," but because Undershaft's foundry has employed him. And the foundry can employ only a small proportion of the nation's working class: it is not a real solution to the problem of poverty. The play shows both the best and the worst effects of capitalism, and clearly implies that the blighted lives of the unfortunates at the Salvation Army shelter are more representative than those of the comfortable residents of Undershaft's garden city.

Undershaft, then, has achieved neither the religious nor the political goals of the play. He has not saved souls, in Barbara's and Shaw's sense, and he has not abolished poverty. Nor has he put an end to war. The Armorer's Faith—"to give arms to all men who offer an honest price for them, without respect of persons or principles"—has caused him to provide only the means for the waging of war, not the means for its abolition. His weapons serve no higher purpose of his own, but the lower purposes of "the most rascally part of society," as Cusins points out. Undershaft seems to be quite unaware of these limitations, and yet he is drawn to Barbara and Cusins, who may be able to accomplish what he has not accomplished. His attitude toward them is contradictory: some of his speeches suggest that he sees them as followers, who will carry on his work for him. But in other speeches he challenges them to do work which is profoundly different from his own, and which would entail the overthrow of himself, his foundry, his class, and his gospel.

He tells Cusins in act 2 that Barbara will be his follower, that she will give up her religion for his:

> UNDERSHAFT: . . . I shall hand on my torch to my daughter. She
>   shall make my converts and preach my gospel—
> CUSINS: What! Money and gunpowder!

> UNDERSHAFT: Yes, money and gunpowder. Freedom and power.
> Command of life and command of death.

In act 3 he continues to talk as if Barbara must give up her religion and practice his. He says, as we have seen, that he has saved the souls of his men; if this is the case, then there is no place for Barbara's religion at the cannon works. But on the following page he issues his challenge to Barbara: not to give up her religion for his, but to preach her own gospel to his employees. "Try your hand on *my* men," he says; "their souls are hungry because their bodies are full." The change now is to be not from one religion to another but from the hungry to the well-fed, in line with Shaw's view that material well-being must precede spiritual improvement. Yet Undershaft is contemptuous of Barbara's concept of salvation:

> CUSINS: I . . . want to avoid being a rascal.
> UNDERSHAFT [*with biting contempt*]: You lust for personal right-
>   eousness, for self-approval, for what you call a good con-
>   science, for what Barbara calls salvation, for what I call
>   patronizing people who are not so lucky as yourself.

Undershaft, then, invites Barbara to convert his men to a religion that he appears to reject, a religion that could supplant his own.

His challenge to Cusins contains a similar contradiction. It is not clear whether he intends him to carry on precisely as he himself has done, or to bring about a new era at the cannon works. The particular question is whether Cusins will remain true to the Armorer's Faith: whether he will sell weapons to anyone who can pay for them, or whether he will provide them only to those who will use them for the benefit of mankind. Undershaft insists that Cusins "must keep the true faith of an Armorer, or you dont come in here." But then on the next page he says to him: "If you good people prefer preaching and shirking to buying my weapons and fighting the rascals, dont blame me." That Undershaft is inviting Cusins to gain control of the weapons in order to fight the rascals is clear from his final challenge to him, "Dare you make war on war? Here are the means." Now, one cannot both sell weapons only to those who can pay for them and at the same time make war on war. If you are loyal to the Armorer's Faith, then you continue to sell arms to the ruling classes—that is, to those who now have them anyway—and society does not change significantly.

These contradictions can be partly accounted for by the fact that Undershaft, a master of irony, is unscrupulously and cleverly appealing to Barbara and Cusins on their own terms. "It is through religion alone that we

can win Barbara," he tells Cusins in the scene in act 2 in which he declares
that she will preach his gospel of money and gunpowder. Similarly, it is only
through high-minded political goals that he can win Cusins. And so he
invites Barbara to save the souls of his men and challenges Cusins to make
war on war, confident that once they have joined the foundry they will
succumb to the spirit of the place and continue as he has done.

But the contradictions are not entirely explained in this way. For they
are connected not only with Undershaft's conscious irony, but with contradictions within his own mind of which he is not conscious. His hatred of
poverty is genuine. "I hate poverty and slavery worse than any other crimes
whatsoever," he says. "And let me tell you this. Poverty and slavery have
stood up for centuries to your sermons and leading articles: they will not
stand up to my machine guns. Dont preach at them: dont reason with them.
Kill them." This is not ironic but impassioned; Undershaft sounds here like
a serious revolutionary, and soon after this he is saying to Cusins, "Come
and make explosives with me. Whatever can blow men up can blow society
up."

Undershaft considers himself bound by the Armorer's Faith, as he considers himself bound by the firm's Antonine tradition of inheritance. He and
his six predecessors have all been true to the Armorer's Faith, with the result
that poverty and slavery have stood up not only to the sermons and leading
articles written by people like Barbara and Cusins but to the seven generations of Andrew Undershafts. What is needed now—and Undershaft seems
unconsciously to recognize this—is a new Andrew Undershaft who will
reject the Armorer's Faith and sell arms only to those who will use them to
fight against war, poverty, and slavery. The play implies that at some level
he knows that he himself is inadequate for the task of creating a better
society: that powers very different from his own are required as well. In act
2, in his first Dionysiac conversation with Cusins, he proposes an alliance
between himself, Cusins, and Barbara: "I am a millionaire; you are a poet;
Barbara is a savior of souls. What have we three to do with the common
mob of slaves and idolaters? . . . We three must stand together above the
common people: how else can we help their children to climb up beside us?"
The implication here, whether Undershaft consciously intends it or not, is
that the three of them together might be able to do what he alone cannot do.
And there are other hints in the play that Undershaft has some sense of his
limitations. He tells Lady Britomart that the cannon works "does not belong to me. I belong to it"; and he admits to Cusins that he has no power
of his own. Even more significant is his challenge to Barbara and Cusins,
which follows Cusins's statement that Undershaft has no power: "If you

good people prefer preaching and shirking to buying my weapons and fighting the rascals, dont blame me. I can make cannons: I cannot make courage and conviction." In this speech he is saying in effect that he must rely on "good people" like Barbara and Cusins to reform society, that he cannot do it alone.

Undershaft shows an awareness of the value of dialectical conflict in his desire for strong opponents. He tells Barbara near the end of the play that he loves only his "bravest enemy. That is the man who keeps me up to the mark." When Mrs Baines mentions that in 1886 the poor broke the windows of clubs in Pall Mall, Undershaft replies, *"gleaming with approval of their method,"* that this forced the rich to contribute to the relief of poverty.

He also tells Mrs Baines that he is giving money to the Salvation Army "to help you to hasten my own commercial ruin." "It is your work to preach peace on earth and goodwill to men . . . Every convert you make is a vote against war." He is, of course, being ironic; his purpose in giving the money is to win Barbara from the Salvation Army. But there is a double irony here. By bringing Barbara and Cusins into his cannon works, he *is* hastening his ruin, in that he is handing over the works to people whose values are profoundly different from those on which the foundry rests. And this is what, at his deepest level, he may wish to do.

Undershaft's position is like that of Wotan in Wagner's *Ring of the Nibelung*. Wotan, bound by his treaty with Fafnir, is unable to accomplish his own goal, the retrieval of the ring from him, just as Undershaft, bound by the Armorer's Faith, is unable to fight poverty. Wotan's desire for a hero who will not be bound by the god's treaty and will be able to carry out the deed which he himself cannot is comparable to Undershaft's desire for Cusins to succeed him at the foundry. The relevance of this parallel between Wotan and Undershaft is made clear by the way in which Shaw discusses *The Ring* in *The Perfect Wagnerite*. Before he begins his analysis of *The Valkyre* he tells his readers that "above all, we must understand—for it is the key to much that we are to see—that the god, since his desire is toward a higher and fuller life, must long in his inmost soul for the advent of that greater power whose first work, though this he does not see as yet, must be his own undoing." Wotan, Shaw says earlier, looks for a higher race which will "deliver the world and himself from his limited powers and disgraceful bargains." On every side he is shackled and bound, dependent on the laws of Fricka and on the lies of Loki, forced to traffic with dwarfs [the instinctive, predatory, lustful, greedy people] for handicraft and with giants [the patient, toiling, stupid, respectful, money-worshipping people] for strength." This reminds one of Cusins's statement, which Undershaft does not really deny, that Undershaft is driven by the cannon works, which in turn is driven "by the most rascally part of society, the money hunters, the pleasure hunters, the military promotion hunters." Undershaft's reply, which is the invitation to Cusins and Barbara to use his weapons to "fight the rascals," is comparable to Wotan's hope that a hero will defy those who limit his power.

IV

In selecting Cusins as his successor, Undershaft is in a sense putting into practice his view that his best friend is his bravest enemy; he chooses his opposite—his anti-self. Cusins is humane, hates war, loves the common people, refuses to accept the Armorer's Faith, and—contrary to the Undershaft tradition—is middle class, of respectable background, and highly educated. According to Shaw, Undershaft decides on Cusins's merit in act 2, just before the first Dionysiac scene. Shaw wrote to Calvert, "The change comes from the line 'And now to business.' Up to that, Undershaft has been studying Cusins and letting him talk. But the shake-hands means that he has made up his mind that Cusins is the man to understand him; and he therefore takes the lead in the conversation and dominates Cusins at once." What has presumably impressed Undershaft is not that Cusins has agreed with any of his views (which he hasn't) but that Cusins has declared, in reply to Undershaft's implied objections to him as a suitor for Barbara, that nothing will stop him from marrying her. And just before the handshake, Cusins responds to Undershaft's "You are a young man after my own heart" with "Mr Undershaft: you are, as far as I am able to gather, a most infernal old rascal." This is the way in which Cusins refers to Undershaft for the rest of the play, and while he is incapable of defending his own point of view against Undershaft's energy and arguments, he insists until the end of the play that he loathes Undershaft's principles. In reply to G. K. Chesterton's statement (in his book on Shaw) that Cusins puts up an "incredibly weak fight" against Undershaft's arguments, Shaw wrote, "As to the professor making no fight, he stands up to Undershaft all through so subtly and effectually that Undershaft takes him into partnership at the end of the play."

The most important difference between Cusins and Undershaft is the difference between the kind of power that each possesses and represents. Undershaft's power, as we have seen, is in the main akin to that of Ann and Violet in *Man and Superman*. Cusins's power is like that of Tanner and Don Juan: the power of imagination and intellect. Shaw's usual view of professors of Greek was not very favorable, but Cusins is based on Gilbert Murray, a close friend whom Shaw admired and respected. He says in the play's prefatory note on Murray that his "English version of The Bacchae came into our dramatic literature with all the impulsive power of an original work," and in *Major Barbara* itself Cusins is presented as a poet, an artist, a thinker (which the true Shavian artist always is). Like all of Shaw's Realists, he has a desire to improve the world around him. As a teacher of Greek he has tried to do this in Tanner's way, through thought, through spirit. He says in the play that his purpose in teaching Greek was to "make spiritual power," and this is amplified in an earlier draft, with the addition to Cusins's speech of the statement that "I am no mere grammarian: if I had not believed that our highest faculties would kindle and aspire at the touch of Greek poetry and Greek thought, I should never have wasted an hour in a class room." In the final version of the play Shaw let the audience infer Cusins's sense of high purpose as a teacher of Greek from the sentence about "spiritual power" and from Cusins's character as a whole.

Cusins's interest is not confined to the university classroom. He tells Undershaft in act 2 that his attachment to the Salvation Army is genuine, in the sense that the Salvation Army inspires people with joy, love, and courage: "It picks the waster out of the public house and makes a man of him: it finds a worm wriggling in a back kitchen, and lo! a woman!" And he objects to Undershaft's contemptuous dismissal of "the common mob of slaves and idolaters." "Take care!" he replies. "Barbara is in love with the common people. So am I." This love of the common people is a characteristic which Cusins shares with his original. Gilbert Murray wrote of himself that as Professor of Greek at Glasgow he tried to combine "an enthusiasm for poetry and Greek scholarship with an almost equal enthusiasm for radical politics and social reform." But he found that the two causes did not always go well together. "Throughout history it has been hard to combine the principles of culture and of democracy, the claims of the few who maintain and raise the highest moral and intellectual standards with those of the masses who rightly do not want to be oppressed." Whereas Gilbert Murray felt that he was able to reconcile these two principles, Cusins is forced to choose one or the other. He chooses the claims of "the masses who rightly do not want to oppressed"; he decides that it is better to give weapons to the many than civilization to the few. It is not that civilization is necessarily useless, but that it can affect only a minority, while the mass of society is left in the condition of the unfortunates in the Salvation Army shelter. "The world can never be really touched by a dead language and a dead civilization. The people must have power; and the people cannot have

Greek." The only kind of power that can be of use to the majority is not the higher power of the spirit but the primitive, physical power of gunpowder. "As a teacher of Greek I gave the intellectual man weapons against the common man. I now want to give the common man weapons against the intellectual man. I love the common people. I want to arm them against the lawyers, the doctors, the priests, the literary men, the professors, the artists, and the politicians, who, once in authority, are more disastrous and tyrannical than all the fools, rascals, and impostors. I want a power simple enough for common men to use, yet strong enough to force the intellectual oligarchy to use its genius for the general good."

In the language of *The Quintessence of Ibsenism*, Cusins, the Realist, wants to provide the common people with Philistine power to use against the Idealists—an idea which is prefigured in Shaw's preface (1900) to *Three Plays for Puritans*. If "the democratic attitude becomes thoroughly Romanticist," he predicts there, "the country will become unbearable for all realists, Philistine or Platonic. When it comes to that, the brute force of the strong-minded Bismarckian man of action, impatient of humbug, will combine with the subtlety and spiritual energy of the man of thought whom shams cannot illude or interest. That combination will be on one side; and Romanticism will be on the other." The implication in Cusins's speech is that the really dangerous people are not those with no ideas—the money hunters, the pleasure hunters, the military promotion hunters—but those with the wrong ideas. Cusins's speech presents the same pattern that we found in *Man and Superman:* the Realist will use aimless Philistine power for a higher purpose, and the real enemy of progress is the Idealist. Cusins will use gunpowder as Tanner will use sex, although Tanner's role is more passive, and he is largely unconscious of it.

In *Man and Superman* the dangers of Idealism are made to seem much greater in the discussion in the Hell Scene than they are in the presentation of life in the Comedy. Similarly, Cusins's discussion here of the misuse of spiritual power has little basis in the rest of the play. The only significant Idealists in the play are Stephen and Lady Britomart, and neither of them seems to represent much of a threat to society. Stephen, as the aspiring politician, comes closest to Cusins's speech, but Undershaft's statement in the first part of act 3 that "*I* am the government of your country," which is confirmed in the second part of the act when the political man is the only member of the visiting party who praises the cannon works unreservedly, would seem to dispose of the political Idealist as an important factor. What one gathers from the play as a whole is that there is no effective "government of your country," that control is in the hands of those who have no social goals: that society is not guided by any purpose, good or bad, but by the primitive acquisitive instincts of those in whom these instincts are strongest. Both *Man and Superman* and *Major Barbara* tell us about the danger of Idealist illusions but make us feel that Philistine power is much more significant. It is not until *Saint Joan* that Shaw's intellectual fear of Idealism becomes something deeply enough felt to be given dramatic expression in characters like the Inquisitor, Cauchon, and de Stogumber. Cusins's speech, in fact, applies much more directly to *Saint Joan* than to *Major Barbara*. It would seem more to the point to arm the common people against the Inquisitor than against Stephen Undershaft.

In spite of this element of contradiction, Cusins's aims are basically clear enough. He will try to create a society which is run for the benefit of the majority by providing the common people with weapons so that they can insist on such a society. Only the threat of revolution, the play implies, will cause the ruling classes to do something about the state of society. In determining to arm the common people, Cusins is determining to reject the Armorer's Faith: he will provide weapons for that part of the community which without his intervention would never acquire them. When Undershaft first tells him of the Armorer's Faith, which (says Undershaft) he must keep if he is to succeed to the cannon works, he unhesitatingly rejects it: "As to your Armorer's Faith, if I take my neck out of the noose of my own morality I am not going to put it into the noose of yours. I shall sell cannons to whom I please and refuse them to whom I please. So there!" Undershaft's reply is that "from the moment when you become Andrew Undershaft, you will never do as you please again." So one is left, as one is in so many of Shaw's plays, with a conflict which will continue after the play ends; Cusins intending to depart from the Armorer's Faith, and struggling against Undershaft, "the place," and presumably the "rascals" for whom the weapons are now produced. Whether or not he succeeds fully, a vital step has been taken: the man of intellect has united with the physical power of the Philistine world.

As in *Man and Superman,* this is in one sense a defeat for the man of intellect and in another sense a victory. It is a defeat in that the intellectual life is given up for the Philistine life: the teaching of Greek for the manufacture of cannons—as in *Man and Superman* the philosopher's activities are given up for those of the father and husband. But as Tanner's submission to Ann may also be seen as a step toward the control of Ann's kind of power by Tanner, so in *Major Barbara* Cusins submits to the foundry so that he can control it. Despite his agreement with Barbara's comment that he will have no power when he enters the foundry, his next speeches, about arming the common people, indicate that he plans to exercise a power which Undershaft has never had: the power of directing the weapons which are made at the foundry. He will put the power of thought to practical use, and his power, like Tanner's, will increase rather than diminish when it combines with that of the Philistine world.

Neither Cusins's kind of power nor Undershaft's is of much use when it exists alone. Undershaft's view that spiritual power without cannons is impotent ("If you good people prefer preaching and shirking to buying my weapons and fighting the rascals, dont blame me") is balanced by Cusins's view that cannons without spiritual power are impotent. His remark to Undershaft that "*You* have no power" equates the maker of cannons with the cannons themselves; the Armorer's Faith reduces Undershaft to an instrument. "I have more power than you, more will," Cusins claims; that is, at least I have the power of mind which designs, seeks conscious goals, and is not a blind force with no purpose of its own. The mild-mannered professor of Greek has more significant power than the tough millionaire cannon manufacturer. This is the same kind of paradox that one finds in *Candida,* in which Marchbanks turns out to be stronger, more manly, and more religious than Morell. Shaw wrote to Gilbert Murray while he was writing act 3, "I have taken rather special care to make Cusins the reverse in every point of the theatrical strong man. I want him to go on his quality wholly, and not to make the smallest show of physical robustness or brute determination. His selection by Undershaft should be a puzzle to people who believe in the strong-silent-still-waters-run-deep hero of melodrama. The very name Adolphus Cusins is selected to that end."

But although Cusins's kind of power may be more meaningful than Undershaft's, Cusins has done no more than Undershaft to improve society. Each of them has benefited only a relatively small number of people: Cusins his students, Undershaft his employees. And the improvement they have caused in these people has been only partial: Cusins has improved only men's minds, while Undershaft has improved only men's bodies. Cusins and Undershaft, when acting separately, have achieved little of real significance. Only when the spiritual and the material join together can society be improved. "Society cannot be saved until either the Professors of Greek take to making gunpowder, or else the makers of gunpowder become Professors of Greek."

Even this combination of Cusins and Undershaft is not sufficient, however. Cusins, in taking over the foundry, will try to provide "the people" with weapons and hence money, but this could only bring the population up to the level of the employees at the foundry. He would be using his spiritual power in giving the weapons a purpose, a direction, but in order to do this he is giving up the making of spiritual power. In order for men to be saved as well as fed, Barbara's power is required.

Barbara, like Cusins and Undershaft, has been almost—but not quite—ineffectual when working by herself. She does have an effect on Bill Walker, and the play implies that although her attempt to save his soul is frustrated by Undershaft, she has brought about a real change in him. When Barbara tells Bill that she will replace his pound, he replies, in a suddenly improved voice and accent, that he will not be bought by her. And when in the next act she reproaches Undershaft for taking Bill Walker's soul from her, he convinces her that Bill's soul is not entirely lost:

> UNDERSHAFT: Does my daughter despair so easily? Can you strike a man to the heart and leave no mark on him?
> BARBARA [*her face lighting up*]: Oh, you are right: he can never be lost now: where was my faith?

Bill Walker, however, is quite unlike the others whom Barbara is trying to save at the Salvation Army shelter. He has come to the shelter not to beg bread but to demand his girl-friend. He is not noticeably hungry or poor; and he has been able to save two pounds "agen the frost." In fact, he is not very different from Undershaft's "fullfed, quarrelsome, snobbish, uppish" employees, and it is therefore most significant that Barbara converts him, while she has no effect whatever on the others at the shelter, who have come only to satisfy their bodily hunger.

Neither Barbara nor Cusins, then, can have much effect on society while relying exclusively on spiritual power. They (and all those higher beings who want to improve society, of whom Barbara and Cusins are symbolic) must ally themselves with Undershaft, and the forces that he represents. And Undershaft cannot have much effect on society while he relies exclusively on physical power; he needs Barbara and Cusins as much as they need him. What is required is a marriage of intellectual power, religious power, and physical power. This is the real meaning of the alliance which Undershaft proposes in act 2, although no single character in the play is fully aware of the implications of the synthesis. It is left (as usual in Shaw's plays) for the audience to draw the threads together.

Nothing less than a fusion of all three will achieve the implicit goal of the play: a nation of what Barbara would call the saved—a nation of fully developed men and women. Cusins and Barbara without Undershaft would achieve no significant results: political advance is impossible without weapons and religious advance is impossible without money. Cusins and

Undershaft without Barbara would achieve, as we have seen, only a nation of Philistines—an extension of the society at the foundry. Barbara and Undershaft without Cusins would achieve only a minority of the saved. Barbara recognizes this: when Undershaft challenges her to convert his employees, her (unanswered) reply is, "And leave the east end to starve?"

The aspect of this union which the play concentrates on is the decision of the two characters with spiritual power to unite with Undershaft: his need for the two of them is only implied, as Ann's dependence on Tanner is indicated only in the Hell Scene of *Man and Superman*. The counterpart in *Major Barbara* of the Hell Scene is the crucial scene between Barbara and Cusins near the end of the play, for it is here that the importance of the more highly developed person is made apparent. Barbara and Cusins seem at the beginning of this scene to have been utterly defeated by Undershaft; but now both of them declare triumphantly that they have found their new purpose, and their speeches in this scene should make it plain that the victory in *Major Barbara* is not Undershaft's alone, just as the Hell Scene should make it plain that the victory in *Man and Superman* is not Ann's alone. Neither Barbara nor Cusins is really converted to Undershaft's gospel of money and gunpowder. They retain their own goals, but see that money and gunpowder are necessary if these goals are to be attained. They see that the higher can be achieved only through the lower. This is an idea which is found in many forms in *Major Barbara*. "Then the way of life lies through the factory of death?" Cusins asks after Barbara has discovered her new role at the end of the play; and Barbara replies, "Yes, through the raising of hell to heaven and of man to God, through the unveiling of an eternal light in the Valley of The Shadow." Similarly, the way of the spirit lies through the flesh (Barbara will convert the well-fed) and the way of peace lies through the sword (Cusins will "make war on war," using weapons to create a world in which war would presumably disappear). The idea is also made explicit in Cusins's defense to Barbara of Undershaft's weapons.

> BARBARA: Is there no higher power than that [*pointing to the shell*]?
> CUSINS: Yes; but that power can destroy the higher powers just as a tiger can destroy a man: therefore Man must master that power first.

This is parallel to Barbara's realization that although there is a higher power than money, men must have money first.

Cusins's analogy between Undershaft's weapons and the tiger calls to mind Blake's treatment of wild, destructive power in the *Songs of Experi-*

ence. The imagery of Blake's "The Tyger" is that of the foundry, with particular emphasis on fire ("My sort of fire purifies," says Undershaft in act 1). And Blake's poem evokes the combination of terror and attraction that Shaw intends Undershaft and his weapons to produce in Cusins and in the audience—although Blake can create a much greater sense of terror than Shaw. If we assume that Blake's tyger represents the power necessary to overthrow the fallen world of Experience, then the parallel between the poem and the play becomes closer still. Maurice Bowra, who interprets the poem in this way, says that Blake

> sought some ultimate synthesis in which innocence might be wedded to experience, and goodness to knowledge. . . . The true innocence is not after all that of the *Songs of Innocence,* but something which has gained knowledge from the ugly lessons of experience and found an expanding strength in the unfettered life of the creative soul. . . .
>
> Blake knows well that such a consummation will not come simply from good will or pious aspirations and that the life of the imagination is possible only through passion and power and energy. That is why he sometimes stresses the great forces which lie hidden in man and may be terrifying but are none the less necessary if anything worth while is to happen. . . . The tiger is Blake's symbol for the fierce forces in the soul which are needed to break the bonds of experience.

Almost everything which Bowra says here about Blake applies precisely to *Major Barbara.* The tiger, like Undershaft, symbolizes a force from which "good men" recoil, but without which progress is impossible.

This same emphasis on the necessity of the terrifying is found in *The Marriage of Heaven and Hell.* That "the tygers of wrath are wiser than the horses of instruction" (Plate 9) is exactly what Cusins discovers in *Major Barbara. The Marriage of Heaven and Hell* asserts, like *Major Barbara,* that both forces are necessary: heavenly controlling power and hellish violent, destructive power must exist together. And in both works the heavenly is the conventionally good, while the hellish is the conventionally evil. *The Marriage of Heaven and Hell* tries to break down and confuse rigid distinctions between heaven and hell, good and evil, soul and body. It is not true, says the voice of the Devil, that "Energy, call'd Evil, is alone from the Body; & that Reason, call'd Good, is alone from the Soul." The truth is that "Energy is the only life, and is from the Body; and Reason is the bound or outward circumference of Energy" (Plate 4). Barbara makes a similar discovery: "Turning our backs on Bodger and Undershaft is turning our backs on life . . . There is no wicked side [of life]: life is all one."

Blake's technique of ironic reversal of heaven and hell is an important element in *Major Barbara*. Undershaft is the representative of hell: Cusins calls him the Prince of Darkness, a devil, Mephistopheles, a demon, an infernal old rascal; and says that at the Salvation Army meeting the "brazen roarings" of his trombone "were like the laughter of the damned." He calls the foundry "this Works Department of Hell," and Barbara says before the visit that she has "always thought of it as a sort of pit where lost creatures with blackened faces stirred up smoky fires and were driven and tormented by my father." The foundry, which is the center of hellish activity in the play, turns out to be heavenly ("It only needs a cathedral to be a heavenly city instead of a hellish one," Cusins observes; while the center of heavenly activity, the Salvation Army shelter, is truly hellish. Undershaft's hell—his diabolical assertive values, his money, and his gunpowder—is the true road to heaven. "You may be a devil; but God speaks through you sometimes," Barbara says after her father has dispelled her despondency about Bill Walker's soul. This parallels Cusins's exclamation near the end of the play that "the way of life lies through the factory of death."

Blake, it is true, values hellish energy more than Shaw does, but both of them present hell as a state just as necessary as heaven in our imperfect world. The unpleasant or frightening cannot be dismissed as evil; Stephen and Lady Britomart are the equivalent of Blake's "Bibles or sacred codes" (Plate 4)—the representatives of conventional absolute morality, whose position is demolished in both works. The moral of the final act of *Major Barbara*, Shaw wrote to Gilbert Murray, "is drawn by Lomax 'There is a certain amount of tosh about this notion of wickedness.' " Morality in both *Major Barbara* and *The Marriage of Heaven and Hell* is relative to the situation and to the individual: "There is only one true morality for every man; but every man has not the same true morality" (Undershaft in *Major Barbara*); "One Law for the Lion & Ox is Oppression" (*The Marriage of Heaven and Hell*, Plates 22–24). *Major Barbara* asserts the necessity of accepting and combining good and evil, heaven and hell; and the best brief statement of its central idea is the aphorism from *The Marriage of Heaven and Hell*: "Without Contraries is no progression. Attraction and Repulsion, Reason and Energy, Love and Hate, are necessary to Human existence" (Plate 3).

SALLY PETERS VOGT

Ann and Superman:
Type and Archetype

Despite the voluminous criticism devoted to *Man and Superman*, Ann Whitefield, Shaw's most persuasively feminine heroine, continues to be an enigma. Most critics would agree with Arthur H. Nethercot that Ann is Shaw's "prototype of predatory females," but assessments of her specific role vary. Thus Barbara Bellow Watson celebrates Ann's vitality and originality; Margery M. Morgan denounces her calculating conventionality; and Elsie Adams find that Ann is merely "a composite of traditional types" of heroines. Nor is this surprising, since within the play itself Ann appears in many guises, so that her fellow *dramatis personae* perceive her from their own narrowly circumscribed perspectives. But while the characters' restricted views of Ann provide a major source of the comedy, a coherent assessment of her role requires a broader viewpoint that will discern the genesis of apparent discrepancies in her characterization.

Curiously, the implicitly mythic nature underlying much of the dramatic action has been largely ignored, although a number of studies have focused on the relation between the Don Juan legend and the play. Yet Shaw's use of both the Don Juan legend and his philosophy of Creative Evolution is an ordering of once powerful mythic patterns that, even though now attenuated, continue to survive and function in the modern world. Once the presence and function of these mythic patterns are revealed, Ann's role will be clarified. It will then be possible to assess the ways in which Ann is a typical, and not so typical, Victorian heroine, and the ways in which her role demands archetypal formulation. Since Ann's characterization suspends

From *Fabian Feminist: Bernard Shaw and Woman*, edited by Rodelle Weintraub. © 1977 by Pennsylvania State University. Pennsylvania State University Press, 1977.

from mythic elements, this dimension of *Man and Superman* will be explored in an effort to uncover the ultimate face behind Ann's many masks. While all four acts of the play will be considered, it is in the crucial third act that mythic elements are most clearly discernible.

That Shaw was aware of and sympathetic to the possibilities of myth is evident from both his admiration of Wagner and his symbolic reading of *The Ring* in *The Perfect Wagnerite,* a reading that supports Shaw's own evolutionary view. Underlying this affinity to myth is Shaw's essentially religious nature, which manifested itself in his lifelong evangelicalism. Shaw's devotion to his own particular view, however, did not prevent him from recognizing basic similarities between diverse phenomena that function as hierophanies, that is, to reveal what is "sacred" to the believer. In the preface to the *Plays Pleasant* he can thus assert of the times:

> Religion was alive again, coming back upon men, even upon clergymen, with such power that not the Church of England itself could keep it out. Here my activity as a Socialist had placed me on sure and familiar ground. To me the members of the Guild of St Matthew were no more "High Church clergymen," Dr Clifford no more "an eminent Nonconformist divine," than I was to them "an infidel." There is only one religion, though there are a hundred versions of it. We all had the same thing to say; and though some of us cleared our throats to say it by singing revolutionary lyrics and republican hymns, we thought nothing of singing them to the music of Sullivan's Onward Christian Soldiers or Haydn's God Preserve the Emperor.

A hundred versions of one religion—this is the view of the comparative religionist and the cultural anthropologist. Shaw's version emerges in the harmonies of Creative Evolution scored for both virtuoso performance and background music in *Man and Superman.* Inquiry into this implicitly mythic and religious play can be enriched by a widening of critical perspective, so that our range of vision more closely approximates Shaw's. Consequently, in order to reevaluate Ann, the mythic dimension of the play will be explored, using the insights of scholars who approach myth from the viewpoints of the history of religions (Mircea Eliade), anthropology (Joseph Campbell), psychology (Carl G. Jung), symbolism (J. E. Cirlot) and literary criticism (Northrop Frye). In addition, these insights will facilitate a wider frame of reference in describing certain formal properties of the play.

It is noteworthy at the outset that the action of *Man and Superman* is located in two different structures: the immediately apparent dramatic surface reveals the familiar action of comic romance, with its stereotypic pursuing and pursued characters; this in turn derives from a conceptual deep structure, mythic in both content and origin, whose forward thrust directs the surface action. The two structures, therefore, do not merely coexist; they are hierarchically related, with the second grounding the first. But the specific relationships between the two are by no means self-evident. In fact, it is precisely the reduction and deletion of much of the overtly mythic material in three of the four acts that has led to the apparently anomalous surface form of the play. Thus, in acts 1, 2 and 4, the romantic comedy of Ann's pursuit of John Tanner is so much to the fore that the mythic deep structure appears to be, if not entirely eliminated, then at least largely submerged. Conversely, in the crucial third act, the formerly latent deep structure surfaces with almost startling clarity, while the action of the romantic comedy is held in abeyance. Both these structures must be understood and explicitly correlated, if Ann is to emerge in her totality, and if the pattern behind the woman-dominated, woman-motivated dramatic action is to be clearly perceived.

Before the underlying mythic pattern and Ann's place in this pattern can be revealed, however, we must first examine the familiar surface structure. Female domination of the male is one of the most obvious characteristics of the surface structure, a truly remarkable paradox since the women have no outlet for their energies outside their narrowly and traditionally defined social and biological roles. Biology is indeed destiny in the not always comic world of Ann Whitefield and Violet Robinson. Nevertheless, within the confines of their roles, these women exert a powerful, though always decorous force. The consequence is remarkable: *the men are defined through their relationships with women*. Thus, despite Tanner's protests against marriage and his pretensions to being a utopian philosopher, we view him as a frightened male fleeing from Ann. Similarly, Roebuck Ramsden may be a *"president of highly respectable men,"* as the stage directions inform us, but we see only what Ann calls "Annie's Granny," a pompous and ineffectual man. Just as Ramsden is rendered powerless by his myopic view of Ann, so the aspiring poet Octavius is paralyzed by a romanticized conception of Ann, which pervades all his speeches and actions.

But Ann is not the only strong woman in the play. Both Hector Malone, Sr., and his son are dominated by Violet's desire to have money as well as marriage—Malone Jr. at the outset; Malone Sr. finally. Nor, as we discover in the dream frame, must the women necessarily be present to shape their men's lives. Unrequited love for the absent Louisa has made a mountain brigand out of the urbane waiter Mendoza. Romantic longing impels

Mendoza to reveal his love to the supremely rational Henry Straker. As the long arm of comic coincidence would have it, Straker is Louisa's brother, and Mendoza's news strips him of rationality, goading him into an emotional reaction at odds with his scientific outlook. In hell, of course, what we already know of Don Juan, and what we will know, centers on his former susceptibility to and present disdain of feminine charms.

Since women exercise such powerful role-defining influence, it is perfectly consistent that the surface structure of the comedy charts Tanner's reactions to women in great detail. In one sense, woman-initiated thought or action is responsible for all the actions, physical and discursive, of Tanner and Don Juan. Thus the entire first act shows Tanner in a series of reactions, first to Ann's insistence on retaining him as her guardian, second in his embarrassing defense of Violet, and finally in his confession to Ann of "the birth in [him] of moral passion." Tanner, in his reactive role, has much in common with the passive hero of melodrama. The stupid conventionalism of the melodramatic hero becomes, paradoxically, converted in Tanner into the opaque brilliance of a would-be revolutionist uttering panegyrics on the Life Force.

Act 2 shows Ann adroitly manipulating Tanner, who, in response, leaps into *"a sociological rage,"* only to be neatly deflated. Not yet daunted, Tanner replies with the outrageous challenge that Ann race across Europe with him; she stuns him by accepting. Once he learns from Straker of Ann's matrimonial inclinations, Tanner is forced into a frantic dash from her in hopes of preserving his single state. But Ann successfully pursues him into the Sierra Nevadas; even while yelling "Caught!" he continues to react against the idea of marriage, not verbally acquiescing until the very end of act 4. Still he valiantly tries to persuade himself and his auditors that he is in command of the hour, precisely, though fruitlessly, outlining his spartan terms for the marriage ceremony and its accoutrements. Unruffled, Ann assures him that he should "go on talking," to which Tanner can only indignantly sputter "Talking!"—his final reaction to Ann and, fittingly, the final speech of *Man and Superman.*

It is obvious, therefore, that in the surface structure of the romantic comedy, women not only influence but actually control the action. Though stoutly fending off marriage until the very end of the play, Tanner speaks of the inevitability of his reaction by alluding, in Schopenhauerian terms, to the intangible force that directs men's lives: "We do the world's will, not our own." Thus Tanner's reactions culminate in his engagement to Ann because, as he so deterministically puts it, "It is the world's will that [Ann] should have a husband."

Just as the surface structure of the romantic comedy is a comic inversion of the pursuit of the heroine by the hero, so the dramatically slender surface of the dream symposium revolves around the comic inversion of the Don Juan theme. Don Juan, the arch libertine, becomes the pursued prey who seeks only a meditative respite from the rigors of ever-pursuing, ever-amorous women. Because of a duel over a woman Don Juan is in hell, and even there Woman continues to direct his destiny, a result of having on earth "interpreted all the other teaching" for him, consequently revealing the extent of his susceptibility to irrational life. Thus, in a perverse parody of Descartes's *cogito ergo sum,* he confesses, "It was Woman who taught me to say 'I am; therefore I think.' And also 'I would think more; therefore I must be more.' "

On one level, then, the play seems to exist merely to dramatize Shaw's joke about women who pursue. Much of the humor of the joke lies in Shaw's manipulation of conventional melodramatic roles. As an example of type, Ann resembles the heroine less than she does the siren of melodrama, but high passion has been channeled into its single respectable course, which leads—however lively the wooing—to marriage. Part of the waywardness Ann radiates can therefore be attributed to the tension resulting from the intertwining of two radically different melodramatic types: the intriguing siren and the forever chaste heroine. Consequently, Ann appears fascinating to those who admire energetic clever women, or hypocritical to those who are shocked by the covert operation of the marriage trap.

An analysis of the deep structure of the play, however, eliminates the need for such either/or judgments, since it becomes apparent that the complexities engendered by Ann's multiple guises are grounded in her universal-mythic role. This role may at first be difficult to discern, for the play's cosmic focus has been blurred by the use of the traditional, albeit inverted, romantic comedy. The action of the romantic comedy stems, nevertheless, from a mythic base. Ironically, the dialectical structure of the dream symposium (heaven versus hell, reality versus illusion, optimism versus pessimism) has had a similar obscurantist function: first because of its ambiguous relationship to the rest of the play; second because its brilliant rhetoric attracts attention to *lexis,* not *praxis,* verbal meaning seemingly overwhelming any function as action this rhetoric might serve. Shaw's brilliant display in the dream symposium is not mere pyrotechnics, however, but is rooted in a fundamental mythic rhythm. The organizing rhythm of dialectic is, as Frye has shown, as basic a unifying pattern as the cyclical rhythm customarily encountered in mythic works. Thus the major phases of human experience revealed by the action—birth and death, initiation and marriage—are set against the moral dialectic which pits the affirmative Life Force against the negating ignorance and vice of the world. And since unending dialectic is but another name for process, and since process is the essence of Creative Evolution, Shaw constantly suggests his theory through his method.

But even though the third act is dialectically structured, the cyclical nature of the whole of human history is explicitly suggested by the Devil and assented to by Don Juan: "An epoch is but a swing of the pendulum; and each generation thinks the world is progressing because it is always moving." And in Tanner's view, what has so far been applauded in history is just "goose-cackle about Progress." This tendency toward cyclical rhythm is evident in the play as a whole, but it is strongly counterbalanced by dialectical rhythm, especially in the dream symposium, which reveals the mythic deep structure most forcefully. In contrast, the surface realism of the other three acts—where the action is more cyclically oriented—conceals the play's mythic nature through the addition of specific incidents, psychologically plausible motivations and a setting in the very mundane world of Victorian England. Shaw's real joke, therefore, is that he has indeed given the world a Don Juan *play,* not merely a Don Juan *scene.*

In the dream symposium in hell, Shaw presents a void peopled with incorporeal characters. This conscious movement away from the particulars of a given scene is a method of universalizing, since the action is abstracted from concrete time and place, thereby creating a zone in which action becomes ceremony, and actors, archetypes. Instead of Tanner, Ann, Mendoza and Ramsden, Ann's guardian, we find hero, goddess, the Devil and Holdfast, the guardian of the status quo. Hell, with its ease of access to both heaven and earth, becomes, in effect, Shaw's satiric version of a sacred center of the universe. Using ritual techniques, Shaw expresses the philosophy of Creative Evolution, which becomes inclusive in that the major planes of experience are accounted for—the biological, the spiritual and the psychological. The hope for a superman is but another of the messianic visions that characterize many religions and which, like Creative Evolution, look forward to future generations. This belief in a messiah can also be correlated with Shaw's socialistic fervor since, as Eliade points out, "at the end of the Marxist philosophy of history lies the age of gold of the archaic eschatologies."

The age of gold Shaw envisions is possible only through evolution in a future time suggested by the play but not encompassed by the action. Thus, in order to make Creative Evolution dramatically viable, Shaw uses the Don Juan legend as his pre-eminent vehicle. Frequently occuring in musical and literary treatment, the legend has been raised to the level of myth through its reappearance apart from any historical context. Though our popular culture bears witness to the degeneration of many mythic patterns, these same patterns may revivify and function creatively for man. The changing character of Don Juan in treatments subsequent to Tirso de Molina's *El Burlador de Seville* attests to the vigor of this myth. The reason for this vigor is clear, for the myth expresses man's perennial longing for an earthly paradise. But the mundane form of the Don Juan myth does not disguise its similarity to Shaw's myth of Creative Evolution, which also has an earthly paradise as goal. Both Creative Evolution and the Don Juan myth express the same basic human desires, differ though they may in form and level of spirituality. In addition, the appropriateness of the Don Juan myth to Shaw's dramatic needs lies in its protean nature, evidenced in the multiple transformations undergone by the Don Juan figure in succeeding works of art. More important than the specific transformations the unfolding legend provides is the very fact of change itself. Thematically, the fluid Don Juan myth becomes a favorable milieu for Creative Evolution: the evolving form of the sexually based Don Juan myth becomes intimately associated with Shaw's evolutionary myth, which depends on the power of sexual energy for its ultimate triumph. Consequently, the legend—which Shaw alluded to in his first novel through the hero Don Juan Lothario Smith, and later in the short story "Don Giovanni Explains" through the ghost of Don Juan—becomes in *Man and Superman* the vehicle through which Shaw communicates his cosmic philosophy. And the Don Juan character, which has evolved and will evolve in yet uncreated works of art, becomes the logical complement to the elusive and variable Ann.

Against this mythic background, the woman-dominated action becomes at once more comic and also more necessary. It is more comic because, though the frivolity masks the profundity, the cosmic nature of Ann's very mortal quest calls forth the indulgent laughter of the kind that concludes the play. We look at the surface structure and witness, amused, a moral, unmarried woman, afraid to flout convention openly, yet determined to usurp the male prerogatives of choice, chase and capture. Ann's far from original actions place her in a long line of heroines from Shakespeare's Rosalind, as Shaw acknowledges in the Epistle Dedicatory, to Tennessee Williams's Maggie the Cat—women who *will* have their way. Ann's typicality, however, in no way supplants her archetypicality, which is based on the structural simplicity and range of her universal role. But the typicality of her modern role suggests that the role has undergone degeneration, thereby setting up an unrelieved comic tension in the play. Oblivious to this incongruity, Ann plays out her attenuated modern role against the awesome background her mythic precursors have erected.

The mythic background also makes the woman-dominated action more necessary, because the movement of the Life Force toward a more highly evolved human being requires the active participation of the female in capturing the male. If it is to serve Shaw's philosophical purpose, the Don Juan myth *must* be inverted. Of course, the inversion is apparent in both the romantic comedy and the dream symposium. Tanner's participation in a pattern that exactly imitates the acts of his ancestor thus endows with a ritualistic character his simultaneous fascination with and flight from Ann, while the act of repetition makes Tanner a contemporary of Don Juan in mythic terms.

Given this need for active women and, as a consequence, relatively passive men, Shaw's strict observance of the traditional man-woman/mind-body dichotomy is itself an inversion, since that dichotomy assumes the passivity of women and their corresponding domination by men. In examining this traditional phenomenon, J. C. Flugel observes that "there exists a very general association between the notion of mind, spirit or soul, and the idea of the father or of masculinity; and on the other hand between the notion of body or of matter (materia—that which belongs to the mother) and the idea of the mother or of the feminine principle." In general, the Victorians believed that women were passive. Faith in Woman's essential passivity encouraged Victorian men to relegate spiritual and moral concerns to her, thereby freeing the men to assume their aggressive and superior roles as captains of industry.

Shaw ignores this contemporary division in male-female roles in favor of the ahistorical view so vehemently asserted by Nietzsche. Nietzsche's simplistic avowal that "everything in woman hath a solution—it is called pregnancy," however, is modified by Shaw's Schopenhauerian belief in will. Ann, heir to this will, is consequently endowed with certain aggressive tendencies popularly thought to be masculine. But, psychologically, this is not necessarily so, according to the twentieth-century symbolist J. E. Cirlot, who believes that Western man is currently "dominated by the feminine principle." Thus, in her unrelenting desire to have her way, Ann, the representative of the feminine principle, is the antithesis of the fondly held Victorian view of Woman martyred upon the wishes and demands of others. Yet Ann's willingness to sacrifice her life for her maternal duty delineates ultimately an emotional similarity to the most docile Victorian wife. The means may differ; the end is the same. And what we see is Ann's manipulation of the means available to her, a trait that marks her as an unmistakably Shavian character. Through this manipulation Ann emerges supreme in a way Tanner does not even approximate, since her instincts transcend her limited awareness, while Tanner's intellect is by definition inferior to that of the evolving superman and by nature less forceful than Ann's will.

Although she lacks the higher intellect the superman will supposedly possess, Ann is more than an instrument of the Life Force, for she becomes identified with the essence of Creative Evolution itself. Her elusive nature, ever-changing, ever-various, is symbolic of the unending process involved in Creative Evolution. Such a process defies easy definition. Therefore the characters around her are able to discriminate only those qualities they most desire in a woman or expect to see. To Ramsden she is an inexperienced young woman; to Tanner she is a predatory animal; to Octavius she is a romanticized Earth Mother. These views of Ann all rely on the conception of Woman implicit in the mythic deep structure, making increasingly apparent the truth of Shaw's seeming jest in the Epistle Dedicatory: "every woman is not Ann; but Ann is Everywoman."

Ironically, it is Octavius's view of Ann that synthesizes these qualities and most directly refers to a mythic origin: *"To Octavius* [the stage directions assert] *she is an enchantingly beautiful woman in whose presence the world becomes transfigured, and the puny limits of individual consciousness are suddenly made infinite by the mystic memory of the whole life of the race to its beginning in the east, or even back to the paradise from which it fell."* The effete Octavius, because of his excessively romantic disposition an object of Shaw's satire and Tanner's pity, becomes a vehicle through which Shaw playfully incorporates mythic motifs; simultaneously, Shaw delights in Tanner's own romantically charged view of himself as *raisonneur* and Life Force advocate. The real humor is that Tanner, who warns Octavius of Ann, is ultimately vanquished by his own romantic temperament. When he recognizes imminent defeat, Tanner characteristically rationalizes his predicament by attributing to the Life Force his personal desires, and "renounc-[ing] the romantic possibilities of an unknown future."

Plagued as he is by chronic pragmatic astigmatism, Tanner's perception of Ann can only be partial, and therefore distorted. Octavius's view is also distorted, as long as it is limited to the transfiguring enchantment of a beautiful woman, but the implications of his view are far richer. Paradoxically, the illusion-blinded Octavius sees more of the total configurative pattern surrounding Ann than Tanner, who prides himself on his perception of the order of things. This pattern, which is not perceived in its totality by any single character, subsumes a startling array of roles: daughter, sister, virgin, temptress, bride and mother—all within the mythological role of Queen Goddess of the World, the archetypal goddess who consumes as well as nourishes. Ascribing this role to Ann implies both the humor inherent in all myth, as it perpetually renews itself in strange and marvelous forms, and Shaw's very special sense of the absurd. That the decorous Ann Whitefield, whose name suggests commonplace innocence and nubility, should rise, by means of her vitality, to genius and hence to godhead, is, of course, comically incongruous. But this very incongruity affirms the inexhaustible nature of the mythological experience, which is never naturalistic, but is rendered in fantastic and exaggerated shapes. From the broad comic viewpoint of joy in exuberant life, Ann as a large figure representing such life is eminently plausible. She is archetypal Woman, carrier of the Life Force, Shaw's embodiment of the Blakean credo of celebration: "Energy is eternal delight."

With Ann as goddess, and therefore lure and guide to the hero Tanner, comedy erupts as she tries to lead Tanner from *dianoia* to *nous,* from merely rational knowledge to the unifying wisdom possible only through determined will and faith. But Tanner, like many a mythic hero, does not know a goddess when he sees one. Consequently, he responds to Ann in a classic way, recognizing in her only the temptress, a role he disdains on intellectual grounds. Though Tanner is wonderfully unsuccessful in convincing Ann of anything, his limited view of her role has largely prevailed with the critics. What is amazing is the extent to which Ann's actions are defined through Tanner's labeling. It is the age-old power ploy of manipulation through categorization. Not content to compare Ann to one or two familiar predatory animals, Tanner refers to her variously, but not necessarily imaginatively, as "cat," "boa-constrictor," "lioness," "tiger," "bear," "spider," "bee," and "elephant." Ann, however, is merely amused as she becomes a veritable one-woman zoo. And we may wonder if Shaw has not *for once* overdone a good thing.

Yet Shaw has not arbitrarily chosen these unlikely animals only to allude outrageously to Ann's hunting instinct, as has been commonly assumed: These comic epithets playfully underscore a wide range of Ann's attributes. In mythic lore, the lioness is held to be a symbol of the *Magna Mater,* while the queen bee is associated with both the mother goddess and the Virgin Mary. These three roles represent the extreme of views held by Tanner, Octavius and Ramsden, respectively. Similarly, the creativity, aggressiveness and illusion associated with the spider are traits that Ann exhibits as she pursues and persuades, as much as she exhibits the strength and powerful libido which tradition accords the elephant.

But it is the snake epithet that occurs most often, at least four times. In addition, there is the stage business of the feather boa coiled around Tanner's neck. Inextricably identified with Eve—with whom Ann is linked in the stage directions—the snake more than any other creature symbolizes the feminine principle. With its sensuous movements, tenacious strength and glittering coloration, the snake is closely allied to the alluring, vividly garbed Ann, whose power lies in her insinuating charm, which Tanner suggests when he labels her "my dear Lady Mephistopheles." Even Ann's facile movement from young innocent to chaste seductress to unscrupulous huntress is reflected in the snake image, bringing to mind the periodic shedding of skin that gives the snake the appearance of becoming a new and different creature. Once again the evolutionary process, with which Ann is clearly associated, is suggested. Moreover, the snake is regarded as a symbol of energy, thereby epitomizing one of Ann's essential qualities.

The importance of the animal imagery extends beyond these affinities to Ann's portraiture. In the symbolic interpretation that makes the play's deep structure meaningful, the majority of the animals are considered lunar animals. The significance of the lunar relationship increases when we note that the cat (sacred to the Egyptian goddess of marriage), the bear (companion to Diana) and the tiger (symbolic of darkness and Dionysus) all have specific associations with the moon in various mythologies. In addition, there is an implied connection between these animals and basic instincts which preclude spirituality. Ann's powerful instincts and indifference to certain intellectual and spiritual qualities should therefore be viewed within the implied metaphorical framework of the moon, perennially evocative of desire.

The aptness of the lunar metaphor is readily apparent. Thought to be passive because it reflects the sun's light, the moon is traditionally associated with the feminine principle. Indeed, the physiological functioning of the female is viewed as in some way dependent on the fertility-controlling lunar cycle. Consequently, the additional feminine qualities of maternal love and protection are attributed to the moon, even while its half light creates an aura suggestive of danger and the unconscious. These lunar qualities surface in Ann's inability to explain her motives consciously. Nevertheless, she risks all to be wife and mother, even "perhaps death." More pointedly, Shaw's portrait of Ann is directly consistent with the major characteristic imputed to the moon, a felicitous ability to appear as both the chaste Diana and the sorceress Hecate. And the incessant modifications in its apparent shape that the moon undergoes are reflected in Ann's constant role-changing.

Ann's characterization, which is immediately exhibited in the play's surface structure and greatly affects the progress of the action, is, therefore, actually dependent on the mythic substructure. The entire surface structure itself is in fact regulated by the deep structure, which determines Ann's centrality and her metaphorical identification with the moon. For this identification to be in any way conclusive, the body of lunar myths must be taken into account, and they must effectively increase our understanding of the play.

Eliade has shown "the importance of lunar myths in the organization of the first coherent theories concerning death and resurrection, fertility and regeneration, [and] initiation." This is especially significant for *Man and Superman*, since the play's structure expresses Shaw's satiric view of societal interpretations of a number of rites of passage—birth, death, marriage and initiation. The opening of act 1 is actually a mock celebration of death, as family and friends manipulate the legal will of the deceased Mr. Whitefield so they can assert their own personal wills. Octavius and Ramsden luxuriate in their sorrow, trade sentimental clichés and gravely discuss Ann's future. The bereaved daughter, beautifully dressed in black and violet silk, *"which does honor to her late father,"* and expressing all the proper sentiments, uses the occasion to begin to have her way. This terrestrial view of death is reflected in Doña Ana's conventional views in the opening scene in hell, integrating the surface structure of the dream symposium with the romantic comedy. Don Juan, believing all such conventions to be masks of reality, disdains the code of conduct, just as Tanner ignores it. But both Ann and Doña Ana instinctively eschew death, being supremely concerned with life.

Dialectically balancing this mock celebration of death is the comic mourning of birth. The disclosure that the supposedly unmarried Violet Robinson is pregnant initiates the parody. In defending Violet, Tanner preaches the triumphant language of the Scriptures, strengthening the scene's ritualistic ties: " 'Unto us a child is born; unto us a son is given.' " This passage is paralleled by the segment in hell in which the superman subject is constantly implied as Don Juan speaks "of helping Life in its struggle upward." The possibility of change, which is evidenced in the restlessness of the characters, becomes all-important in hell's changeless environment. Don Juan wants to exchange his infernal residence for a heavenly one; the Statue wants to trade the tedium of heaven for the illusion of romance that hell provides; and the Devil claims to move back and forth between the two realms, citing the Book of Job as evidence. Implied in the desire for change are natural and supernatural birth, which are alluded to or examined in both structures of the play. Thus, in the romantic comedy, Tanner confesses to the birth of moral passion within him. Thematically, this description of the origin of Tanner's moral consciousness prefigures the discussion in hell, which posits the need for the advent of an intellectually superior being, by drawing attention away from the merely biological aspect of birth.

Having inverted the conventional rituals surrounding death and birth, Shaw inverts the rituals of wooing, with Ann pursuing Tanner on earth and Doña Ana pursing a father for the superman: "For though by her death she is done with the bearing of men to mortal fathers, she may yet, as Woman Immortal, bear the Superman to the Eternal Father." Shaw thus reinterprets, for the purposes of his myth, essential parts of the cycle of human experience, which satirically illuminate the community he is portraying.

But beneath the surface structure, Tanner moves through a series of adventures, which form a necessary prelude to his marriage to Ann. These adventures, though comic, are akin to the journey of the mythic hero as he is initiated into the mysteries of life. As hero, Tanner implicitly embodies those qualities complementary to Ann's lunar nature. Because of his courageous and vigorous renewal of the world order, the hero has frequently been considered a human analogue of the sun, the sun itself being allied with the masculine principle. In addition, the sun early was identified with the rational intelligence and, hence, with the philosopher. Tanner's characterization, of course, relies on his philosophical aspirations and his faith in the rational intelligence. The single god, however, that is most closely associated with the virtue of judgment is not Apollo, as might be expected. Rather it is Jupiter. The stage directions introducing Tanner are explicit. Not only is he *"prodigiously fluent of speech, restless, excitable"* with *"snorting nostril and . . . restless blue eye,"* but he also has an *"Olympian majesty,"* suggesting *"Jupiter rather than Apollo."* Tanner's belief that strength of judgment should forge destinies is immediately suggested by the analogy, since tradition grants Jupiter this mythical power. Despite such power, it was his union with the Great Goddess that made Jupiter sacred, although—unlike many sky gods—marriage did not diminish his ability to guarantee universal order. Tanner's view of marriage as a muffin-like affair may not be the *only* possibility.

These implicit mythic ascriptions to Tanner prepare us for his nightlong journey into hell, a journey, according to mythic lore, the sun makes each night. Tanner's metaphorical descent into his unconscious is a journey through the labyrinth of his own disordered thoughts and emotions, as he seeks through his pilgrimage an initiation into "absolute reality," what can be called the mystic center of his spirit. This journey takes place largely within the third act. The call to adventure is instigated by Ann's insistence, shocking to the blustering Tanner, that they motor across Europe together. *"Wildly appealing to the heavens,"* Tanner heeds the call, which indicates that he is on the threshold of new experience. Just as Goethe's Mephistopheles guides Don Juan's "cousin Faust," Tanner's supernatural guide is the Devil himself, who will attempt to win over the life-worshiping Tanner-Don Juan.

The Devil is first encountered as the bandit leader, Mendoza. His band of brigands, living in the seclusion of the Sierra Nevadas, is a transmutation of the dangerous creatures of mythology found in isoloated places. Whether generally described as dragons, ogres or monsters, or specifically defined like Pan and his satyrs or like the enticing Sirens—all these creatures represent tests for the hero who enters their domain. The kind of geographical isolation in which such creatures are found is fertile ground for the unconscious to project its fantasies, so that frequently in mythology the hero crosses the first threshold into a mysterious zone through a dream.

Tanner's dream—framed by Mendoza's suggestion that "this is a strange country for dreams," and his later question, "Did you dream?"—follows an ancient pattern. As the dream begins, the scene fades into the extraordinary world of hell, which functions as a sphere of rebirth attainable only after self-annihilation and hence metamorphosis have occurred. During the course of the dream, Tanner moves back in time to become his ancestor Don Juan, who, paradoxically, is more advanced spiritually than he. Don Juan's commentary, largely a response to Doña Ana, externalizes the long woman-dependent educational process he has undergone. As a result of this commentary, we glimpse his unrevealed soul, which, in the fashion of a medieval morality play, becomes the prize multiple adversaries vie for. Viewed from the standpoint of the play as a whole, Tanner articulates through his dream those psychological and intellectual obstacles which impede his struggle toward enlightenment. His reincarnation as Don Juan leads to his subsequent rebirth as a more mature individual, one better able to assume the responsibilities of fatherhood and the vagaries of life with Ann.

That this assumption of parental obligation is a *raison d'être* for the dream symposium is evident from the commentary in hell. There such subjects as civilization, morality and progress appear to be disparate. But actually all of the subjects are related to those posited in the romantic comedy—love, marriage, sex and Woman—since all contribute to an understanding of Creative Evolution, through which fathers are fashioned and, ultimately, supermen ascend. The theme of Creative Evolution is further reinforced by the physical and spiritual metamorphoses the characters undergo in hell, where the setting transforms earthly time and space. In the process of metamorphosis, the characters lose extraneous personal traits exhibited in the romantic comedy, leaving only the quintessential qualities necessary for the creation of the superman, fertility and energy in Doña Ana, and intellectual and spiritual striving in Don Juan. Doña Ana and Don Juan typify these qualities—or type them in the nineteenth-century vitalist sense—placing them in the line of inheritance. The entire play moves toward this evolutionary change that is at once supremely symbolized by Ann in her many guises and championed by Tanner-Don Juan, for the mythological hero heralds the Life to Come.

Theme, philosophy, action and psychology intersect, all levels of dramatic action indicating that the flux of life can be integrated, assimilated and regenerated through the union of the world-embracing goddess-mother and the world-renouncing hero-saint. This union can occur only after Tanner, as hero, has traveled to the underworld and brought back the boon of his life-restoring private insight to the waiting community. Very often in myth, because the hero fails to return unaided or refuses to abandon the joy he has found, the society which he has left must seek him, as is true in Tanner's case. He cannot, as Don Juan, be allowed to find his contemplative bliss in heaven; he must be brought back to the earthly world of practical reality and coerced by Ann into enriching the social community.

To the mythic journey of the hero, the presentation of rites of passage and the identification of the characters with archetypal figures must be added a fourth element of the mythic deep structure—setting. The first two acts are set in the present of Victorian England, suggesting the beginning of a pattern of growth, whose mature fruit will be evident in the Spanish Sierras of act 4. But before that happens, act 3 moves toward spatial freedom, opening in the uncertain light of evening and therefore signaling uncertain space amid the inhospitable arid landscape of the Sierra Nevadas. Scattered patches of olive trees, Jupiter's sacred tree, impart an ancient and religious aura. The mountains dominate the action; Tanner refers to the "august hill," and much stage movement involves climbing or sitting on rock formations. The symbolism of the mountains foreshadows the movement into the void of hell, for "the Sacred Mountain—where heaven and earth meet—is situated at the center of the world."

It is not only in act 3, though, that the center of the world is suggested. Again in act 4, the mountains overshadow the action. The universality of the action to ensue is indicated by the opening description of the setting which could *"fit Surrey as well as Spain,"* except for the *"Alhambra, the begging, and the color of the roads."* But the little drama that Tanner and Ann could act out on English soil is elevated and made more inclusive by the presence of the Alhambra in the background. Taking its name from the red of its clay bricks, the Alhambra, by means of its color, symbolizes passion, blood, fire

and sublimation. The dualism suggested by the opposition of passion and sublimation is specifically supported by the history of the Alhambra. This fortress
palace was originally constructed in the thirteenth century by Moorish mon-
archs, who were expelled some two and a half centuries later. Soon after, the
already damaged structure was partially demolished by the Spanish Charles
V to make room for a Renaissance palace of Italian style. Ravaged in the early
nineteenth century by Napoleon's army and then an earthquake, the building
remained standing. Man's blood lust and his spiritual ascendancy through
created art fuse in the history of the Alhambra, just as ages and cultures fuse
in its design. These evidences of the best and worst of man's intentions, which
are set against the expansive background of centuries, underscore the Alhambra's symbolic meaning and relate it to the "architectonic symbolism of the
Center." Eliade observes that "every temple or palace—and, by extension,
every sacred city or royal residence—is a Sacred Mountain, thus becoming
a Center. Being an *axis mundi,* the sacred city or temple is regarded as the
meeting place of heaven, earth, and hell."

As a center, the Alhambra reflects cosmic images, but it illuminates
Tanner's earthly struggle as well. The building is dominated by the famed
Fountain of the Lions, and it is the lion that is the animal most closely
associated mythologically with the sun and the masculine principle, and
therefore with Tanner. Also striking is the unusual architectural design,
which includes the ubiquitous use of water in both static and dynamic
forms, signifying death and rebirth. This strongly suggests that Tanner's
encounter in hell has revitalized him in the manner of a religious discipline;
his former self is annihilated as the result of the psychological rigor he has
undergone, and a new life awaits him.

At the same time that the action moves toward new life, it expands
outward into atemporality. Act 1 is set indoors, closed within Ramsden's
study, which is itself a symbol of outmoded liberalism and narrow perspective. Act 2 moves outdoors to *"the park of a country house."* In act 3 the
cultivated regions give way to an unknown mountainous zone, and finally
to the timeless eternity of hell. The force of the atemporality of act 3 carries
over into the fourth act, partially through the symbolism of the Alhambra
and partially through the hilly garden landscape. The setting stresses *"a
circular basin and fountain in the centre, surrounded by geometrical flower
beds, gravel paths, and clipped yew trees in the genteelest order,"* from
which steps lead to *"a flagged platform on the edge of infinite space at the
top of the hill."* This extremely ordered landscape signals the return to the
rational, conscious world, while the steps symbolize the spiritual evolution
Tanner has achieved. The flagged stone platform functions as an *omphalos,*

a ritualistic center, uniting heaven and earth and signifying the presence of the superhuman. Often the *omphalos* bears witness to a covenant—even such as will be made between Ann and Tanner. The fountain, imitative of the Alhambra's fountain, suggests the omnipresence of the Life Force and is situated at the absolute center of the sacred zone. Representing the symbolism of the center of the world is the presence of the yew trees, since these trees are considered a particular symbol of immortality and regeneration. And the implicit greenness of vegetation and water supports the suggestion of fertility and the life process.

This movement into atemporality and regeneration, which the setting traces, crucially depends on the existence of the dream symposium, the movement corresponding to Jung's hypothesis on dreams. Summarizing Jung's concept, Campbell states that archetypal themes appearing in dreams "are best interpreted ... by comparison with the analogous mythic forms.... Dreams, in Jung's view, are the natural reaction of the self-regulating psychic system and, as such, point forward to a higher, potential health, not simply backward to past crises." Thus Tanner's dream, which transposes a personal relationship into a universal fable of evolution and creation, powerfully affirms the possibilities for a regenerated society, even while it satirizes vice and folly. And Tanner, by means of the labyrinthine dream that has unfolded his hopes and beliefs, has simultaneously attained the center and knowledge of himself. Having journeyed successfully from hell, he has traveled the route Eliade shows the hero eternally traversing, "from death to life, from man to divinity." He has completed his initiation, becoming a worthy mate for Ann. Tanner may pun on being "sacrifice[d] ... at the altar," still believing he is "scapegoat" and sacrificial lamb, as Ann works her "magic" with "siren tones," but the humor really lies in his wry realization that the Life Force is triumphant. Tanner cries out: "The Life Force. I am in the grip of the Life Force." Soon after, *the echo from the past,* based on dialogue from the dream symposium, like the "echo from a former existence" which Ann earlier experienced, brings the dream of the third act directly into the romantic comedy: "When did all this happen to me before? Are we two dreaming?"

In terms of the play's deep structure, the promised marriage becomes a mystical marriage, which unites the contrary qualities of heaven and earth, sun and moon, representing Tanner's apprehension of life through Ann, who *is* life. This unique personal action of Ann and Tanner is so intimately connected with the community at large that only the sudden arrival of family and friends accomplishes the betrothal. The reluctant Tanner is finally brought into the social unit, the anticipated marriage ceremony serving to keep the community intact, thereby ostensibly reinforcing the status quo; however, the hoped-for birth of the superman, issuing from the union of Ann and Tanner, promises a new society rising above the morally archaic, absurdly flawed, human institutions of the present. The chorus of universal laughter attests to the transcendent nature with which life itself is endowed in vitalist philosophies. While Tanner protests that he is not a happy man, and Mendoza claims that life is a tragedy whether or not one gets one's heart's desire, the myth of Creative Evolution overcomes these petty tribulations, clothing Ann's uncertain fate as mother, and Tanner's pretensions, with the dark glory of a modern Divine Comedy.

And undoubtedly the quality of a Divine Comedy so permeates Ann's characterization that to perceive her in any shallow or less complex way is really not to perceive her at all. Once the essential relationship of the mythic deep structure to the surface comedy is revealed, many of the apparent problems and discrepancies in Ann's characterization fall away; indeed her portrait achieves a startling clarity of focus. Far more than merely a strong-willed young woman who overpowers a somewhat foolish bachelor, Ann, as Woman Incarnate in Shaw's dramatic version of evolutionary myth, becomes nothing less than the hope of the race in the movement toward a superman. Certainly Shaw's Everywoman is no less than the complete woman, the perfect realization of womanhood, what Kenneth Burke, after Aristotle, would call the *entelechialization* of woman. For there is that about Ann which can only be termed perfection—perfection of charm, of fascination, of endless complexity married to single-minded drive. Embodying all female biological drives in a plenary way, she is not merely the average woman with average instincts. Nor is she the stereotypical woman who is reduced to caricatured simplicity as mere predator or abortive mother-woman. She is archetypal Woman, whose role subsumes all roles. Biologically she may serve the species and socially she may seem to serve men, but psychologically she is free to woo and win as she chooses. And instead of Octavius, who plays at love and life and poetry, she chooses Tanner, who, infused with moral passion, can tell her he adores creation "in tree and flower, in bird and beast, even in you." Just as she rescues Tanner from his private inferno of self-doubt, thus enabling him to function unseparated from society, so she urges the passions in his soul and psyche to be expressed within the societal framework as he seeks order and renewal. Paradoxically identified with both the origin of life and the end toward which life aspires, Ann is a culminant figure, epitomizing an entire spectrum of related qualities and exemplifying Shaw's art of dramatic imitation in all the richness of its symbolizing and universalizing aspects.

NICHOLAS GRENE

Shavian History

There is a story (apocryphal no doubt) of a Cecil B. deMille epic in which the troops were roused by the stirring line, "Men of the Middle Ages, let us now rise up and go out and fight the Hundred Years War." Anachronism is of the essence in any dramatisation of history. We can only see what we can from where we are. To us the Middle Ages are the Middle Ages, after the Dark Ages, before the Renaissance; however little aware the soldiers at Crécy or Poitiers were of the fact, we know that the war they were fighting was to last on and off for roughly a hundred years. To ask modern actors to play the parts of historical figures, to write for them lines which will be intelligible to contemporary audiences, to make of the complicated and half-known facts of the past an immediate and dramatic present, is and must be anachronism enacted. Indeed, one of the commonest forms of inauthenticity in historical drama derives from a superficial concern with the accurate recreation of period. Scrupulously faithful costumes and décor, careful historical background research, can often do no more than make us aware that what we are watching is a shell of past action conspicuously empty of reality. If the history play or film is going to convince us, it must create its own reality which lives in our here and now.

But with the greatest history plays—and in English this means Shakespeare and nobody else—there is a profound sense of an encounter with the past. We all know the jokes about the conspirators in *Julius Caesar* with their very un-Roman hats plucked down over their faces. Yet T. S.

From *Bernard Shaw: A Critical View.* © 1984 by Nicholas Grene. Macmillan, 1984.

Eliot was surely right when he argued that "Shakespeare acquired more essential history from Plutarch than most men could from the whole British Museum." The Roman tragedies are very much plays of their own time, but they represent a vision of Roman history which is not merely a projection backwards of Renaissance England. There is in *Coriolanus* a vivid evocation of the atmosphere of the emergent Republic, in *Julius Caesar* and *Antony and Cleopatra* a compelling view of the power politics through which the Republic was turned into the Empire. Whether or not they represent historical truth, the plays show us Shakespeare's imagination inhabiting a milieu which is identifiably not his own, reaching out to a past which he authenticates by his capacity to imagine it.

Shaw in *Saint Joan* measured himself against Shakespeare, not obtrusively and aggressively as in *Caesar and Cleopatra,* but without diffidence either. In the preface he explained his procedure in conceiving the historical characters who surrounded Joan:

> I really knew no more about these men and their circle than Shakespear knew about Falconbridge and the Duke of Austria, or about Macbeth and Macduff. In view of the things they did in history, and have to do again in the play, I can only invent appropriate characters for them in Shakespear's manner.

But, he went on to claim, he was in a position to understand the medieval period as Shakespeare, living still too close to it in time, never could. That understanding, moreover, was an understanding of the significance of historical events which, he complained, Shakespeare never attempted: "a novice can read his plays from one end to the other without learning that the world is finally governed by forces expressing themselves in religions and laws which make epochs rather than by vulgarly ambitious individuals who make rows." His *Saint Joan* was to be more than a Shakespearean clash of characters, much more than a conventional costume drama:

> Those who see it performed will not mistake the startling result it records for a mere personal accident. They will have before them not only the visible and human puppets, but the Church, the Inquisition, the Feudal System, with divine inspiration always beating against their too inelastic limits: all more terrible in their dramatic force than any of the little mortal figures clanking about in plate armor or moving silently in the frocks and hoods of the order of St Dominic.

Shaw's object was to write a play in which what he took to be the historical significance of the life of the fifteenth-century saint would be manifest to a twentieth-century audience. What sort of dramatic reality was the result?

One answer is supplied in the preface, where Shaw speaks of *Saint Joan* as showing "the romance of her rise, the tragedy of her execution, and the comedy of the attempts of posterity to make amends for that execution." The play is in turn romance, tragedy and comedy, the three modes corresponding to its three movements: scenes 1–3 concerned with the rise of Joan up to the climax of the relief of the siege of Orléans; scenes 4–6 showing not only the trial and execution but the chain of circumstances which led up to it; and the epilogue which evokes the five-hundred-year-long rehabilitation which ended with Joan's canonisation in 1920. To try to define the quality of *Saint Joan* we need to consider the nature of these three modes and movements and how far they blend together to give us something which is both genuinely Shaw and genuinely a play about Joan of Arc.

Again and again in the preface and elsewhere, Shaw stressed that in writing the play he had done no more than dramatise the transcript of her trial and the later fifteenth-century enquiry which reversed the trial's verdict: "I took the only documents that are of the smallest value—the report of the process and that of the rehabilitation. I simply arranged what I found there for the stage, relying on Joan to pull me through, which she did." This is, of course, Shavian overstatement, but Brian Tyson has made clear how very closely Shaw did stick to his main source, T. Douglas Murray's edited and translated version of J. E. J. Quicherat's *Procès de Jeanne d'Arc*. In returning to the original documents, in rejecting the romantic legends which had grown up about Joan, Shaw felt that he could realise upon the stage the much more dramatic drama of the real-life events.

To a large extent, therefore, even the romance of Joan's rise to power which is represented in the first three scenes of the play is intended to be anti-romantic romance. Joan, Shaw stresses, was not good-looking, not the beautiful Maid of perfervid imagination. Taking as his model instead the head of St Maurice in Orléans, reputedly a portrait of Joan, he describes her as having "an uncommon face: eyes very wide apart and bulging as they often do in very imaginative people, a long well-shaped nose with wide nostrils, a short upper lip, resolute but full-lipped mouth, and handsome fighting chin." Jeanne, from Lorraine in the North of France, in Shaw becomes a rough-speaking country girl with a somewhat dubious North-country dialect. Most annoyingly, and most unconvincingly, Shaw gives to Joan the mannerism which he so frequently gives to his masterful young

women, that of calling the other characters by nicknames. Just as Octavius
Robinson and Roebuck Ramsden are Ann's Tavy and Granny, as Adolphus
Cusins and Charles Lomax become Barbara's Salvation Army recruits Dolly
and Cholly, so Joan makes a Jack of Sieur Jean de Metz, a Polly of Bertrand
de Poulengy, and a Charlie of the Dauphin. The more resounding the name,
the more Shaw delights in reducing it to a nursery-like familiarity which
bespeaks the effortless and humiliating control exercised by his strong
heroines.

Throughout Shaw is bent on demystifying the figure of Joan. She is to
be seen as plain-speaking, buoyant, unabashed, unreverent. Shaw could
never conceive "a great man as a grave man," and his Saint Joan, as much
as his Caesar, was to have little time for conventional gravity. But Eric
Bentley is exactly right when he claims that Shaw's intention was not only
to "show Joan as a credible human being" but to "make her *greatness*
credible." He was determined to remove the glamour of the legendary Joan
because by making her apparently ordinary, he could all the more effectively
highlight what was truly extraordinary in her character—the energy, the
resolution, the unswerving will. Throughout the first three scenes of the
play, the romance section, we see her steadily imposing her will on others.
Robert de Baudricourt, her first and easiest victim, is characterised as
"handsome and physically energetic, but with no will of his own" and when
the play opens he "is disguising that defect in his usual fashion by storming
terribly at his steward." The unfortunate steward, with his deficient hens, is
there to represent the bottom of a heap which Joan will swiftly climb to the
top. In the second scene her success is all the more remarkable because it is
the Dauphin, with his tenacious instinct for survival by the line of least
resistance, whom she must inspire with her fighting spirit. There is a significant replay in the interview between Joan and the Dauphin of the encounter between Caesar and Cleopatra. Just as Caesar taught Cleopatra
queenliness, Joan, by a similar mixture of harrying and coaxing, gives the
Dauphin a crash-course in kingliness. Both are lessons in the use of the will.
But the reversal of roles, by which it is the adolescent girl who teaches the
older man, makes Joan's achievement all the more striking and enforces
Shaw's point that the vital genius, the figure of outstanding will, may appear
in any human shape or form.

In the opening scenes of the play Shaw thus goes far towards establishing Joan an an anti-romantic Shavian superwoman. Yet he does not
altogether deny to the audience the Maid of romance with her voices and
miracles. The voices were clearly a problem for Shaw, as he made clear in
the preface:

I cannot believe, nor, if I could, could I expect all my readers to believe, as Joan did, that three ocularly visible well dressed persons, named respectively Saint Catherine, Saint Margaret, and Saint Michael, came down from heaven and gave her certain instructions with which they were charged by God for her. Not that such a belief would be more improbable or fantastic than some modern beliefs which we all swallow; but there are fashions and family habits in belief, and it happens that, my fashion being Victorian and my family habit Protestant, I find myself unable to attach any such objective validity to the form of Joan's visions.

Shaw accordingly interpreted the voices as "the dramatisation by Joan's imagination of that pressure upon her of the driving force that is behind evolution." In the opening scene he shows Joan herself aware of this interpretation:

> JOAN: I hear voices telling me what to do. They come from God.
> ROBERT: They come from your imagination.
> JOAN: Of course. That is how the messages of God come to us.

And later she admits that they may be "only echoes of my own commonsense." But there can be little doubt that Jeanne d'Arc believed in her communication with the saints at a much more literal level than this. At her trial attempts were made to suggest that she suffered from hallucinations brought about by fasting, or even perhaps from erotic fantasies which might be the sign of demonic possession (as in the authentic question, which Shaw borrows, about whether St Michael appeared to her as a naked man), but Jeanne countered them all with solidly detailed testimony as to the nature of her supernatural visitations. There is an uneasy tension within *Saint Joan* between the representation of the historical Joan's real belief in her voices and Shaw's desire to credit her with something more like his own rationalistic attitude.

Shaw's treatment of Joan's miracles is even more ambiguous, and in some ways less defensible. The Archbishop of Rheims in the second scene gives a non-miraculous account of miracles. He explains to La Trémouille in advance that Joan will be able to spot the substitution of Gilles de Rais for the Dauphin: "She will know what everybody in Chinon knows: that the Dauphin is the meanest-looking and worst-dressed figure in the Court, and that the man with the blue beard is Gilles de Rais." But this, he goes on to add, will not make it any less of a miracle.

A miracle, my friend, is an event which creates faith. That is the purpose and nature of miracles. They may seem very wonderful to the people who witness them, and very simple to those who perform them. That does not matter: if they confirm or create faith they are true miracles.

This concept of the miracle as a faith-creating conjuring trick might seem to be Shaw's own. Several critics have assumed that we are not intended to accept Joan's miracles at their face value, but instead to witness their effect on those more credulous than ourselves. However, when we consider the dramatic use to which the miracles are put, it is hard to sustain this view.

The miracle of the eggs in the first scene was, as Shaw himself explained, an invention to take the place of the real event which convinced or converted Robert de Baudricourt:

The apparent miracle which impressed him was the news of the Battle of Herrings. Joan learnt this from the mouth to mouth wireless of the peasantry. She was therefore able to tell him what had happened several days before the news reached him by the official routine of mounted messenger. This seemed to him miraculous. A much simpler form of miracle has been substituted in the play to save tedious and unnecessary explanations.

In giving a sceptical explanation of the real-life "miracle" here, Shaw would seem to imply that the invented substitute is of a similar order. But this is hardly the effect of the strong ending of the first scene:

> *The steward runs in with a basket.*
> STEWARD: Sir, sir—
> ROBERT: What now?
> STEWARD: The hens are laying like mad, sir. Five dozen eggs!
> ROBERT [*stiffens convulsively; crosses himself; and forms with his pale lips the words*]: Christ in heaven! [*Aloud but breathless*] She did come from God.

This is pure ham, but it is surely unironic ham, intended to send shivers of excitement up the spine in the theatre. Similarly with the changing of the wind before Orléans in scene 3.

> DUNOIS [*looking at the pennon*]: The wind has changed. [*He crosses himself*] God has spoken. [*Kneeling and handing his baton to Joan*] You command the king's army. I am your soldier.

In performance it is impossible to respond at this moment with sceptical detachment, to smile at Dunois's naïveté (he is not naïve) in seeing supernatural meaning in a natural event. To claim that Shaw, at moments like these, is "satirising popular religious psychology" is like the neo-classical critics who defended Homer's (otherwise improper) inclusion of the marvellous in *The Odyssey* by explaining that all those stories of the Cyclops and the Sirens were simply fantasies invented by Odysseus for the benefit of the gullible Phaeacians.

Each of the first three scenes of *Saint Joan* ends with a similar high-point, as the miracles of the Maid create faith in those around her. The audience is surely intended to share this excitement. And yet at some level we must be affected by Shaw's partial scepticism, his awareness that what he is writing is "romance." Sybil Thorndike recounts how when Shaw first read the play to her, after she had listened spell-bound to the opening three scenes, he remarked "That's all flapdoodle up to there—just 'theatre' to get you interested—now the play begins." One suspects that the comment may have been partly a matter of embarrassment at the romantic nature of these scenes, but there is nevertheless a damning ring of truth to it. The romance section of the play is skilfully crafted—Shaw had not worked in the theatre for thirty years for nothing—but, with its blend of farcical comedy and drama, its atmospheric kingfishers on the Loire, it seems often more a knowing exploitation of theatricality than an action of real dramatic integrity.

And Shaw's real business does begin in scene 4. The tent-scene is a brilliant and wholly Shavian invention which is crucial to the play's structure. It gives Joan herself a much-needed break from the stage and in her absence makes possible a broad and generalising discussion of the meaning of her life and (in anticipation) of her death. Shaw chooses for his interlocutors the Earl of Warwick, who commanded the English forces at the time of Joan's capture and execution, and the Bishop of Beauvais who presided over her trial. They represent in this scene the viewpoint of the feudal nobility and of the Church, as Shaw saw it the two great forces to which Joan was opposed. They are characterised only to the limited extent that they need to be contrasted. It scarcely matters if we agree with Desmond MacCarthy that Warwick "is a purely eighteenth-century nobleman." There is no effort made to pretend that Cauchon and Warwick are "in period" in this scene; rather they self-consciously expound what they are about in a conversation which is necessarily out of normal historical time. The principle involved is the cardinal one for Shaw, advanced in the preface: "it is the business of the stage to make its figures more intelligble to themselves than they would be in real life; for by no other means can they be made intelligible to the audience." The third party to the conversation in the tent-scene, the English chaplain De Stogumber, has been very commonly written off as one of Shaw's mistakes in the play. However irritating we may find Shaw's crude and silly caricature of the chauvinist Englishman, he does to some extent turn that irritation to account by making of De Stogumber the butt of Cauchon and Warwick as well as our butt, by using his clownish interruptions to vary and punctuate the main formal debate.

The purpose of the debate is to establish the essential principles of Protestantism and nationalism for which Shaw claimed Joan stood. In a cleverly choreographed dialogue, Warwick the feudalist and Cauchon the Catholic churchman diagnose the two ideas associated with Joan which they are resolved to combat. On the one hand, as Warwick says, there is "the protest of the individual soul against the interference of priest or peer between the private man and his God. I should call it Protestantism if I had to find a name for it." On the other, as Cauchon puts it, for Joan "the French-speaking people are what the Holy Scriptures describe as a nation. Call this side of her heresy Nationalism if you will." There were, inevitably, protests against this interpretation of Shaw's as eccentric and wildly anachronistic, but he had more than a little support for it in his source. He might well have taken his cue for Joan's nationalism from a comment in T. Douglas Murray's Introduction:

> Nations in the modern sense had not fully arisen. The State was everything. Whether a great Anglo-French monarchy sitting in Paris ruled over France, England, Ireland, and Wales, or a more domestic French line only ruled over France itself, was a question on which upright men might well take opposite sides. Jeanne's special merit was that she saw the possibility of a great French nation, self-centered, self-sufficient, and she so stamped this message on the French heart that its characters have never faded.

Her "Protestantism" is illustrated on page after page of the transcript of her trial, as she refused categorically to accept that the Church Militant was a higher authority than her own sense of her divine mission. When she was asked, "Will you submit your actions and words to the decision of the Church?," she replied, "My words and deeds are all in God's hands: in all I wait upon him," or again:

"Will you refer yourself to the decision of the Church?"
"I refer myself to God Who sent me, to our Lady, and to all the
  Saints in Paradise. And in my opinion it is all one, God
  and the Church; and one should make no difficulty about
  it."

The rehabilitation enquiry was at pains to try to establish that Joan had been willing to submit her case to the Pope or to a General Council of the Church, refusing to accept the judgement only of the ecclesiastical court which was packed with her political enemies. That was the view, also, of Shaw's friend the Irish priest, Father Leonard, who acted as his "technical adviser" while he was writing the play. But the occasional references in the trial itself to the possibility of an appeal to the Pope appear to be ambiguous at best, and there is much to support Shaw's reading of Joan as unable to accept any authority which would deny the truth of her personal inspiration by God.

Whether we accept Joan as proto-nationalist, proto-Protestant or not, there is a remarkable detachment in the presentation of the arguments in the tent-scene. Shaw has perhaps relatively little real sympathy for Warwick's point of view, the feudal barons' fear of a centralised monarchy which would break their power deriving from Joan's idea of the king as God's deputy, but Warwick is allowed to present it articulately and with force. But to Cauchon the Catholic Shaw gives real eloquence:

> What will the world be like when The Church's accumulated
> wisdom and knowledge and experience, its councils of learned,
> venerable pious men, are thrust into the kennel by every ignorant
> laborer or dairy-maid whom the devil can puff up with the mon-
> strous self-conceit of being directly inspired from heaven? It will
> be a world of blood, of fury, of devastation, of each man striving
> for his own hand: in the end a world wrecked back into barbar-
> ism.

With all the "holy wars" of the Reformation and Counter-Reformation to look back on, not to mention the nationalist conflicts which had culminated in Shaw's day in the First World War, the identification of Joan as Protes-tant and nationalist was no doubt intended to give us pause. Robert Whitman scarcely puts it too strongly when he says that Shaw's Joan appears as the "saint of emergent capitalism." And yet we are made to feel that the attitude of Cauchon and Warwick, however deeply understandable, is a reactionary one, and that the spirit of Joan, however terrible its historical consequences, must be supported against them. Shaw was an internationalist politically, and the medieval idea of a supranational state and church should have had much to recommend it to him. Elsewhere in his work, most notably in *John Bull's Other Island,* he appeals to a concept of fully catholic Catholicism transcending national barriers as an ultimate ideal. But he resisted the common nineteenth-century socialist tendency to sentimentalise medieval feudalism, and instead celebrated Joan as one of those exceptional historical figures whose mission is to move the world on, even if it was to move it on to other terrible eras.

If scene 4 shows us the full force of Joan's enemies and what they stood for, scene 5 gives the equivalent picture of how little support she was to expect from her friends. Just as he left Joan immediately before the triumph for the relief of Orléans, it was a real dramatist's instinct which made Shaw return to her in Rheims cathedral immediately after the great climax of the crowning of the Dauphin. With Joan praying in the empty cathedral, we catch a glimpse of a private moment between two public shows, the coronation and the appearance to the people outside. In this behind-the-scenes atmosphere, Shaw builds up naturally and effectively the sense of her isolation. Once again the individual characters who warn Joan stand for more than themselves. If she is captured, she will not have the support of the monarchy—Charles will not ransom her; though the Archbishop of Rheims is on her side politically, he will not use the authority of the Church to help her against Cauchon and the Inquisition; Dunois, her closest friend and companion in arms, yet speaks firmly for the army that he will not risk the life of a single soldier to save her. With immense skill Shaw creates out of the individual voices a formal chorus of renunciation.

That chorus is designed to bring out the developing emotions of Joan. She begins in the affectionate intimacy of a conversation with Dunois who, for all his feeling for her, cannot really understand when she tries to tell him about her voices: "You make me uneasy when you talk about your voices: I should think you were a bit cracked if I hadnt noticed that you give me very sensible reasons for what you do, though I hear you telling others you are only obeying Madame Saint Catherine." To which Joan can only retort "crossly," "Well, I have to find reasons for you, because you do not believe in my voices. But the voices come first; and I find the reasons after: whatever you may choose to believe." It is almost as though in Dunois Shaw parodied his own inclination to rationalise Joan's voices—he too uses the mocking "Madame Saint Catherine" in the preface. The relationship between Joan and Dunois remains an affectionate one, but limited in understanding. When they are joined by the other main characters, Joan makes a rather half-hearted offer to the King to return to her village now her mission to crown him in Rheims has been accomplished, and is visibly hurt and taken aback by the alacrity with which the offer is accepted. She is stung to vociferous and belligerent opposition by talk of treaties and an unwillingness on the part of the French to press home the advantages she has won for them. She attacks the faint-hearts with rough arrogance: "I tell you, Bastard, your art of war is no use, because your knights are no good for real fighting." It is only by degrees that she registers the full force of the animus against her and her arguments, and in the rhetorical clash the other voices in the chorus come to dominate hers. She is horrified and bewildered by the threats that are made against her.

And yet out of that horror and bewilderment, out of the relisation that she is alone, she draws the strength which is expressed in one of the greatest speeches in Shaw. It must be quoted at length:

> Yes: I am alone on earth: I have always been alone. My father told my brothers to drown me if I would not stay to mind his sheep while France was bleeding to death: France might perish if only our lambs were safe. I thought France would have friends at the court of the king of France; and I find only wolves fighting for pieces of her poor torn body. I thought God would have friends everywhere, because He is the friend of everyone; and in my innocence I believed that you who now cast me out would be like strong towers to keep harm from me. But I am wiser now; and nobody is any the worse for being wiser. Do not think you can frighten me by telling me that I am alone. France is alone; and God is alone; and what is my loneliness before the loneliness of my country and my God? I see now that the loneliness of God is his strength: what would He be if He listened to your jealous little counsels? Well, my loneliness shall be my strength too; it is better to be alone with God: His friendship will not fail me, nor His counsel, nor His love. In His strength I will dare, and dare, and dare, until I die. I will go out now to the common people, and let the love in their eyes comfort me for the hate in yours. You will all be glad to see me burnt; but if I go through the fire I shall go through it to their hearts for ever and ever. And so, God be with me!

The scriptural echoes of so much of this speech are made all the more effective for the development of the pastoral image from literal to meta-phorical level. The two main rhetorical movements are separated by a nicely judged piece of commonsensical colloquialism: "But I am wiser now; and nobody is any the worse for being wiser." The touch of childish petulance— "You will all be glad to see me burnt"—is turned into a ringing affirmation of the meaning of martyrdom. It is here that we truly see what Shaw meant by calling Joan a Protestant. As Brian Tyson has pointed out, the speech draws upon the final lines of Stockmann in *An Enemy of the People,* "the strongest man in the world is he who stands most alone." There is a strain of absolute individualism in Ibsen, however hedged round with ironies it may be in the figure of Stockmann, and it is this Protestant individualist stance which Shaw attributes to Joan: "it is better to be alone with God."

In the trial-scene Shaw did, very nearly, what he claimed he had done, that is to dramatise and arrange the events, even the very words, which he found in the original documents. Many of the questions and many of Joan's replies are taken all but verbatim from Murray and, though Joan's recantation and subsequent retraction of the recantation happened over a period of days, what Shaw gives is only a theatrically heightened image of what actually took place. The main Shavian invention in the trial-scene is the figure of the Inquisitor and the immensely long speech he is given in defence of his role. Shaw's insistence, against all the traditional prejudices, that the judges who tried Joan were fair-minded and reasonable men is, of course, one of the key features of the play and provoked the most controversy (as no doubt it was intended to do). The Inquisitor's apologia might seem to be the ultimate achievement in Shavian devil's advocacy. Certainly Murray, his main source from whom he derived so much, took the conventional view of the authorities who tried Joan. "The worst of these servile churchmen was the wretched Bishop of Beauvais, Pierre Cauchon. Many other prelates were Caesar's friends, but he sits exalted in solitary infamy." Yet it was not merely perversity which made Shaw try to reverse this verdict on Joan's accusers. Reading through the account of the trial and the rehabilitation enquiry, one can see why Shaw saw it as he did. There can be little doubt that the Bishop of Beauvais, as supporter of the English, under constant pressure to find Jeanne guilty, must have to some extent been biased against her. Yet the trial lasted over three months, Jeanne was very comprehensively examined and frequently exhorted to repent, and though some anecdotal evidence suggests that Cauchon was determined to find a means to convict her even after the recantation, there is also a suggestion—on which Shaw built—that he refused to act merely as an ecclesiastical stooge for the English. It was not a kangaroo-court that tried Jeanne d'Arc; if it was, obviously, in some sense a political trial, the rehabilitation proceedings were

every bit as political, perhaps more evidently bent on redeeming the reputation of Jeanne than the original judges were on convicting her.

Shaw acknowledged in the preface that he flattered the character of
Cauchon, virtually invented the character of the Inquisitor, who is a very
shadowy figure in the account of the trial. But he argues that such were the
"inevitable flatteries of tragedy," that in order to make the trial of Joan fully
significant, he had to make her judges the best possible representatives of the
system that found her guilty:

> It is, I repeat, what normally innocent people do that concerns
> us; and if Joan had not been burnt by normally innocent people
> in the energy of their righteousness her death at their hands
> would have no more significance than the Tokyo earthquake,
> which burnt a great many maidens. The tragedy of such murders
> is that they are not committed by murderers. They are judicial
> murders, pious murders; and this contradiction at once brings an
> element of comedy into the tragedy.

This is a very significant passage. It is typical of Shaw in his refusal to be
interested in evil, his belief that most of what is wrong in the world is caused
by misguided people acting according to their lights. It explains why he
lavishes on Cauchon and the Inquisitor such evident sincerity, such reasoning force and eloquence. They are serious men who fervently believe in their
principles; they are only terribly, tragically mistaken. And yet, as Shaw
admits, there is comedy in that tragic conviction and in the clarity with
which it is seen. One of Shaw's greatest comic gifts was to show the inevitable clash of impenetrable argumentative attitudes. In the trial-scene in
Saint Joan he put that comic gift to the service of tragedy:

> CAUCHON: . . . Joan: I am going to put a most solemn question
>   to you. Take care how you answer; for your life and salva-
>   tion are at stake on it. Will you for all you have said and
>   done, be it good or bad, accept the judgement of God's
>   Church on earth? More especially as to the acts and words
>   that are imputed to you in this trial by the Promoter here,
>   will you submit your case to the inspired interpretation of
>   the Church Militant?
> JOAN: I am a faithful child of the Church. I will obey the Church—
> CAUCHON [*hopefully leaning forward*]: You will?
> JOAN: —provided it does not command anything impossible.
>   *Cauchon sinks back in his chair with a heavy sigh. The*

> *Inquisitor purses his lips and frowns. Ladvenu shakes his head pitifully.*

Joan's reply here is taken more or less directly from the trial transcript— "On all that I am asked I will refer to the Church Militant, provided they do not command anything impossible." But Shaw in building up the solemnity of Cauchon's question, in breaking Joan's reply, makes of this a moment of anticlimax which is basically a comic technique. Joan cannot understand what seems so appallingly heretical to the judges in what she has said; the judges cannot for a moment enter into Joan's view of things. In another context we might be able to laugh; here the gap in understanding is too wide, the consequences too terrible, to make it a laughing matter.

Shaw talks of the tragedy of Joan's execution, coming after the romance of her rise. Is it in fact tragedy as he represents it? It has been a much argued question. The common view at the time of the play's first production was that Shaw, for once, had written a true tragedy, but had then ruined it by the addition of his comic excrescence of an epilogue. Arland Ussher has argued just the opposite, that it is rather the burning of Joan which is anomalous, out of key with the rest of the play and that the purpose of the epilogue is "in fact, to restore the easy argumentative note which the intrusion of the brutal historical facts has a little disturbed." This is perhaps somewhat unfair—the clash of irreconcilable points of view in the trial is in some sense experienced as a tragic clash—but it is true to the extent that Shaw is unwilling to face the full horror of Joan's execution. He could never bear really to imagine the idea of pain, and one of the reasons that he opposed what he called "Crosstianity" so vigorously was that he could not accept suffering as redemptive. It is not accidental, therefore, that he chooses to register the effect of the burning through the buffoon turned grotesque figure of De Stogumber. The English Chaplain, the most vehement opponent of Joan, who earlier declared his willingness to burn her with his own hands, is utterly horrified by the sight itself. His broken and hysterical words are intended to demonstrate the degree to which cruelty is merely lack of imagination. But this is hardly a full apprehension of the tragic nature of Joan's death, and Shaw keeps De Stogumber's comic chauvinism to the end: "Some of the people laughed at her. They would have laughed at Christ. They were French people, my lord: I know they were French." We pity De Stogumber, we are even moved by his "conversion," but we are left with enough detachment to smile at his unconverted partisanship.

From the moment of Joan's exit at the end of the trial, we can see Shaw tuning the play back towards the serio-comic tone of the epilogue. Even the appearance of the Executioner involves a joke (lifted directly from Shakespeare's Abhorson in *Measure for Measure*):

> WARWICK: Well, fellow: who are you?
>
> THE EXECUTIONER [*with dignity*]: I am not addressed as fellow, my lord. I am the Master Executioner of Rouen: it is a highly skilled mystery.

At certain moments Shaw is prepared to risk drastically lessening the impact of the trial we have witnessed in order to achieve this retuning of tone. As Cauchon is about to hurry out to stop the English dragging Joan straight to the stake without formal sentence by the secular authorities (as they in fact did), the Inquisitor holds him back: "We have proceeded in perfect order. If the English choose to put themselves in the wrong, it is not our business to put them in the right. A flaw in the procedure may be useful later on: one never knows." There is a similar effect with the last line of the scene; when the Executioner assures Warwick that he has "heard the last of her," he replies, "The last of her? Hm! I wonder!" Shaw here prepares us for the reappearance of Joan in the epilogue, prepares us for the continuation of her story into the "comedy of the attempts of posterity to make amends" to her. But the knowingness of these lines given to the Inquisitor and to Warwick seems a real indecorum in context. The whole force of the trial-scene depends on the assumption that Joan's judges, and the Inquisitor especially, are men of complete probity. The suggestion that in fact the Inquisitor has one eye on the future when a technical loophole might be desirable, surely comes close to sabotaging altogether the integrity of the character. There is a theatrical slickness in Warwick's curtain-line which again seems to betray the seriousness of what we have just seen. Shaw's irresistible urge to turn his characters into smart-alecs rarely served him worse.

The epilogue was essential to the play from Shaw's point of view: "I could hardly be expected to stultify myself by implying that Joan's history in the world ended unhappily with her execution, instead of beginning there. It was necessary by hook or crook to shew the canonised Joan as well as the incinerated one." And hence we get a dream-sequence like that in *Man and Superman* with a similar comic eschatology: the Soldier describing the jolliness of Hell—"Like as if you were always drunk without the trouble and expense of drinking. Tip top company too: emperors and popes and kings and all sorts." This vein of schoolboy facetiousness, so irritating and yet in a way rather endearing, is very characterisitic of Shaw. The English soldier, in fact, had figured in his first fantastic sketch of what he might do with a "Joan play"—"beginning with the sweeping up of the cinders and orange peel *after* her martyrdom, and going on with Joan's arrival in heaven." The epilogue is anti-tragic in that it allows us to escape the finality of death, so fundamental to the sense of tragedy, into a region of cosy immortality in which the characters can congregate amicably to discuss the action.

But the epilogue is not merely Shaw the joker taking over after the self-restraint of the tragic drama. There is more to it than the opportunity for Joan to exchange bantering repartee with all the other characters, to give her shrewd comments on all that happened after her death. It is a real attempt to show Joan's tragedy in the ultimate light of divine comedy. The epilogue is intended as a salute to the spirit of Joan and what it achieved both in the short term—the freeing of France, and the firm establishment of Charles VI on the throne—and in the long term—the inspiration to later generations recognised finally in the canonisation in 1920. This is formally expressed in the litany of praise from her assembled friends and enemies who kneel to her, in thanks for showing them their limitations. But this is followed by a deliberate anticlimax:

> JOAN: . . . And now tell me: shall I rise from the dead, and come
> back to you a living woman?
> *A sudden darkness blots out the walls of the room as they*
> *all spring to their feet in consternation.*

One by one, in a pattern of denial to match the previous paean of praise, they refuse to accept the idea of her return. Shaw's design here is to repeat in little the basic structure of the play as a whole: the inspiring force of Joan which occupies the first half, met by the worldly sources which in the second half doom her to death. Projected on to a scale of eternal recurrence this figures what for Shaw is the ultimate tragedy of Joan, that the heroic can never be accepted in its own time, by implication the earth will never be ready to receive its saints.

"Joan of Arc as the subject of a historical hypothesis, as Shaw would have it, an exponent of certain ways of thinking—there is something annoying about it. In her irreducible uniqueness she can be understood only by means of a sense of sympathetic admiration." We may well be inclined to agree here with the medieval historian Johan Huizinga. For all the extraordinary skill of Shaw's dialectic in identifying Joan with emergent Protestantism and nationalism, there *is* something annoying about it. It is hard to repress a feeling that this is no more than Shavian cleverness. And yet, as Huizinga himself admits, what is remarkable is that Shaw did respond to

Joan with the necessary "sense of sympathetic admiration," was inspired by "her irreducible uniqueness." There was in this an element of personal identification with Joan, as many critics were quick to point out. Joan's single-mindedness, her militant spirit, her directness in cutting through forms and ceremonies to the heart of the matter, all of these were essentially congenial to Shaw. He may well also have been attracted to her asceticism and her chaste asexuality. Earlier playwrights had romanticised Joan's relationship with her followers, particularly La Hire. Shaw instead lays great emphasis on her fellow-soldiers who testified to her lack of sexual attractiveness. Joan at last gave Shaw a subject without what was for him the distracting nuisance of sex. Above all where he felt an affinity with Joan was in the capacity to be right when everyone else was wrong. There is a splendid anecdote told by Archibald Henderson—so well-turned that one suspects Shaw ghost-wrote it—about a lecture on Joan of Arc in which Shaw summed up all the various ways in which Joan "knew everybody's business better than they knew it themselves." He worked up to the deliberately provocative peroration: "After pondering over the matter for a time, I finally hit upon the perfect word which exactly describes Joan: *insufferable*." He got the reaction he was looking for from the lady who moved the vote of thanks, who pointed out "the one fundamental error into which Mr Shaw had fallen: it is not Joan of Arc, but Mr Bernard Shaw who is insufferable." From Shaw's point of view, they were both insufferable because they told the truths that nobody wanted to hear. Arland Ussher sees an element of "nostalgia" in this identification: "The hero who is laughed at, tolerated, petted, cannot conceal a certain envy for the heroine who is taken seriously and killed." Perhaps—Shaw, though courageous enough, was not the stuff of which martyrs are made. But he was convinced that he was, like Joan, if not a martyr at least a witness to an understanding of the world which could only come after him. Whether or nor this now seems like a delusion, it was a real emotional source for *Saint Joan*.

To emphasise the element of personal identification might be to suggest, what some people have felt, that what we get is really a Joan cut down to Shavian size. Negatively it is true that there are aspects of Jeanne d'Arc that Shaw could not engage with imaginatively and which he omits from his representation. One of the most poignant features of the trial transcript is Jeanne's repeated pleas to be allowed to hear Mass, repeatedly refused except on the condition that she abandon her masculine dress. Although Shaw alludes to her devoutness in the preface, this very Catholic need to participate in the ritual of the Mass could not be made part of his "Protestant" Saint Joan. The certainty and resolution of Joan's faith were central for Shaw. As a result he could not really render the moving sense of humility expressed in the phrase Jeanne used so frequently in the trial: "I wait on Our Lord." Shaw's religion is a rational irrationalism without mystery and in making Joan a saint of Creative Evolution, he could scarcely present her with the attributes of a canonised saint of the Roman Catholic Church. Hence the ambiguity of the treatment of the voices and the miracles. But Shaw's imagination did go out to Joan, he did dramatise something of the extraordinary quality of her life. *Saint Joan* may not be tragedy; there is a deliberateness, a clarity about its form and significance which seem to take away the sense of awe and bewilderment which tragedy at its most profound evokes.

BARBARA M. FISHER

Fanny's First Play: *A Critical Potboiler?*

Fanny's First Play opened in London on April 19, 1911, after a hasty two weeks of rehearsal. It continued to run, first at the Little Theatre and then at the Kingsway, for a total of 622 performances—the longest unbroken run of any Shaw play. *Fanny* had a "rapturous reception," comments C. B. Purdom, "not in the least diminished by the pretence that the play was not, perhaps, by Bernard Shaw." When Shaw handed the script to Lillah McCarthy, who was to play Margaret, he told her he hadn't put his name to it and urged her to "do everything to suggest the play is by Barrie." Theatergoers who attended the opening performance, that Wednesday afternoon, found the author displayed on the playbill as "Xxxxxxx Xxxx."

Shaw clearly did not anticipate the tremendous popular appeal of the play or the run that extended for nearly two years. In the preface (a mere page-and-a-half in the Bodley Head edition), he introduces the piece as a "potboiler"—that is, written purely for the purpose of turning a buck. Exactly five months to the day after the opening, Shaw wrote from France to his friend and fellow playwright Harley Granville-Barker, coldbloodedly inquiring if *Fanny* were not "dead at last?" But as Hesketh Pearson recalls, Shaw did not enjoy being told that the play was beneath his genius. He defended the "potboiler" vigorously: "I do not waste my time writing potboilers," he wrote to Pearson, "and even my *pot au feu* has some chunks of fresh meat in it."

Airily tossed together as it might appear, *Fanny* does have meat in it—

From *Shaw: The Neglected Plays*, Vol 7., *SHAW: The Annual of Bernard Shaw Studies,* edited by Alfred Turco, Jr., © 1987 by Pennsylvania State University. Pennsylvania State University Press, 1987.

substantial chunks of critical content. The play within the play focuses a critical lens on the older generation. It is written with the pen of a nineteen-year-old; its heroine is a candid young woman about the same age, and its philosophy is the philosophy of youth. But the Shavian view of youth is hardly fatuous. "The young," says Shaw in the preface, "had better have their souls awakened by disgrace, capture by the police, and a month's hard labor, than drift along from their cradles to their graves doing what other people do for no other reason than that other people do it, and knowing nothing of good and evil, of courage and cowardice." In fact, Shaw's pot-boiler comments sharply on the unwisdom of immaturity, its conventional idealism, rigid opinions, and cocksure attitudes. But *Fanny* goes further than that. It serves up a Fabian critique of nearly every major phase of English life during the first decade of the century. Nothing escapes the Shavian X-ray vision. Shaw's "Easy Play for a Little Theatre" registers middle-class respectability, the business sector, religion, the home, prostitution, the aesthetic sensibility, class hierarchies, the generation gap, police brutality, political insularity, and the gentlemanly code of *noblesse oblige*. As A. B. Walkley wrote seventeen years earlier of *Arms and the Man*, "In the form of a droll, fantastic farce, it presents us with a criticism of conduct, a theory of life."

The induction and epilogue that girdle the three acts of the play proper contain a sort of cadenza, a bravura piece of critical decanonization. In the Middle Ages, it is recorded, the Islamic philosopher Algazali published a refutation of various Aristotelian doctrines entitled "The Incoherence of the Philosophers." His points were rebutted by Averroës in a treatise which restated the case for the Aristotelians: "The Incoherence of the Incoherence." On a less exalted plane perhaps, but in much the same spirit, Shaw contrived in the framing sections of *Fanny* a Criticism of the Criticism. Spicing the *pot au feu* is an in-house critique of current theater coverage, and a lampoon of several London drama critics (including A. B. Walkley, quoted above).

Between its outer frame and the inner vehicle, *Fanny's First Play* draws upon a range of dramatic modes; and it is worth taking note that what we are dealing with is a carnival of forms seldom brought together in one continuous action. There are elements of the morality play, the comedy of manners, of stark Ibsenist realism. There is the ritual violence of Punch and Judy, the fantastic harlequinade plottings of commedia dell'arte, a dash of Socialist allegory, and more than a hint of Gilbert and Sullivan light opera. Indeed, the first character we meet in the induction is a fetchingly vulgar entrepreneur called "Savoyard."

At the upper end of the scale *Fanny* recalls the aristocratic structures of the court *masque*. The inner play is meant to be performed privately, at a noble house, and only once. It is an occasional piece commemorating Fanny O'Dowda's birthday, and it dispenses both poetic fictions and saturnine surrealism. The inner play turns upon an ethical center, a moral "device"; it provides innocent entertainment, a crisis of confrontation, and a *deus ex machina* in the magical figure (after Barrie) of the footman/aristocrat. In the 1916 version, the "authoress" played a major role in the inner play, reflective of the easy crossing of boundaries between creator and performer and audience which is markedly characteristic of the *masque* form. Finally, echoing the vision of a debased dancehall debacle in the play within the play, the framing sections with their outspoken yet tightly contained satirical content set up a critical crossfire and in themselves constitute a species of *antimasque*. To use the language of Russian formalist M. M. Bakhtin, *Fanny's First Play* can be read as a densely interwoven "dialogic" enterprise.

Bakhtin uses the term *dialogic* to express the ideological warfare that obtains between culturally opposed modes of language as well as the effect wrought upon one by the other, or others. Michael Holquist glosses *dialogism* as the "characteristic epistemological mode of a world dominated by heteroglossia. Everything means, is understood, as part of a greater whole—there is a constant interaction between meanings, all of which have the potential of conditioning others." When we turn from the language of modes to the modes of language in Shaw's deceptively-styled "easy play," it becomes evident that *Fanny* provides a brilliant example of Bakhtinian *polyglossia*—the coexistence of multiple socially-determined dialects (Bakhtin would say "Words") within a given culture.

This is not always the case in Shavian drama, where elegance of language and speed of wit often sweep over class lines and serve to obscure distinctions of origin, whether of caste or place. On the other hand, one recognizes the energetic dialogic interaction in the earlier *Candida* (1895), for example, where the social levels of the characters are finely calibrated—and, one may add, in almost perfect inverse ratio to the scale of their ages. Here, styles of language range from the working-class canniness of Burgess, and Prossy's "lower middle class . . . pert and quick of speech"; to the Reverend Morell's educated but unctuously humanitarian overtones; to the extreme end of the socio-linguistic scale—the public school Word of the young poet and gentleman of noble birth, Marchbanks.

But it was in *Pygmalion* (1912), which followed hard on the heels of *Fanny*, that Shaw cast language itself in the star roles. For it is not so much Higgins and Eliza who are in conflict in this dramatic arena; after all, they

both want the flower seller to "talk like a lady." In *Pygmalion,* language
assumes the function both of protagonist and antagonist. Mapped out in
their respective languages are two economically and socially distinct
worlds—with distinct attitudes, experience, abilities, training, perceptions,
expectations—that are engaged in a violent polyglossic power struggle. An
exchange in the opening scene presents the essential conflict, particularly if
we understand that Liza's "I" includes her spoken language. With feeble
defiance, she tells Higgins: "Ive a right to be here if I like, same as you." And
Higgins replies:

> A woman who utters such depressing and disgusting sounds has
> no right to be anywhere—no right to live. Remember that you
> are a human being with a soul and the divine gift of articulate
> speech: that your native language is the language of Shakespear
> and Milton and The Bible; and dont sit there crooning like a
> bilious pigeon.

Shaw asserted in the preface to *Pygmalion* that it was "impossible for an
Englishman to open his mouth without making some other Englishman hate
or despise him." In dialogic terms, he is referring to a linguistically stratified
island "dominated by heteroglossia," and pointing to the innate hostility of
each class-sprung Word toward the other.

In *Fanny,* the dialogic texture is rather more complex than in either
Candida or *Pygmalion. Fanny* stands to these much as three-dimensional
chess stands to the single-level game. As noted earlier, various dramatic
modes in themselves set up a dialogic interplay on the structural level, just
under the surface of the action. Again, as in the other two plays, the socially
determined dialects engage in a sometimes outspoken, sometimes subtle
polemic, on a level we will call above the action—that is, beyond the personalities of the individual characters who speak the lines. In addition, the
subject matter, the very plot of the inner play, lends itself to Bakhtin's
construct, for the young authoress is propounding a political problem with
a bluntly Socialist resolution: in Fanny O'Dowda's play, the revolutionary
discourse of each outside person or group threatens the position of the
entrenched inside group.

Finally, I should like to suggest that apart from the play's evident
socio-political concerns, its dialectics of inside/outside extend beyond the
planes of pure structure into an abstract ethical sphere. The play as it stands
is fashioned to provide points of overlap, a meeting ground between the
inner dramatic action and the critical framework. More specifically, the
question raised at these points has to do with the relation of ethical prin-

ciples to aesthetic values. Mr Xxxx is bringing up a corollary to the long-vexed problem of whether the ventures of art are bound in any way to moral considerations and constraints. He is asking, in effect, whether the way one talks about art is to be considered "pure art" in itself, and hence exempt from ethical criteria, or if critical discourse is subject to ethical principles. And while Shaw does little more than raise the question and adopt a stance, this may very well be the most intriguing metaphysical problem advanced in *Fanny's First Play*. Keeping it in mind, we can turn most usefully now to the players, the plottings, and the plot.

As the curtain opens, a footman is admitting Savoyard to the country house of Count O'Dowda, a wealthy Irishman whose title, it turns out, harks back to the Holy Roman Empire. Fanny, the Count's cherished only child, wants to stage a play for her birthday and Savoyard has engaged to supply actors, a director, and professional drama critics for the event. With some difficulty the entrepreneur has persuaded three London critics to attend, and bribed a reluctant fourth. These gentlemen are expected to arrive shortly, for dinner before the play.

O'Dowda is the quintessential aesthete and Shaw has cartooned the character with a certain stylish freedom. The Count spends most of the year in a Venetian palazzo and listens by preference to Pergolesi. The stage directions tell us he is a *"handsome man of fifty, dressed with studied elegance a hundred years out of date."* While he loathes industrial England and the nineteenth century (and refuses to recognize the twentieth) his hero, ironically, is the iconoclastic Byron. As St. John Ervine put it, O'Dowda is "a Peter Pan of fifty." Fanny's play is to be a surprise for him but he confidently and quite erroneously informs Savoyard that the production will resemble a "Louis Quatorze ballet painted by Watteau." Believing his daughter to be as firmly planted in the eighteenth century as himself, the Count enlarges on this vision of *delicatesse:*

> The heroine will be an exquisite Columbine, her lover a dainty Harlequin, her father a picturesque Pantaloon, and the valet who hoodwinks the father and brings about the happiness of the lovers a grotesque but perfectly tasteful Punchinello or Mascarille or Sganarelle.

The Count will be severely disenchanted, of course. Fanny, who has just completed two eye-opening years at Cambridge and joined the young Fabians there, has no intention of presenting a Louis Quatorze series of tableaux. On the contrary, she has engineered an up-to-date three-acter with scandalous modern views, a Fabian solution, and a stern critique of parental obliquity. It is as remote from the eighteenth century as she can make it. After we have become involved in Fanny O'Dowda's little comedy of errors, however, it may be borne in upon us that we are looking at something remarkably like the pantomime sketched above. For Fanny is as romantic as her father. Although she has clothed her players in modern dress, the action of the valet who "hoodwinks the father and brings about the happiness of the lovers" quite precisely conforms to the Count's script.

The critics arrive: Mr Trotter, Mr Vaughan, Mr Gunn, and Flawner Bannal. There is no flourish of trumpets, but one has the distinct sense of a parade. Each represents an age group as well as a separate "dialect" of dramatic criticism. Trotter, the Count's contemporary, is conservative and gentlemanly. Savoyard warns O'Dowda that Trotter is touchy on the subject of Aristotelian poetics; a play that departs from the Stagirite's formulations is no play at all for him, but a staged "discussion." Vaughan, forty, is unimpeachably honest but "has no sense of humor. . . . it's not that he doesnt see a joke: he does; and it hurts him." Gunn, at thirty, is a cynical and blasé young Intellectual for whom the most recent experiments in theater are boringly passé. He is useful, Savoyard explains, largely because "he pitches into the older Intellectuals." Bringing up the rear is Flawner Bannal, the oracle of the populace. He is twenty years old, knows nothing about drama and has no taste; he has been bribed to come. But as Shaw somewhat acidly informs his audience through Savoyard's mouth, "Flawner Bannal's your man. Bannal really represents the British playgoer." His is the review that makes or breaks a play.

Shaw scholarship has identified the models for three of the critics. "Trotter" is Shaw's good friend Walkley of *The Times*. "Vaughan" is E. A. Baughan of the *Daily News,* while "Gunn" is Gilbert Cannan of *The Star.* Walkley, reviewing *Fanny* in *The Times,* coyly refused to recognize himself: "We rather like Mr. Trotter," he wrote, "probably for the usual reasons that we are all apt to admire our opposites. He is a genuine invention of Mr. X . . . a pure figment of the imagination, wholly unlike any actual person." In fact, Claude King who played Trotter had picked up the elder critic's appearance, manner, and style of speech—his peculiar decorum—all with Walkley's good-humored help. But Walkley's review asserted that "Mr. Claude King . . . had evidently modelled his diction and demeanor upon Mr. Bernard Shaw." We can see that on some level the tone of voice of the play has determined, or shaped, the critical response. An invitation to join in the fun has been extended; the reviewers have permission—indeed, they are urged—to become part of the action, as it were. The result of this complicated banter passing publicly between critical author and authorial critic is that fictions, counterfictions, and reality become entangled—not only inside but outside the confines of the play proper. Thus players, plottings, and plot have reached into the review. The Word of the playwright has conditioned if not contaminated the critical Word.

The character of "Flawner Bannal" may have been modelled on Clement Scott of *The Daily News.* E. J. West tells us that in 1894 (when *Arms and the Man* was first produced), "Clement Scott . . . prided himself as dramatic critic on being the *vox populi;* he had a tremendous photographic memory and could describe accurately what he saw and heard in performance, but he had absolutely no critical judgment or philosophic principles."

Shaw must have reserved a warm spot in his heart for the scandalously unprincipled Bannal. At the time *Fanny* was moving to the Kingsway Theatre to continue its run, the magazine *Play Pictorial* put out a special issue devoted to the play (Souvenir Number 114). In it, Shaw addressed a letter to the editor and signed it "Flawner Bannal." It continued the fiction—and the reality—of a powerfully anti-intellectual *vox populi.* Shaw wrote:

> As you well know I write for the *Matutinal Meddler* and represent "the man in the street." We are the biggest publicity medium in the world and if my original notice was somewhat guarded . . . you . . . will understand that it was not policy on my part to put forward, however vaguely, any original view as to the play in question.
>
> Trotter may write with his tongue in his Grecian cheek . . . but I am simply a plain, straight-forward Englishman, with a plain straight-forward duty to multitudinous readers who like to assimilate my opinions with their bacon and eggs.

Three things snare the attention in this passage: the raw power and prerogative invoked in the "biggest publicity medium in the world"; the leveling of taste implied in the common-denominator policy not to "put forward . . . any original view as to the play in question"; and the punning reference to Trotter, who "may write with his tongue in his Grecian cheek." That these statements point to antithetical ideologies is clear. That they represent an interlocking of political, aesthetic, and ethical concerns is also clear. We do not have to ask: is this a political statement? Is this statement about art? Shaw makes the connections for us. But he has also taken the dialogic ripple effect of the play a step further. As we have seen, Walkley reviewed *Fanny* in a playful, responsive way, actually bending the critical function to the service of the dramatist's art. Shaw, in his letter to the editor, springs two characters out of the play into the non-fiction world, into real-life controversy. He is using the dramatist's art to roundly criticize the "system."

The system, of course, is young Fanny's target. Her play (left untitled by Mr X) unfolds in three acts and is scored for a range of social dialects. Although the inner play purports to be a young woman's serious attempt at serious criticism, a carnival atmosphere insinuates itself in the tone and the pacing while characters such as Juggins, Duvallet, and Darling Dora are the familiar personae of operetta and farce. Fanny's plot straightforwardly combines social commentary with romantic notions and an earnest condemnation of parental narrowness. Shaw, however, has framed the scenes of the inner play in a complex series of perspectives that range from the impersonal to the intimate. The inner play is, after all, the central action. It is watched by the actual audience in the actual theater, and by the professional reviewers in that audience. It is observed by the four critics of the induction and epilogue and by the father at whom these scenes are aimed. The characters who convey the action of the inner play have the "inside" perspective. Fanny notes the effect of the action on her audience as she sits and watches on stage; Mr Xxxx does the same offstage. One could go on enumerating points of view. The proliferation of perspectives seem to spring from the dialogic nature of the play. I have in no way exhausted the possibilities. Perhaps it will be most useful, now, to look at the family structures that Shaw has taken so much trouble to frame.

Unlike the Montagues and Capulets, the respectable Gilbeys (act 1) and the god-fearing Knoxes (act 2) wish to cement their families' business relations by the marriage of their children. The young people have become engaged, but Bobby Gilbey is smitten with Darling Dora, a streetwalker of merry disposition and indelicate speech; while Margaret Knox finds Bobby less stimulating than Duvallet, a Frenchman on holiday, and far less attractive than Juggins, the Gilbeys' footman. Their footman serves the middle-class Gilbeys with tact and finesse and the gracious condescension of a duke. And, as it turns out to the astonishment of all but the audience, "Juggins" is in truth the brother of a duke. He has entered domestic service to atone for a sin of unkindness—so much for young Fanny's attempt at hard-core realism.

The plot turns upon another remarkable coincidence. Unknown to their parents, or to each other, both Bobby and Margaret have run afoul of the law and spent some weeks in jail. Bobby was merely a drunken accessory to Darling Dora's impertinence to a "copper," but Margaret not only resisted but assaulted the arresting officer when she found herself part of a crowd being forcibly ejected from a dancehall. This episode has crowned Margaret's transformation from the docile child who was awarded the good conduct prize three years running to the emancipated young woman who is Fanny's heroine. Margaret's description of the episode powerfully conveys her sense of the encounter as a rite of passage. She tells her shocked mother how she visited a dancehall with Duvallet, and how tipsy students invaded the place and began to smash things so that the police were called:

> The students fought with the police; and the police suddenly got quite brutal, and began to throw everybody downstairs. . . . Two more attacked me and gave me a shove to the door. That quite maddened me. I just got in one good bang on the mouth of one of them. . . . I was rushed through the streets to the police station. They kicked me with their knees; they twisted my arms; they taunted and insulted me; they called me vile names . . . [N]ext morning . . . the police were quite jolly; and everybody said it was a bit of English fun.

The Gilbeys and Knoxes want to keep the news of their children's disgrace quiet, each family fearing the other will want to break off the engagement. Bobby remains sullen and introverted but Margaret, whom Ervine calls "one of the finest young women in all Shavian drama," is in a mood to publicly celebrate her deliverance—both from jail and from conventional morality. She has come of age by being forced to share the treatment of the unprotected and the deviant. Her gift is to recognize a common humanity with her cell mates. "Ive been shoved and bullied," she tells Mrs Knox. "Ive been flung into a filthy cell with a lot of other poor wretches. . . . And the only difference between me and the others was that I hit back." She flings down the challenge to her upbringing, to the conventional Word: "I wasnt ladylike. I cursed. I called names." By the end of act 2, Margaret is a solid candidate for the bad conduct medal. Her pious mother is unable to pray; Mr Knox has switched from ordering his daughter out of the house to begging her—on his knees—"not to let it out." Margaret brings down the second-act curtain by threatening to destroy her father's respectability. She will publish the revolutionary Word: "I'll tell everybody."

The third act opens with a lesson in manners. Perhaps it would be nearer the mark to say that it focuses attention on the contrast between Bobby's conventional hypocrisy and the candid nature of gentlemanly courtesy. This is an important scene, for the question of a viable morality is the central issue, the problem that beats at the heart of Shaw's play. Bobby asks advice of Juggins in this scene. He wants to break his engagement with

Margaret but, as he tells the servant, would like to "give it a gentlemanly turn." Juggins speedily rules out this approach: "If you wish to spare her feelings, sir, you can marry her. If you hurt her feelings by refusing, you had better not try to get credit for considerateness at the same time." Bobby persists in seeking a way to squirm out of his contract with his ego intact and is informed with imperial certitude: "I assure you, sir, theres no correct way of jilting. It's not correct in itself."

It has been suggested that Shaw was "more than a little proud of his genteel origin." In *Fanny's First Play,* the Irish nobleman O'Dowda represents a comic extreme of aestheticism. His world of Art is an escapist realm that is militantly moral. It is the nobleman of the inner play—having humbled himself to serve others—who sets the tone and establishes the true standard of moral behavior. It is presented as an efficient code for living with other people rather than a recipe for "goodness." Juggins lets us know that the gentlemanly thing to do is the decent thing to do, requiring simple honesty and an intelligent consideration for others. Opposed to the murky respectability prized by the Gilbeys and Knoxes of Denmark Hill is the footman's radical notion of granting choice to the other and assuming responsibility for oneself. Juggins concludes the lesson to Bobby with a little homily:

> I have noticed, sir, that Denmark Hill thinks that the higher you
> go in the social scale, the less sincerity is allowed, and that only
> tramps and riff-raff are quite sincere. Thats a mistake. Tramps
> are often shameless; but theyre never sincere. Swells—if I may
> use that convenient name for the upper classes—play much more
> with their cards on the table.

Shaw has introduced the problem of establishing a socially consistent ethic through the charming but improbable figure of Juggins. On the one hand Juggins, like Marchbanks, represents the public school Word; that is to say, they each convey an ideal mode of conduct. But where the shy young aristocrat in *Candida* is imbued with reality, Juggins is not: he is the personification of an abstract moral code, clearly a code which traces its lineage back through knightly romance to the rule of chivalry. On the other hand, what we see through the double lens of Shaw/Fanny is essentially a *parable.* Juggins and Count O'Dowda are characters in a tale that could be entitled "The Lesson of the Wise and Foolish Nobleman."

In the third act of Fanny's play, the wrong couples are separated, the right couples brought together, and a general leveling brought to pass. Bobby and Margaret tell each other they have been in jail. Bobby is irritated at the news and Margaret contemptuous of him. Darling Dora arrives and immediately recognizes Margaret as her cellmate: "Why, it's never No. 406!" The girls are delighted at the reunion, but Bobby is discomfited by the equitable relations that obtain between the good girl and the bad girl. They quarrel until Juggins ushers in Duvallet. Margaret explains to Dora—in her own language—that Duvallet is her "bloke" and that he has paid her fine "like a gentleman." When the Gilbeys are spotted returning home, Juggins squirrels the lot of them in the servants' kitchen. There they have tea, giggle, sing, joke and generally cut up while the Gilbeys entertain the Knoxes in a more staid fashion above-stairs.

Just before the Knoxes arrive, Juggins has given notice and revealed his identity. The Gilbeys are understandably appalled to learn that they have been served, and observed, by a duke's brother. In the kitchen the symbolic unification of class, gender, nationality, and income level brought about by Juggins below-stairs corresponds to an unusual openness between the older folk on the floor above. Mrs Knox takes this opportunity to deliver her views on family life and morality, which, we find, are notably close to the views set forth by Shaw in the preface. Says Mrs Knox:

> We dont really know whats right and whats wrong. . . . We bring our children up just as we were brought up; and we go to church or chapel just as our parents did; and we say what everybody says; and it goes on all right until something out of the way happens: theres a family quarrel, or one of the children goes wrong, or a father takes to drink, or an aunt goes mad, or one of us finds ourselves doing something we never thought we'd want to do. . . . With all our respectability and piety, weve no real religion and no way of telling right from wrong. Weve nothing but our habits; and when theyre upset, where are we? Just like Peter in the storm trying to walk on the water and finding he couldnt.

This is a truly poignant moment in the inner play, poignant because the motherless Fanny has put this sadly resigned but truthful speech in the mouth of Mrs Knox, the "spiritual" mother. Hard on this revelation the downstairs party is uncovered and brought together with the older group. With the mingling of generations the social unification is complete: every mountain and hill has been made low, the crooked have been made straight, and the rough places plain.

Having accomplished the impossible, Juggins/Rudolph declares his feeling for Margaret. He presents his suit, not as a nobleman, but as "a

sober, honest, and industrious domestic servant . . . a man with a character." At this point the young people also learn of Juggins's double identity,
but as Dora is to be taught manners and it appears that both young couples
are to be united with the consent of their parents, everybody is happy. Thus,
the knottiest difficulties are resolved in the time-honored fashion of comedy—but Duvallet has the last word. And one hears in it yet another dialectical reverberation, an echo of the elder dramatist calmly assessing the
work of the newcomer: "In France it would be impossible. But here—ah . . .
la belle Angleterre!" And with this we are dropped into the epilogue.

The final frame contains a bang-up critical cadenza introduced by the
arpeggios of the affronted father. "This play implies obscure, unjust, unkind
reproaches and menaces to all of us who are parents," he moans. Bewildered and horrified, he appeals to the critics—"the choice and master spirits
of this age"—to render an opinion. A heated controversy ensues. Bannal, as
usual, finds it impossible to form an opinion; he cannot tell if he has seen a
farce or a melodrama, tragedy or comedy. The Count presses for a judgment: "But is it a good play, Mr Bannal? Thats a simple question." Bannal
responds circularly:

> Simple enough when you know. If it's by a good author, it's a
> good play, naturally. That stands to reason. Who is the author?
> Tell me that; and I'll place the play for you to a hair's breadth.

Gunn, true to his young Intellectual bias, declares the piece a "rotten old-
fashioned domestic melodrama." Vaughan agrees only to the extent that it
is "intensely disagreeable" and therefore cannot have been written by Barrie.

This precipitates an argument about the author. Is it Barrie? Pinero?
Granville-Barker? Bannal brilliantly suggests Shaw. But Vaughan holds on
two counts that the play cannot be Shaw's. It has a note of passion, and
Vaughan has "repeatedly proved that Shaw is physiologically incapable of
the note of passion." He follows this quasi-sexual slur with the observation
that the characters in this play are distinct from one another while "all
Shaw's characters are himself: mere puppets stuck up to spout Shaw."
Clearly the audience is being treated to a rare author-baiting and, to carry
the point home, to an equally rare critic-baiting. We should note that Trotter does not enter the dialogue here. But something else is afoot. We have
arrived at one of those points of overlap where the inner and outer plays
usefully comment upon one another.

Two ethical issues can be discerned at this meeting ground and they are
not entirely unrelated. First, the morality of *life* question of the inner play is
reflected in the morality of *criticism* issue of the outer frame. Just as the

Gilbeys and Knoxes make questionable ethical assumptions and think in rigid categories, so do the satirized critics proceed on questionable aesthetic grounds and entertain equally rigid notions about what constitutes "good" and "bad" drama. Is it right to decide whether a play has merit by asking who the author is? And isn't such complacency analogous to a general tendency to accept dubious actions if they are performed by people assumed to be "good"?

Secondly, this scene brings the issue of critical discourse itself to stage center. Shaw the critic stands in the wings, divided from the gesticulating author ("Shaw" is repeated some thirteen times during the short dialogue) and from the image he has invented of an egomaniacal dramatist. Close to this familiar fiction hovers Shaw the experienced drama critic, music critic and art critic. Together they raise one of the more difficult questions attaching to interpretive discourse. Put most simply it comes to this: *Is it possible to talk usefully about art or does criticism always end up talking about talk?* Surely the squabble among Bannal, Vaughan, and Gunn is meant to indicate in boldface the WRONG WAY—indeed, three fruitless paths. But has Shaw implied a right way? Only the sage Trotter has guessed who the real author is, and we should note that he remains silent during this exchange.

The struggle of critical discourse to elucidate and condition the art it criticizes has been reduced to an illustration: the (fictional) critique of a fiction within a fiction. The twist is that the inner play is a perfectly focused satire on the way things are; as social commentary it recommends realistic changes in attitudes and behavior. The fictional exposé of the fictional critics is methodologically different, for here Shaw relies on an *artful* parody to drive home his Criticism of the Criticism. I do not wish to proliferate dizzying regressions in the infinite mirrors of discourse and art, but I do want to point out what Shaw seems to be telling us in this section—apart from "irresponsibly" drawing attention to himself. Isn't Shaw suggesting that imaginative modes (such as this fictional scene) are as useful as the purely analytical when it comes to honest and effective criticism? And isn't he, with an impish glitter in his steely blue eye, really saying: "I've shown you it's possible because I've just *done* it"?

Maurice Valency has remarked that the "pleasantly impudent" framework around *Fanny's First Play* was intended to "satirize the critical reception" of Shaw's plays (as for example the previously panned *Misalliance*). But the parody's deeper significance lies, he thinks, in Shaw's advocacy of a new theater with new dramatic modes—specifically, "the type of discussion-drama he was attempting to naturalize in the English theater." While Valency rightly points out that several larger principles are invoked—e.g., questions of order and freedom, the problem of permissible deviance within a given social milieu—he is clear that lack of communication between parents and children is the play's central theme. This is certainly so; and before concluding, I should like briefly to consider a second point of overlap between inner play and frame. As noted above, only Trotter has remained aloof during the critics' debate in the epilogue; he knows that Fanny has written that play. In the induction, Fanny has revealed to him her membership in the young Fabians, at which the elder critic makes the connection. "Impertinent little kittens," he snorts, and predicts that the play they are about to see is one in which "members of Fabian Societies instruct their grandmothers in the art of milking ducks." A meeting ground has been established here so that we can see the generational tensions of the inner play reflected in the frame—in reverse perspective.

The parent–child relation is central to Shaw from *Mrs Warren's Profession* to *Heartbreak House*. *Misalliance*, written just prior to *Fanny*, is prefaced with a treatise on "Parents and Children" which illustrates both sides of the generational barrier. In this essay one finds, for instance, if not an *apologia* for Count O'Dowda's uninformed parenthood, at least a recognition of his genuine distress: "Children are extremely cruel without intending it; and in ninety-nine cases out of a hundred . . . they do not conceive their elders as having any human feelings." As usual, Shaw is refreshingly unsentimental on this point, but he also evens up the score immediately: "Serve the elders right, perhaps, for posing as superhuman!"

In the frame, Trotter is shown to possess the older person's conventional narrowness and superciliousness toward the young when he attributes to Fanny's fellow Fabians a penchant for gratuitous instruction of their wiser elders. Conversely, young Fanny's (and her heroine Margaret's) insensitivity to the feelings of all but her contemporaries is also mapped out in the preface to *Misalliance*—and with the same ironic edge. The treatise exposes the same generational dynamics revealed in the inner play. The parents, says Shaw,

> have none of the illusions about the child that the child has about the parents; and the consequence is that the child can hurt its parents' feelings much more than its parents can hurt the child's, because the child, even when there has been none of the deliberate hypocrisy by which children are taken advantage of by their elders, cannot conceive the parent as a fellow-creature.

It follows that Monsieur Duvallet, a parent who acts with the irresponsibility of a child, cannot function as a mediator in Fanny O'Dowda's play. It takes a miracle in the form of a noble servant to effect the reconciliation of young and old. But the generational warfare is mediated in quite another way for the real audience behind the footlights, for Shaw has prepared a neutral meeting ground—a critical island so to speak—on which the dialogically embattled age groups may be observed and compared. Thus Shaw attempts to *draw his entire audience within the critical circle*—which brings us to the last question to be considered here, the question of objective and subjective critical modes.

Is it odd, one may ask, that a man whose critical writing is pungently visceral should periodically require of his audience a cerebral distancing from the action on stage? In the epilogue to *Fanny*, Shaw achieves this result very simply by introducing his own name into the critical discussion, thus collapsing the flimsy-at-best illusion of reality. In one of his studies of Shaw, Stanley Weintraub analyzes the structured distancing that forces an audience into critical objectivity:

> By destroying stage illusion and by inhibiting the possibilities of empathic identification between audience and characters, the playwright . . . creates a distance which forces the spectator to look at the action on stage in a detached and critical spirit: what Brecht called, years later, his "alienation effect."

It is no easy task to engage an audience completely, and it is demanding a great deal to expect an audience that is being entertained to snap out of it and start to think. As Weintraub notes, "the audience . . . is given little opportunity to absorb itself imaginatively into the play [when] the playwright jests directly with his audience"—which is exactly what Shaw does in the epilogue to *Fanny*. Bernard Shaw fully intended to jolt us out of the near-hypnotic receptivity that attends the willing suspension of disbelief; he was tactically dedicated to bringing our rational equipment onto the field. But when he forced the members of the audience to exercise their critical faculties he did not expect them to remain coldly remote: he was hoping to contact their feelings by way of their minds, and to have both mind and heart invaded at once.

Shaw, by nature a critical animal, was fiercely subjective but also fiercely protective of an ethical code in criticism. As drama critic for the *Saturday Review*, says Weintraub, Shaw in the years 1895–98 "had become the most feared and respected, as well as the most entertaining, columnist in London." He was one of the most gifted of music critics and his extensive and astonishingly readable music criticism is well known, but it would be hard, I think, to find another music critic—or any critic in any time—who would admit to such flagrant subjectivity. As a music critic in 1890 Shaw had already published his critical manifesto:

> Criticism written without personal feeling is not worth reading.
> It is the capacity for making good or bad art a personal matter
> that makes a man a critic.

This is not a philosophy that stops at delicate impressions or indeed at anything short of total destruction when it comes upon "bad art," for Shaw continues: "when people do less than their best, and do that less at once badly and self-complacently, I loathe them, detest them, long to tear them limb from limb."

However, when a young critic wrote to Shaw abusing Oscar Wilde, the older man answered severely: "You must give up detesting everything appertaining to Oscar Wilde or to anyone else. *The critic's first duty is to admit, with absolute respect, the right of every man to his own style.*" As protective of artistic freedom as he was vexed by social and critical hypocrisy, Shaw was handing down to Golding Bright the first critical precept of Pope's famous Essay:

> A perfect judge will read each work of Wit
> With the same spirit that its author writ.

We would do well to apply Pope's critical yardstick to *Fanny's First Play*. Or, to stretch Shaw's own terms a wee bit, to grant the right of every play to its own style, its own Word. *Fanny* represents a lighthearted but necessary experiment. If it is not one of the major plays, neither is it trivial. Isn't it a way station or testing ground where an intricately knotted problem of morality and art can be turned this way and that, inspected if not resolved, thoughtfully noted if not—like its great Gordian predecessor—cloven neatly apart?

Chronology

1856   Born on July 26, in Dublin, Ireland.

1876   Moves to London in the hopes of professional advancement and becomes a small-time journalist.

1879   Hired by the Edison Telephone Company and completes his first novel, *Immaturity*.

1880   Writes a second novel, *The Irrational Knot*. Joins the Dialectical Society.

1881   Becomes a vegetarian in an attempt to cure migraine headaches and takes lessons in boxing. Writes *Love among the Artists*.

1882   Converts to socialism and completes his best novel, *Cashel Byron's Profession*.

1884   Falls among the Fabians. *An Unsocial Socialist* is serialized.

1885   Father dies.

1886–88   Works as an art critic and music critic for various journals.

1889   Publishes *Fabian Essays*.

1890   Begins work as a music critic for *The World*. Lectures to the Fabian Society on Ibsen.

1891   Publishes *The Quintessence of Ibsenism*.

1892–93   *Widowers' Houses, The Philanderer, Mrs Warren's Profession*.

1894   *Arms and the Man, Candida*.

1895   Starts as drama critic for the *Saturday Review; The Man of Destiny, You Never Can Tell.*

1896   *The Devil's Disciple.*

1898   Marries Charlotte Payne-Townshend. *Caesar and Cleopatra, The Perfect Wagnerite.*

1899   *Captain Brassbound's Conversion.*

1903   *Man and Superman.*

1904   *John Bull's Other Island.*

1905   Visits Ireland. *Major Barbara.*

1906   Meets Ellen Terry. *The Doctor's Dilemma, Our Theatre in the Nineties.*

1908   *Getting Married.*

1909   *Misalliance, The Shewing-up of Blanco Posnet.*

1911   *Fanny's First Play.*

1912   *Androcles and the Lion, Pygmalion.* Friendship with Mrs. Patrick Campbell.

1914   *Common Sense About the War.*

1916–19   *Heartbreak House.*

1920   *Back to Methuselah.*

1923   *Saint Joan.*

1926   Receives the Nobel Prize for literature—uses the prize money to support the publication of translations from Swedish literature.

1928   *The Intelligent Woman's Guide to Socialism, Capitalism, Sovietism, and Fascism.*

1929   *The Apple Cart.*

1931   *Ellen Terry and Bernard Shaw: A Correspondence.* Travels to U.S.S.R.

1932   *The Adventures of the Black Girl in Her Search for God.*

1933   Goes to America.

1934   *Collected Prefaces.*

1939   *In Good King Charles's Golden Days.*

1943   Wife dies.

1944   *Everybody's Political What's What.*

1950   Dies on November 13.

Contributors

HAROLD BLOOM, Sterling Professor of the Humanities at Yale University, is the author of *The Anxiety of Influence, Poetry and Repression,* and many other volumes of literary criticism. His forthcoming study, *Freud: Transference and Authority,* attempts a full-scale reading of all of Freud's major writings. A MacArthur Prize Fellow, he is general editor of five series of literary criticism published by Chelsea House.

STANLEY WEINTRAUB is Research Professor of English and Director of the Institute for the Arts and Humanistic Studies at Pennsylvania State University. He is author of *The Unexpected Shaw* and *Journey to Heartbreak.*

G. K. CHESTERTON was a prolific novelist, essayist, poet, and, after his conversion in 1922, Roman Catholic polemicist. He is best remembered for his Father Brown detective stories, for his fantasy novel *The Man Who Was Thursday* (1908), and for his critical studies of Chaucer, Dickens, Browning, and Shaw.

ERIC BENTLEY is Katherine Cornell Professor of Theatre at the State University of New York at Buffalo. He has written extensively on contemporary drama. In addition to translating the work of Pirandello and Brecht he has directed such plays as Garcia Lorca's *The House of Bernarda Alba* and O'Neill's *The Iceman Cometh.* His own plays include *The Recantation of Galileo Galilei* and *Expletive Deleted.*

FREDERICK P. W. McDOWELL is Professor of English at the University of Iowa. He is author of *Poet as Critic, Ellen Glasgow and the Ironic Art of Fiction,* and critical studies of Joseph Conrad and Virginia Woolf.

LOUIS CROMPTON is Professor of English at the University of Nebraska. He is author of *Shaw the Dramatist,* and writes extensively on homosexual literature and history. His most recent book is *Byron and Greek Love: Homophobia in Nineteenth-Century England.*

MARTIN MEISEL is Professor of English and Comparative Literature at Columbia University. One of our foremost critics of nineteenth-century drama, he is author of *Shaw and the Nineteenth-Century Theater* and *Realizations: Narrative, Pictorial, and Theatrical Arts of the Nineteenth Century.*

MARGERY M. MORGAN is Reader in English at the University of Lancaster. She is author of *A Drama of Political Man: A Study in the Plays of Harley Granville-Barker* and *The Shavian Playground.*

CHARLES A. BERST is Professor of English at the University of California at Los Angeles. He is author of *Bernard Shaw and the Art of Drama* and editor of *Shaw and Religion.*

MAURICE VALENCY is Emeritus Professor of Dramatic Literature at Columbia University and Director of Academic Studies at Juilliard. He has written extensively on modern drama and is author of *In Praise of Love: An Introduction to the Love Poetry of the Renaissance* and a novel, *Ashby.*

J. L. WISENTHAL is Professor of English at the University of British Columbia and editor of *Shaw and Ibsen: Bernard Shaw's* The Quintessence of Ibsenism *and Related Writings.*

SALLY PETERS VOGT writes on Shaw and modern drama.

NICHOLAS GRENE is Fellow and Director of Studies in Modern English at Trinity College, Dublin. In addition to a critical study of Shaw, he has written *Shakespeare, Jonson, Molière: The Comic Contract* and *Synge: A Critical Study of the Plays.*

BARBARA M. FISHER is Assistant Professor of English at the City University of New York.

Bibliography

Adams, Elsie B. *Bernard Shaw and the Aesthetes.* Columbus: Ohio State University Press, 1971.

Barr, Alan P. *Victorian Stage Pulpiteer: Bernard Shaw's Crusade.* Athens: University of Georgia Press, 1973.

Bentley, Eric. *The Playwright as Thinker.* New York: Reynal & Hitchcock, 1946.

Berst, Charles A. *Bernard Shaw and the Art of Drama.* Urbana: University of Illinois Press, 1973.

Caudwell, Christopher. "George Bernard Shaw: A Study of the Bourgeois Superman." In *Five Approaches of Literary Criticism,* edited by Wilbur S. Scott. New York: Collier, 1962.

Chesterton, G. K. *George Bernard Shaw.* New York: Hill & Wang, 1956.

Crompton, Louis. *Shaw the Dramatist.* Lincoln: University of Nebraska Press, 1969.

Dukore, Bernard F. *Bernard Shaw, Director.* Seattle: University of Washington Press, 1971.

———. *Bernard Shaw, Playwright: Aspects of Shavian Drama.* Columbia: University of Missouri Press, 1973.

Ellmann, Richard, ed. *Edwardians and Late Victorians.* New York: Columbia University Press, 1960.

Evans, T. F., ed. *Shaw: The Critical Heritage.* London: Routledge & Kegan Paul, 1976.

Fiske, Irving. *Bernard Shaw's Debt to William Blake.* London: The Shaw Society (Shavian Tract no. 2), 1951.

Gassner, John. *Ideas in the Drama.* New York: Columbia University Press, 1964.

Gibbs, A. M. *The Art and Mind of Shaw.* London: Macmillan, 1983.

Grene, Nicholas. *Bernard Shaw: A Critical View.* London: Macmillan, 1984.

Harris, Frank. *Bernard Shaw.* Garden City, N.Y.: Garden City Publishing, 1931.

Irvine, William. *The Universe of G. B. S.* New York: Whittlesey House, 1949.

Kaufmann, R. J., ed. *G. B. Shaw: A Collection of Critical Essays.* Englewood Cliffs, N.J.: Prentice-Hall, 1965.

MacCarthy, Desmond. *Shaw.* London: MacGibbon & Kee, 1951.

Mander, Raymond, and Joe Mitchenson. *Theatrical Companion to Shaw: A Pictorial Record of the First Performances of the Plays of George Bernard Shaw.* New York: Pitman, 1955.

Meisel, Martin. *Shaw and the Nineteenth-Century Theater*. Princeton, N.J.: Princeton University Press, 1963.

Mencken, H. L. *George Bernard Shaw: His Plays*. Boston: John W. Luce, 1905.

Mills, John A. *Language and Laughter: Comic Diction in the Plays of Bernard Shaw*. Tucson: University of Arizona Press, 1969.

Morgan, Margery M. *The Shavian Playground: An Exploration of the Art of George Bernard Shaw*. London: Methuen, 1972.

Nethercot, Arthur H. *Men and Supermen: The Shavian Portrait Gallery*. New York: Blom, 1966.

O'Donovan, John. *G. B. Shaw*. Dublin: Gill & Macmillan, 1983.

Ohmann, Richard M. *Shaw: The Style and the Man*. Middletown, Conn.: Wesleyan University Press, 1962.

Quinn, Martin, ed. "Shaw and Dickens: A Special Issue." *The Shaw Review* 20, no. 3 (September 1977).

Roy, R. N. *George Bernard Shaw's Historical Plays*. Delhi: Macmillan, 1976.

Silver, Arnold. *Bernard Shaw: The Darker Side*. Palo Alto: Stanford University Press, 1982.

Smith, Percy J. *The Unrepentant Pilgrim*. Boston: Houghton Mifflin, 1965.

Turco, Alfred, Jr. *Shaw's Moral Vision: The Self and Salvation*. Ithaca: Cornell University Press, 1976.

Valency, Maurice. *The Cart and the Trumpet: The Plays of George Bernard Shaw*. New York: Oxford University Press, 1973.

Weintraub, Rodelle, ed. *Fabian Feminist*. University Park: Pennsylvania State University Press, 1977.

Weintraub, Stanley. *Journey to Heartbreak: The Crucible Years of Bernard Shaw 1914–1918*. New York: Weybright & Talley, 1971.

———. *The Unexpected Shaw: Biographical Approaches to G. B. S. and His Work*. New York: Frederick Ungar, 1982.

Weiss, Samuel A., ed. *Bernard Shaw's Letters to Siegfried Trebitsch*. Palo Alto: Stanford University Press, 1986.

West, Alick. *George Bernard Shaw: "A Good Man Fallen Among Fabians."* New York: International Publishers, 1950.

Williams, Raymond. *Drama from Ibsen to Brecht*. New York: Oxford University Press, 1968.

Wilson, Colin. *Bernard Shaw: A Reassessment*. London: Hutchinson, 1969.

Wilson, Edmund. *The Triple Thinkers*. New York: Oxford University Press, 1963.

Wisenthal, J. L. *The Marriage of Contraries: Bernard Shaw's Middle Plays*. Cambridge: Harvard University Press, 1974.

Woodbridge, Homer E. *George Bernard Shaw: Creative Artist*. Carbondale: Southern Illinois University Press, 1963.

Acknowledgments

"Introduction to Shaw" (originally entitled "Editor's Introduction") by Stanley Weintraub from The Portable Bernard Shaw, edited by Stanley Weintraub, © 1977 by Viking Penguin, Inc. Reprinted by permission.

"The Critic" by G. K. Chesterton from *George Bernard Shaw* by G. K. Chesterton © 1910 by Devin Adair Publishers, Inc.

"Pygmalion: A Personal Play" (originally entitled *"Pygmalion"*) by Eric Bentley from *Bernard Shaw 1856–1950* by Eric Bentley, © 1947, 1957 by New Directions Publishing Co., © renewed 1975 by Eric Bentley. Reprinted by permission of New Directions Publishing Co.

"The Shavian World of *John Bull's Other Island"* (originally entitled "Politics, Comedy, Character and the Shavian World of *John Bull's Other Island"*) by Frederick P. W. McDowell from *PMLA* 82 (December 1967), © 1967 by the Modern Language Association of America. Reprinted by permission of the Modern Language Association of America.

"Caesar and Cleopatra" by Louis Crompton from *Shaw the Dramatist* by Louis Crompton, © 1969 by the University of Nebraska Press. Reprinted by permission of the University of Nebraska Press.

"Shaw and Revolution: The Politics of the Plays" by Martin Meisel from *Shaw: Seven Critical Essays,* edited by Norman Rosenblood, © 1971 by Norman Rosenblood. Reprinted by permission of the editor and the University of Toronto Press.

"The Virgin Mother" by Margery M. Morgan from *The Shavian Playground: An Exploration of the Art of George Bernard Shaw* by Margery M. Morgan, © 1972 by Margery M. Morgan and by the Trustees of the British Museum, Governors and Guardians of the National Gallery of Ireland and the Royal Academy of Dramatic Art. Reprinted by permission.

"*Heartbreak House:* Shavian Expressionism" by Charles A. Berst from *Bernard Shaw and the Art of Drama* by Charles A. Berst, © 1973 by the Board of Trustees of the University of Illinois. Reprinted by permission of the University of Illinois Press and the author.

"*Back to Methuselah:* A Tract in Epic Form" (originally entitled "*Heartbreak House*") by Maurice Valency from *The Cart and the Trumpet: The Plays of George Bernard Shaw* by Maurice Valency, © 1973, 1983 by Maurice Valency. Reprinted by permission of the author and Oxford University Press. All rights reserved.

"The Marriage of Contraries: *Major Barbara*" (originally entitled "*Major Barbara*") by J. L. Wisenthal from *The Marriage of Contraries: Bernard Shaw's Middle Plays* by J. L. Wisenthal, © 1974 by the President and Fellows of Harvard College. Reprinted by permission of Harvard University Press.

"Ann and Superman: Type and Archetype" by Sally Peters Vogt from *Fabian Feminist: Bernard Shaw and Woman,* edited by Rodelle Weintraub, © 1977 by Pennsylvania State University. Reprinted by permission of Pennsylvania State University Press, University Park, Pennsylvania.

"Shavian History" by Nicholas Grene from *Bernard Shaw: A Critical View* by Nicholas Grene, © 1984 by Nicholas Grene. Reprinted by permission of Macmillan Press Ltd. and St. Martin's Press, Inc.

"*Fanny's First Play:* A Critical Potboiler?" by Barbara M. Fisher from *Shaw: The Neglected Plays, Vol. 7, SHAW: The Annual of Bernard Shaw Studies,* edited by Alfred Turco, Jr., © 1987 by Pennsylvania State University. Reprinted by permission of the author and Pennsylvania State University Press, University Park, Pennsylvania.

Index